The US NATO Debate

The US NATO Debate

From Libya to Ukraine

Magnus Petersson

Bloomsbury Academic
An imprint of Bloomsbury Publishing Inc

B L O O M S B U R Y
NEW YORK · LONDON · NEW DELHI · SYDNEY

Bloomsbury Academic
An imprint of Bloomsbury Publishing Inc

1385 Broadway	50 Bedford Square
New York	London
NY 10018	WC1B 3DP
USA	UK

www.bloomsbury.com

**BLOOMSBURY and the Diana logo are trademarks of
Bloomsbury Publishing Plc**

First published 2015

Library of Congress Cataloging-in-Publication Data
Petersson, Magnus, 1972-
The US NATO debate : from Libya to Ukraine / by Magnus Petersson.
pages cm
Includes bibliographical references and index.
ISBN 978-1-62892-452-7 (hardback : alk. paper) – ISBN 978-1-62892-451-0 (pbk. : alk. paper)
1. North Atlantic Treaty Organization–United States. 2. United States–
Military relations–Europe. 3. Europe–Military relations–United States.
4. United States–Military policy. 5. Libya–History–Civil War, 2011-
6. Ukraine–History, Military–21st century. I. Title. II. Title: United States NATO debate.
UA646.5.U5P47 2015
355'.031091821–dc23
2015004237

ISBN: HB: 978-1-6289-2452-7
PB: 978-1-6289-2451-0
ePub: 978-1-6289-2455-8
ePDF: 978-1-6289-2454-1

Typeset by Integra Software Services Pvt. Ltd.
Printed and bound in the United States of America

To my parents, Elisabeth Ling and Eric Petersson

Contents

Foreword

I got the idea to this book when I had the great pleasure to supervise a clever student, Annika Kristin Lønseth Nilsen, at Oslo University during the Academic Year of 2011–2012. Thank you Annika for inspiring me! Then my dear wife, Kersti Larsdotter, brought me to the US during 2012–2013, where I had the opportunity to develop the idea, and where we both had the time of our lives in Boston, Massachusetts. I was a visiting scholar at Boston University's Department of International Relations, and Kersti was a guest researcher at MIT's Security Studies Program. We will always be grateful to our friends that hosted us: Monica Duffy Toft and Ivan Arreguin-Toft, Sallie and Mike Corgan, Julia and Christian Estrella, Cindy Williams and Barry Posen, Noelle and Henrik Selin.

I would also like to thank all the friends and colleagues in the US that I have had the opportunity to speak with during the development of the book: Andrew Bacevich, Nora Bensahel, Nicholas Burns, Damon Coletta, Heather Conley, Patrick Cronin, Charles Kupchan, John Deni, Antulio Echevarria, Jim Goldgeier, Dan Hamilton, Ryan Hendrickson, Jolyon Howorth, Arthur Hulnick, Ben Jensen, Larry Kaplan, Sean Kay, Charles Kupchan, Joe Maître, Rebecca Moore, Wilfrid Rollman, Kaija Schilde, Vivien Schmidt, Andreás Simonyi, Stephen Walt, and Joseph Wippl. Many of them are themselves contributors to the US NATO debate and, as such, actors in the book. They are, however, by no means responsible for the book and its weaknesses.

When I told the US experts that I was doing research on the US NATO debate, their most common reaction was: "What NATO debate?" "Americans seem to take Europe for granted," Stephen F. Szabo at the Transatlantic Academy in Washington, D.C., argues.[1] I think that is the case for NATO as well. And therefore it is perceived in the US that there

---

[1] Stephen F. Szabo, "The Pacific Pivot and the West," Brussels Forum Paper Series, March 2012, http://www.gmfus.org (homepage), date accessed March 12, 2014.

is no NATO debate. But there is, as this book will show. And I am very grateful to my editors, Matthew Kopel and Michelle Chen, for giving me the opportunity to show that.

My fine colleagues at the Norwegian Institute for Defence Studies, and the Norwegian Defence University College, must also be thanked, for giving me such a great academic environment, and the Norwegian Department of Defence for its generous financial support of the NATO in a Changing World Research Program. In particular I would like to thank Paal Hilde and Svein Melby, and Bloomsbury's three anonymous reviewers, who have read the whole manuscript and made the book so much better.

I dedicate this book to my parents, Elisabeth Ling and Eric Petersson. They have always been supportive to my choices in life, and for that I will always be very grateful.

Magnus Petersson

Washington, DC, January 14, 2015

Where is the United States Going with NATO?

What is the present status of NATO in US security thinking? That issue has been debated frequently among politicians, policy advisors, and scholars on both sides of the Atlantic the past years. The Libya War in 2011 gave quite clear indications that the United States wanted to lead NATO "from behind," and that the Europeans were expected to take care of their own problems. The US focus on Asia cemented that impression. According to several experts, NATO had transformed to a "post-American" alliance.[1]

Then, in the spring of 2014, came the Ukraine Crisis. The US reactions were rapid, forceful, and substantial. President Barack Obama took the lead. Money was spent on Europe to bolster US military presence. The president, Vice President Joe Biden, and Secretary of State John Kerry visited Europe— especially several of NATO's "newer" European member states, such as the Baltic States, Poland, and Romania—and American and NATO forces were sent to reassure them that NATO's "Musketeer Paragraph"—"one for all and all for one"—Article V of the North Atlantic Treaty, was reliable. Economic and political sanctions against Russia were implemented. NATO was back in the center of the US security policy debate.[2]

But has the Ukraine Crisis changed the long-term trend? To what degree is the United States actually willing and able to engage in European security

---

[1] Ellen Hallams, "Between Hope and Realism: The United States, NATO and a Transatlantic Bargain for the 21st Century," in *NATO Beyond 9/11: The Transformation of the Atlantic Alliance*, eds Ellen Hallams, Luca Ratti, and Benjamin Zyla, Basingstoke: Palgrave Macmillan, 2013, p. 218. See also Svein Melby, "NATO and U.S. Global Security Interests," in *The Future of NATO: Regional Defense and Global Security*, eds Andrew Michta, and Paal Sigurd Hilde, Ann Arbor: University of Michigan Press, 2014, p. 36.

[2] Magnus Petersson, "The US and the Wales Summit: Washington Is Back, and NATO Is Back to Basics," September 11, 2014, www.europeanleadershipnetwork.org (homepage), date accessed September 16, 2014.

affairs in the future? Were the immediate reactions on the Ukraine Crisis a temporary "rebalancing" to Europe, or did it create more permanent effects on US security policy? Analyzing the content and logic of the US NATO debate can provide answers to those questions. For NATO's European allies, and thereby for European security, these issues are quite important. As Svein Melby, Senior Fellow at the Norwegian Institute for Defence Studies, argues:

> What happens on the Eurasian continent … impacts the relative balance of power internationally, and with it the character of the international system. In other words, this is a discussion of the basic premises for sustaining U.S. global leadership.[3]

From a European perspective it has always been highly relevant to follow, analyze, and understand the longer trends in the US NATO debate and its potential consequences for European and global security. In times of change it is even more important. That is what motivates this book. Where is the United States going with NATO?

I will argue that, despite the Ukraine Crisis, the long-term trend in the debate is that the United States is neither capable nor interested in taking care of Europe's security problems more permanently as it did during the Cold War. The main reason for that is the decreased military ability and political will to engage in regions that are not of first strategic priority for the United States.

The argument is underpinned by a systematical analysis of the content and feature of the US political and policy debate about NATO since the Libya War, supplemented by recent literature on the topic. The conclusion is that Europe will have to take more responsibility for its own security, which should not be an impossible task for the richest, most modern, and most well-functioning region in the world. In the words of Yale Professor Jolyon Howorth, Europeans have to learn to bicycle themselves:

> NATO is like a bicycle that has only ever been ridden by the United States, with the Europeans bundled behind in the baby seat. Now the United States is urging the Europeans to learn to ride the bicycle themselves.

---

[3] Melby, "NATO and U.S. Global Security Interests," p. 43.

The European response has been that they prefer to design their own, rather different, bicycle. It is smaller, slower, and fitted with large training wheels. It is useful for the sorts of missions CSDP [EU's Common Security and Defence Policy] has undertaken, but simply inadequate for serious crisis-management tasks. The Europeans need, sooner or later, to master the adult bike.[4]

NATO's changed role in US security policy

The overall aim of this book is to demonstrate how NATO's importance in US long-term security policy, as manifested in the US NATO debate, has changed since the Libya War. The way of doing that is to analyze the content and logic of the US NATO debate, and to discuss its implications, especially for European security and transatlantic relations. The topic is highly relevant both from a scholarly and practical perspective.

From a scholarly perspective, the theoretical understanding of alliance dynamic is an understudied topic.[5] In addition, most studies of NATO and the transatlantic relations have focused on the East–West conflict, and lately on NATO's operations, and not on the interaction within the alliance. With Georgetown Professor Lawrence Kaplan's words: "Too little attention has been paid to the West–West conflicts that arguably have been more frequent and often more bitter if not more dangerous than the struggle with the Soviet Union."[6]

From a practical perspective the United States is, arguably, Europe's biggest fan. It is not only seen as, with President Obama's words, "the bedrock of America's security."[7] The general US impression of Europe and Eurasia is that it is a region that is culturally close to the United States, that it stands for democratic, liberal, and humanitarian values, and that it is an important

---

4　Jolyon Howorth, "NATO, Bicycles and Training Wheels," Guest Post 20130619, www.foreignpolicy.com (homepage), date accessed July 23, 2014.

5　Stephen M. Walt, "Why Alliances Endure or Collapse," *Survival*, Vol. 39, No. 1 (1997), pp. 156–179.

6　Lawrence Kaplan, *NATO Divided, NATO United: The Evolution of an Alliance*, Westport, CT: Praeger, 2004, p. ix.

7　Barack Obama, "Remarks by President Obama and NATO Secretary General Rasmussen Before Meeting," Speech March 26, 2014, www.whitehouse.gov (homepage), date accessed July 1, 2014.

source for guidance in US foreign policy. As the Assistant Secretary of State for European and Eurasian Affairs in the US State Department, Victoria Nuland, expressed it during her Swearing-in Ceremony in 2013:

> It is the honor of a lifetime to be asked to lead the bureau where I grew up as a diplomat and to have responsibility for America's relationships with the most democratic, prosperous, generous, and globally committed region on Earth.[8]

But the United States has also, since the creation of NATO, been critical to Europe's military ability and political will to use force for political purposes, and to share the transatlantic military burden with the United States. Ironically, the so Euro-positive Nuland became world famous for her anti-EU statement during the Ukraine Crisis, "fuck the EU," revealed by a bugged phone conversation in February 2014.[9]

Furthermore, at least since the Libya War started in March 2011, there has been an underlying assumption that NATO's role in US grand strategy has changed, that Europe's role had diminished because Washington gives Europe less and Asia more strategic priority. The "pivot" toward Asia in US security policy has been very much debated in recent years. However, many analysts agree that it has been ongoing for decades.[10]

Already in an article in *Foreign Affairs* in 1991, US Secretary of State James A. Baker argued that "America's destiny lies no less across the Pacific than the Atlantic." He also noted that the US trade with the region was less than with Latin America in the early 1970s and that the Asia-Pacific region twenty years later was America's largest trading partner, nearly one-third larger than that across the Atlantic.[11]

---

[8] John Kerry, "Secretary's Remarks: Swearing-in Ceremony for Victoria Nuland as Assistant Secretary of State for European and Eurasian Affairs," September 18, 2013, www.state.gov (homepage), date accessed September 25, 2013.

[9] Jonathan Marcus, "Transcript of Leaked Nuland-Pyatt Call," *BBC News Europe*, February 7, 2014, www.bbc.com (homepage), date accessed May 29, 2014; Anne Gearan, "U.S. Official Apologizes for Blunt Remark," *Washington Post*, February 7, 2014.

[10] See, for example, Robert S. Ross, "What the Pivot Means for Transatlantic Relations: Separate Course or New Opportunity for Engagement?," *GMF Policy Brief*, May 2013, www.gmfus.org (homepage), date accessed March 12, 2014, p. 1; Daniel Keohane, "Europeans Less Able, Americans Less Willing?," *GMF Policy Brief*, November 2013, www.gmfus.org (homepage), date accessed February 21, 2014, p. 2; and Hallams, "Between Hope and Realism," p. 28.

[11] James A. Baker, "America in Asia: Emerging Architecture for a Pacific Community," *Foreign Affairs*, Vol. 70, No. 5 (1991), pp. 1–18.

Twenty years later, in November 2011, the US Secretary of State Hillary Clinton published an article in *Foreign Policy* and gave a speech in Honolulu, Hawaii, entitled "America's Pacific Century," in which she coined the concept of the US "pivot" to Asia. "It is becoming increasingly clear," she said in the speech,

> ... that in the 21st century, the world's strategic and economic center of gravity will be the Asia Pacific, from the Indian subcontinent to the western shores of the Americas. And one of the most important tasks of American statecraft over the next decades will be to lock in a substantially increased investment—diplomatic, economic, strategic, and otherwise—in this region.[12]

Furthermore, the US defense strategy that was published in January 2012, *Sustaining US Global Leadership: Priorities for the 21st Century*, stated that the "primary loci" of the threats against the United States and US interests were in South Asia and the Middle East.[13] And National Security Advisor Tom Donilon expressed in a speech at the CSIS November 15, 2012: "We're under no illusions. Our rebalancing toward the Asia Pacific—and within the region— is no short-term effort. It is a long-term undertaking that will continue to demand and receive our focused attention and persistence."[14] Secretary Kerry made a similar description June 18, 2014, in a speech at the US Embassy of New Zealand:

> I want to just emphasize to everybody, America thinks of itself as a Pacific nation and is a Pacific nation proudly ... That is why President Obama made the strategic decision in the first term, to do what has become known as a rebalance or pivot ... President Obama is absolutely committed to continuing to make certain that everybody understands this rebalance is not a passing fancy, it's not a momentary thing ...[15]

---

[12] Hillary R. Clinton, "America's Pacific Century," November 10, 2011, www.state.gov (homepage), date accessed October 26, 2013; and Hillary R. Clinton, "America's Pacific Century," *Foreign Policy*, November 2011.

[13] Department of Defense, *Sustaining US Global Leadership: Priorities for the 21st Century*, Washington, DC: Department of Defense, 2012, p. 2.

[14] Tom Donilon, "Remarks by National Security Advisor Tom Donilon," Speech November 15, 2012, www.whitehouse.gov (homepage), date accessed July 1, 2014.

[15] John Kerry, "Remarks at Pacific Day Policy Seminar," June 18, 2014, www.state.gov (homepage), date accessed June 30, 2014. See also John Kerry, "U.S. Vision for Asia-Pacific Engagement," August 13, 2014, www.state.gov (homepage), date accessed September 6, 2014.

The statements from the Obama administration have also been followed up in practice by less US engagement and military presence in Europe. For example, in 2012 the United States decided to remove two of the four US Army Brigades in Europe, and in the beginning of January 2015, the Pentagon confirmed that it would close an additional fifteen US military bases in Europe. At its peak in 1953, the United States had 450,000 troops in Europe; in the beginning of the 1990s it was reduced from approximately 200,000 to 100,000; and after the latest rounds in the 2010s it will go down to approximately 60,000.[16]

The rebalancing to Asia, and the decreased US interest for Europe, has been reinforced by budget restraints, isolationistic tendencies, and other historical and cultural reasons, for example that a new generation of policy makers in the United States does not have the same Eurocentric worldview that the former generation has, remembering two world wars, and the Cold War. In short, the United States is for many reasons no longer interested in leading NATO activities that mainly concern European conditions. Several experts have suggested that the United States expect that the European security challenges primarily should be handled by NATO's European allies in a new transatlantic burden sharing model, and that the US role should principally be "Article V-focused."[17]

What that means is that Europe and NATO should be more of a traditional military alliance in US security thinking, comparable to what NATO was before the Korean War (1950–1953), with mutual security guarantees but without common permanent military command structures. Several US experts have argued along these lines during the last years. Sean Kay, Professor at Ohio Wesleyan University, is one of them. According to Kay, "it is fair to anticipate dramatic, and highly appropriate, changes in America's role in NATO," which means "placing the US position in NATO in

---

[16] Greg Jaffe, "2 Army Brigades to Leave Europe in Cost-cutting Move," *Washington Post*, January 12, 2012; Luke Coffey, "The Future of U.S. Bases in Europe: A View from America," Lecture, No. 1233, July 15, 2013, http://www.heritage.org (homepage), date accessed January 9, 2015; and BBC, "US Military to Close 15 Bases in Europe," January 8, 2015, www.bbc.com (homepage), date accessed January 9, 2015.

[17] Ellen Hallams and Benjamin Schreer, "Towards a 'Post-American' Alliance? NATO Burden-Sharing after Libya," *International Affairs*, Vol. 88, No. 2 (2012), pp. 313–327.

strategic reserve—hedging against future great power difficulties or shocks to the international system affecting the US and Europe."[18]

MIT Professor Barry Posen is another example. He argues that

> …the United States should withdraw from the military command structure and return the alliance to the primarily political organization it once was. The Europeans can decide for themselves whether they want to retain the military command structure under the auspices of the European Union or dismantle it altogether.[19]

In addition, many analysts believe that the transatlantic interoperability, created by twenty years of operating together in the former Yugoslavia, Afghanistan, Iraq, and Libya, will diminish when NATO's Afghanistan operation ends.[20] These trends in the US NATO debate, which this book confirms, have created concerns, not least in Europe, over the US role within the alliance and it has been argued that NATO is, as many times before, an organization in "crises."[21]

On the other hand, there is, as Wallace J. Thies, Professor of Politics at the Catholic University of America, has pointed out, a "vast literature filled with claims that NATO is in disarray, is about to fall apart, or even has ceased to exist in all but name:"

> If we take these claims seriously, relations between the United States and its European allies fell to the lowest point since the Second World War in 1980, 1981, 1983, and 1987. Predictions that the Alliance was on the verge of collapse or that it had already ceased to exist in all but name found their way into print in 1981, 1982, 1983, 1986, 1987, 1988, 1989, and 1990.[22]

---

[18] Sean Kay, "No More Free-Riding: The Political Economy of Military Power and the Transatlantic Relationship," in *NATO's European Allies: Military Capability and Political Will*, eds Janne Haaland Matlary and Magnus Petersson, Basingstoke: Palgrave Macmillan, 2013. See also Tomas Valasek, "Europe and the 'Asia Pivot'," *New York Times*, October 26, 2012.

[19] Barry Posen, "Pull Back," *Foreign Affairs*, Vol. 92, No. 1 (2013), pp. 116–128.

[20] See, for example, John Deni, "Maintaining Transatlantic Strategic, Operational and Tactical Interoperability in an Era of Austerity," *International Affairs*, Vol. 90, No. 3 (2014), pp. 583–600.

[21] See, for example, Jeffrey Michaels, "NATO After Libya: Alliance Adrift?," *RUSI Journal*, Vol. 156, No. 6 (2011), pp. 56–61.

[22] Wallace J. Thies, *Why NATO Endures*, Cambridge: Cambridge University Press, 2009, pp. 12–14.

As I will argue in this book, despite the Ukraine Crisis and although Thies arguments are strong and well documented, several conditions—not least the argumentation from President Obama's team—are indicating that something more fundamental has happened with the "transatlantic bargain,"[23] and that the war in Libya was a watershed. "Washington is signaling more forcefully than ever to its European allies as well as NATO partners, that they must take on a greater share of Alliance burdens ... and move away from a deeply entrenched culture of dependency," writes Ellen Hallams, Lecturer at King's College, when she talks about a "post-American alliance."[24]

In sum, experts argue Europe has to take control of its own security and rely less on the US resources and leadership, and that will potentially have huge and important practical consequences for European security. How this change is manifested in the US NATO debate is the object of this book.

Analyzing the US NATO debate

To capture the content and logic of the US NATO debate, three general, but central, questions will be asked:

(1) Why do NATO exist (vision)?
(2) What should NATO do (mission)?
(3) How should NATO be led (guidance)?[25]

The answers of those questions from the actors in the US debate—what NATO should be, what NATO should do, and how NATO should be led—has always been decisive for NATO's development. A fruitful way of grasping the current US NATO discussion is therefore to analyze the debate with

---

[23] The term "transatlantic bargain" was coined in the 1960s by the US Ambassador Harlan Cleveland, and has been used frequently by scholars, analysts, and policy makers since then; perhaps most comprehensive, and systematically, by Stanley Sloan. See Stanley Sloan, *Permanent Alliance? NATO and the Transatlantic Bargain from Truman to Obama*, London and New York: Continuum, 2010, pp. xi, and 3.

[24] Hallams, "Between Hope and Realism," pp. x, and 5.

[25] In a recently published article Mark Webber, Ellen Hallams, and Martin A. Smith, for example, proposes quite similar questions when they analyze the present status of NATO. See "Repairing NATO's Motors," *International Affairs*, Vol. 90, No. 4 (2014), pp. 773–793.

those three questions as a point of departure, and to create an analytical instrument on the basis of them.[26]

Vision—military, political, or cultural tool?

Is NATO primarily described as a military, political, or cultural tool in the US debate, and what does that mean? As with the meta-theoretical concepts of realism, liberal-institutionalism, and liberal-constructivism,[27] it is almost impossible to draw distinct lines between what is military, political, and cultural, but that does not mean that the concepts cannot be useful analytical concepts when trying to establish where the main focus is in the debate.

The point of making a distinction—although it might be more like a border area than a border line—between NATO as a military, political, and cultural tool is that it can be argued that if NATO is described primarily as a cultural tool, that is, a tool for spreading "Western" culture such as democracy, in the US debate, the vision of NATO is more comprehensive, or maximalist, and arguably has more importance in US security policy, than if it is primarily seen as a military tool, a tool for generating military power.

Furthermore, a vision of NATO as a cultural tool is implying that NATO is seen as a military and political tool as well, because if NATO is seen as primarily a military tool, it can only have military functions, which is the least comprehensive, or minimalist, vision of NATO. A vision of NATO as a political tool is also implying that NATO is a military tool, but also that it is more than a military tool, that is, a tool for political bargaining, negotiations, and compromises, but not as comprehensive as a cultural tool.

---

[26] See, for example, Nader Chokr, "Prescription Vs Description in the Philosophy of Science, or Methodology Vs History: A Critical assessment," *Metaphilosophy*, Vol. 17, No. 4 (1986), pp. 289–299; Paul Bruthiaux, "Language Description, Language Prescription, and Language Planning," *Language Problems and Language Planning*, Vol. 16, No. 3 (1992), pp. 221–234; Madeline E. Heilman, "Description and Prescription: How Gender Stereotypes Prevent Women's Ascent Up the Organization Ladder," *Journal of Social Issues*, Vol. 57, No. 4 (2001), pp. 657–674.

[27] Theoretically, NATO as a military, political, and cultural tool can be anchored in realism, liberal-institutionalism, and liberal-constructivism. See Damon Coletta and Sten Rynning, "NATO from Kabul to Earth Orbit: Can the Alliance Cope?," *The Journal of Transatlantic Studies*, Vol. 10, No. 1 (2012), p. 27.

The analytical concepts of the US vision of NATO as a military, political, and cultural tool can therefore be illustrated as three concentric circles, or layers, in a globe (see Figure 1.1). The outer, most extensive, layer symbolizes NATO as a cultural tool (the maximalist view), the middle layer NATO as a political tool (the moderate view), and the core layer is NATO as a military tool (the minimalist view):[28]

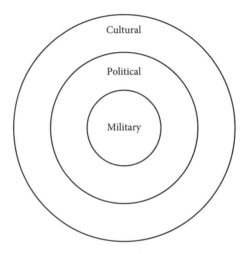

Figure 1.1 The vision of NATO as a military, political, and cultural tool

Although the borders between the layers should be seen as porous rather than concrete, it is possible to decide with some precision where the debate is located and, not less important, how it can move against the surface (centrifugal force) or against the core (centripetal force) over time. For example, during the Cold War, NATO was seen as a military and political tool from a US perspective, but not least as a cultural tool; a way of spreading Western culture in the struggle between communism and liberal democracy.[29]

---

[28] This way of thinking is highly inspired by Richard Betts article "Should Strategic Studies Survive?," *World Politics*, Vol. 50, No. 1 (1997), pp. 7–33. See especially p. 9.

[29] See, for example, John Lewis Gaddis, *Strategies of Containment: A Critical Appraisal of American National Security Policy During the Cold War*, Oxford: Oxford University Press, 2005; and Geir Lundestad, *United States and Western Europe Since 1945: From "Empire" by Invitation to Transatlantic Drift*, Oxford: Oxford University Press, 2005.

Professors Damon Coletta, US Air Force Academy, and Sten Rynning, University of Odense, argue that:

> NATO continues because the Atlantic union is meaningful to national leaders and not merely because power incites cooperation. NATO is significant because it embodies the meeting of Atlantic values and experiences on the one hand, and the framework for action in global politics on the other.[30]

The concept of Atlanticism—the idea of an American–European ["Western"] community founded on political, economic, and social culture—symbolizes, perhaps more than anything, the concept of NATO as a cultural tool.[31] As Szabo argues:

> The struggle with the Soviet Union was both geopolitical and ideological, and Atlanticism was born from this struggle. The United States rediscovered its European roots and overcame its aversion to being involved in the European balance of power during this period and came to regard itself as a European power for the first time in its history. While this reorientation of U.S. policy was based on a realistic assessment of national interest, *it also had a strong cultural component.*[32]

In the 1990s, the political and cultural dimension of NATO was strengthened even more, and the debate moved against the rim, or in a maximalist direction, when NATO became the principal US vehicle for democratization and security building in Europe through NATO enlargement. "The collapse of the Soviet Union in the early 1990s removed the constrains binding those in both the US and Europe who wished to not only protect democracy, but to expand it," Professor Michael Williams, University of London, writes.[33]

---

[30] Coletta and Rynning, "NATO from Kabul to Earth Orbit," p. 39.

[31] Regarding the concept of Atlanticism, see for example R. Judson Mitchell, "Atlanticism and Eurasianism in Reunified Germany," *Mediterranean Quarterly*, Vol. 9, No. 1 (1998), pp. 92–113; Viola Herms Drath, "Toward a New Atlanticism," *American Foreign Policy Interests*, Vol. 28, No. 6 (2006), pp. 425–431; Melby, "NATO and U.S. Global Security Interests," pp. 49–54.

[32] Stephen F. Szabo, "The Pacific Pivot and the West," Brussels Forum Paper Series, March 2012, http://www.gmfus.org (homepage), date accessed March 12, 2014, p. 2. My emphasis.

[33] Michael Williams, *The Good War: NATO and the Liberal Conscience in Afghanistan*, Basingstoke: Palgrave Macmillan, 2011, p. 49.

In fact there was such a large focus on NATO as a cultural tool that the United States "discovered," when NATO launched its first "sharp" military operations in Bosnia and Kosovo, that NATO had become a military tool of limited value.[34]

After 9/11 the US debate moved in the other direction, against the military core of NATO, when NATO more and more became a source for generating military power in the "Global War on Terror." From NATO, the United States could gather "coalitions of willing" for its military operations in Afghanistan and later Iraq.[35] Although NATO also was described as a political and cultural tool, it was seen first and foremost as a "force multiplier."

Mission—promoting interests, collective security, or values?

The mission for NATO can, in a similar way, be expressed as to promote US national interests (a minimalist view), collective security (a moderate view), and central "Western" values (a maximalist view), such as democracy, human rights, the rule of law, and free markets.[36]

"Historically," Melby argues, "NATO has not been an important instrument for the United States in handling direct threats to its national security."[37] During the Cold War, however, NATO's mission from a US perspective was to promote US interests and collective security for the members of the alliance, but not least to defend and promote

---

[34] Rebecca Moore, *NATO's New Mission: Projecting Stability in a Post-Cold War World*, Westport, CT: Praeger, 2007; and Gülnur Aybet and Rebecca Moore, "Missions in Search for a Vision," in *NATO: In Search for a Vision*, eds Gülnur Aybet and Rebecca Moore, Washington, DC: Georgetown University Press, 2010. For an overview of NATO's operations after the end of the Cold War, see *Pursuing Strategy: NATO Operations from the Gulf War to Gaddafi*, eds Håkan Edström and Dennis Gyllensporre, Houndmills: Palgrave Macmillan, 2012, especially Kersti Larsdotter's chapter "The Development of a NATO Strategy in Bosnia-Herzegovina;" Ellen Hallams *A Transatlantic Bargain for the 21st Century: The United States, Europe, and the Transatlantic Alliance*, Carlisle Barracks: US Army War College Press, 2013; Hallams, "Between Hope and Realism," pp. 217–238 and Carl C. Hodge "Full Circle: Two Decades of NATO Intervention," *Journal of Transatlantic Studies*, Vol. 11, No. 4 (2013), pp. 350–367.

[35] Ellen Hallams, *The United States and NATO Since 9/11: The Transatlantic Alliance Renewed*, London: Routledge, 2009; Thies, *Why NATO Endures*; Sloan, *Permanent Alliance?*; and John Allen Williams, "Moving Toward a New NATO?," in *National Strategic Forum Review*, Special Edition: Evaluation of the 2012 Chicago NATO Summit, pp. 12–15, http://nationalstrategy.com (homepage), date accessed October 1, 2012.

[36] Moore, *NATO's New Mission*; and Aybet and Moore, "Missions in Search for a Vision."

[37] Melby, "NATO and U.S. Global Security Interests," p. 37.

important values.[38] The preamble of the foundation of NATO, the North Atlantic Treaty itself, signed in Washington, DC, the April 4, 1949, is a good example:

> The Parties to this Treaty reaffirm their faith in the purposes and principles of the Charter of the United Nations and their desire to live in peace with all peoples and all governments. *They are determined to safeguard the freedom, common heritage and civilisation of their peoples, founded on the principles of democracy, individual liberty and the rule of law.* They seek to promote stability and well-being in the North Atlantic area. They are resolved to unite their efforts for collective defence and for the preservation of peace and security.[39]

In the preamble, the ambition to create stability and peace through collective security is also present, with its explicit connection to the UN Charter signed in San Francisco just four years earlier.[40]

After the end of the Cold War, NATO initially became a very important institution for reaching out to—and integrate—its former enemies in Central and Eastern Europe, and it adopted, as professors Gülnur Aybet and Rebecca Moore express it, a "collective security role," with its peace operations in the former Yugoslavia.[41] After 9/11 and the intervention in Afghanistan it became more and more operations-driven (or mission-driven, as they call it). NATO's mission from a US perspective was to promote US interests through military and political support in the "Global War on Terrorism," and the United States both declared and showed that if NATO could not do that, it would not be very relevant.[42] It could actually be argued that the famous expression "out of area or out of business," coined by US Senator Richard Lugar (R, Indiana) in 1993,[43] actually became more relevant after 9/11 than in the 1990s.

---

[38] Aybet and Moore, "Missions in Search for a Vision."

[39] NATO, *The North Atlantic Treaty*, Washington, DC, April 4, 1949, http://www.nato.int (homepage), date accessed April 22, 2014. My emphasis.

[40] Lawrence S. Kaplan, *NATO and the UN: A Peculiar Relationship*, Columbia, MO: University of Missouri Press, 2010.

[41] Aybet and Moore, "Missions in Search for a Vision," quote from p. 1. See also Karl-Heinz Kamp and Kurt Volker, "Toward a New Transatlantic Bargain," *Carnegie Policy Outlook*, February 1, 2012, http://carnegieendowment.org (homepage), date accessed January 10, 2014.

[42] Hallams, *The United States and NATO Since 9/11.*

[43] Lugar quoted in Jennifer Medcalf, *Going Global or Going Nowhere: NATO's Role in Contemporary International Security*, Bern: Peter Lang, 2008, p. 67.

Anyway, the point is that, from a US perspective, the maximalist view of NATO is that is should promote universal values, and the minimalist view is that it should promote US national interests. If NATO's missions are only—or mainly—to be US centered, its wider importance in US security policy can be interpreted as low, which is visualized in Figure 1.2. The outer, most extensive, layer symbolizes that NATO should promote universal values, the middle layer—the moderate view—that NATO should promote collective security, and the core layer that NATO should promote US national interests.

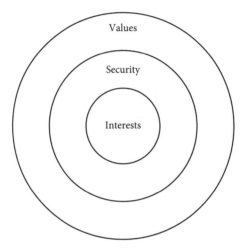

Figure 1.2 NATO's missions as serving interests, collective security, and values

It can be argued that the borders between the layers is even more porous regarding NATO's mission, but even here it is possible to, with some precision, pinpoint where the debate is located and how it changes over time.

Guidance—rational, traditional, or charismatic leadership?

The guidance of NATO, how NATO should be led by the United States, can be expressed with some help of the famous sociologist Max Weber's three forms of legitimate authority: rational, traditional, and/or charismatic authority in different combinations. The concept of legitimacy is useful, and widely used in social science, and may, as Bruce Gilley puts it, "be the most important factor determining outcomes, from democratic stability to international cooperation."[44]

Weber argued that there were three "pure" types of bases for legitimate authority. Rational (or legal) legitimate authority rests on a set of constitutional norms and rules, and the leader/ruler got the authority from these norms and rules. Bureaucratic leadership is a typical example of rational legitimate authority, according to Weber. Traditional (or authoritarian) legitimate authority rests on traditionally sanctioned authority, and the leader/ruler got the authority from custom. Patriarchal or monarchial leadership was a typical example of traditional legitimate authority, according to Weber.[45]

Charismatic (or cultural/ideological/religious) legitimate authority, lastly, rests on "devotion to the exceptional sanctity, heroism or exemplary character of an individual person," and the leader/ruler got the authority from being seen as such an extraordinary person. Cultural, ideological, and religious leadership connected to such an exceptional individual was a typical example of charismatic legitimate authority.[46]

According to Weber, charismatic legitimate authority is the most powerful form of authority, since it is able to transform people's worldviews. But it is also, as Assistant Professor Joshua Derman writes, the most fragile legitimate authority: "If a charismatic individual could no longer demonstrate that he or she possessed special powers, the individual's authority would disappear; thus charismatic rulership required constant demonstrations of wondrous deeds."[47]

It can be argued that the United States through NATO's history has led the alliance in a charismatic way. Hallams argues that there has been a "culture within the alliance of US dominance and European dependency on US leadership and capabilities."[48] During the Cold War, she writes,

> ...the United States consistently spent more on defense than did its European allies, but the U.S. commitment was rewarded with a dominant

---

[44] Bruce Gilley, *The Right to Rule: How States Win and Loose Legitimacy*, New York: Columbia University Press, 2009, p. xii.

[45] Joshua Derman, "Max Weber and Charisma: A Transatlantic Affair," in *New German Critique*, Vol. 38, No. 2 (2011), pp. 55–56; Max Weber, *The Theory of Social and Economic Organization*, New York: The Free Press, 1947, pp. 324–329.

[46] Weber quoted in Derman, "Max Weber and Charisma," p. 56.

[47] Ibid., p. 58.

[48] Hallams, "Between Hope and Realism," p. 224.

leadership role within the Alliance, typified by its occupation of the position of Supreme Allied Commander Europe (SACEUR). The bargain thus gave something to both sides: Europe was provided with a U.S. security guarantee, while the United States established a position of authority and dominance in an alliance that could serve as vehicle for advancing U.S. interests in Europe.[49]

To say that the United States has led NATO in a charismatic way is not to say that the United States has led NATO in an undemocratic way. It is simply that the US leadership within the alliance has been so self-evident and that it has rested exceptional sanctity. Since the Libya war, however, it can be argued that the United States has been leading NATO in a "rational" way (in terms of Weber's concept of authority), and that the United States has wanted the European allies to take a greater responsibility for the leadership of the alliance. This could be interpreted as a minimalist view of US guidance.

The main point is thus that the most extensive view of US NATO guidance is a charismatic US leadership, the moderate view is a traditional guidance, and the least extensive view is a rational US guidance. If NATO is supposed to be guided only—or mainly—in a rational way, its wider importance in US security policy can be interpreted as low. This can be visualized in the following Figure 1.3:

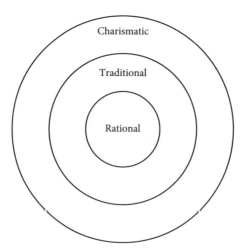

Figure 1.3 The forms of NATO guidance as rational, traditional, and charismatic

[49] Hallams, *A Transatlantic Bargain for the 21ˢᵗ Century*, p. 3.

To summarize:

- A maximalist US view of NATO is when the US views NATO as a cultural tool (vision), when the United States wants NATO to promote "Western" values (mission), and when the United States leads NATO in a charismatic way (guidance).
- A minimalist US view of NATO is when the US views NATO as a military tool (vision), when the United States wants NATO to promote US interests (mission), and when the United States leads NATO in a rational way (guidance).
- A moderate US view of NATO could be *either* when the United States views NATO as a political tool (vision), when the United States wants it to promote collective security (mission), and when the United States wants to lead NATO in a traditional way (guidance)—*or* some sort of combination of a maximalist and minimalist vision, mission, and guidance.

This can be illustrated in the following Table 1.1:

Table 1.1 NATO's level of importance in US security policy

Importance/Issue	Vision	Mission	Guidance
High (maximalist)	Cultural	Values	Charismatic
Moderate	Political	Security	Traditional
Low (minimalist)	Military	Interests	Rational

The analytical instrument created in this sub-chapter—built on the US vision of NATO (Why do NATO exist?), the US view of NATO's mission (What should NATO do?), and the view of how NATO should be guided (How should NATO be led?)—will be used in the empirical chapters of this book to "measure" NATO's importance in US security policy as it is expressed in the US NATO debate.

The actors in the US NATO debate

The actors in the US NATO debate can be identified in several ways. It can be argued that there are three important arenas for the US NATO discussion, as well as discussion on US grand strategy in general: the political debate (Congress and the administration), the policy debate (think tanks and elite media), and the scholarly debate (academic books and journals).[50]

All three arenas overlap, interact with, and influence the others, the policy debate perhaps more than the other two since there are a constant flow of people between think tanks and academia on the one hand, and think tanks and politics on the other. However, the political debate, especially the discussion within the administration, is the most important one, since it represents the actual US security policy, and has the largest impact on US grand strategy.

The NATO discussion within the administration, President Obama's first and second administration, is covered by official speeches and other statements of President Obama, Vice President Joe Biden, Secretaries of State—Hillary Clinton and John Kerry—and Secretaries of Defense—Robert Gates, Leon Panetta, and Chuck Hagel. Those actors' statements and speeches have been analyzed systematically. In addition, statements by representatives of the administration, such as national security advisors, and under secretaries of state and defense, have been analyzed when they have appeared, for example, in hearings in Congress, in elite media, and in other contexts.

The debate in US Congress, the House of Representatives, and the Senate, the elected representatives of the US citizens, is also a part of the political debate. Research has shown that Congress has been an important actor in the "transatlantic bargain," and that it has been a dynamic actor over time. "From the beginning," Stanley Sloan argues, "the powerful American legislative body has played a major role in shaping, as well as critiquing, the deal ... As a result, the bargain is by no means static."[51] Congress also balances the administration in several ways, most important by budget and different types of control mechanisms (such as hearings).

The records of the debate in the House of Representatives and in the Senate—including hearings from both chamber's armed services and foreign

---

[50] Yehudith Auerbach and Yaeli Bloch-Elkon, "Media Framing and Foreign Policy: The Elite Press vis-à-vis US Policy in Bosnia, 1992–95," *Journal of Peace Research*, Vol. 42, No. 1 (2005), pp. 83–99; Stephen F. Larrabee, "The United States and Security in the Black Sea Region," *Southeast European and Black Sea Studies*, Vol. 9, No. 3 (2009), pp. 301–315.

[51] Sloan, *Permanent Alliance?*, p. xi.

committees—have been used to cover the debate, and to some degree the discussion about NATO within the administration (the hearings).[52]

The policy debate about NATO in the United States is in this book understood as the discussion about NATO in the think tank and elite media environment. Think tanks play an important role in US politics, not only in the security and defense sector. There are around 1,500 think tanks in the United States, and around 500 of them are based in Washington, DC. They often play the role of insiders and become an integral part of the political process. The biggest think tanks have enormous resources. For example, in 2003, the RAND Corporation received over $200 million, the Carter Center over $80 million, and the Urban Institute over $75 million.[53]

During the first years after the Cold War, US think tanks were quite influential regarding the formulation of US NATO policy. Ronald D. Asmus, back then based at RAND Corporation in Santa Monica, California, was a witness to that. Along with National Defense University (NDU) and the Atlantic Council (ACUS) in Washington, DC, RAND were, he argues, brought into "normally closed interagency deliberations" and "assisting policy-makers in understanding the issues, options, and tradeoffs": "As a result, a number of think tanks became, for a period of time, an informal but nonetheless real part of an extended inter-agency process and debate within the U.S. government on NATO's future."[54]

Furthermore, there are a continuous flow of people between think tanks and government in the United States, probably more than in any other country in the world. And it is not only on low and middle level positions that people get in and out. In February 2009, James L. Jones, then chairman of ACUS, stepped down in order to serve as President Obama's National Security Advisor. Another Council Member, Susan Rice, left to serve as the

---

[52] The committees hearing's analyzed are the House of Representative's Committee of Armed Services (HCAR), and the Committee of Foreign Affairs (HCFA), and the Senate's Committee of Armed Services (SCAS), and the Committee on Foreign Relations (SCFR). Around 100 hearings from the 112th and the 113th Congress have been analyzed, and in the Congress Records, NATO has been mentioned at least once in around 1,000 occasions.

[53] James G. McGann, *Think Tanks and Policy Advice in the US*, Philadelphia: Foreign Policy Research Institute, 2005.

[54] Ronald D. Asmus, "Having an Impact: Think Tanks and the NATO Enlargement-Debate," *The Quarterly Journal*, Vol. 2, No. 1 (2003), pp. 92–93.

administration's ambassador to the UN, and later also as Obama's National Security Advisor, and, in 2013, the new chairman of ACUS after Jones, Senator Chuck Hagel, stepped down to serve as US Secretary of Defense.

For methodological reasons, the constant flow of actors between think tanks and politics (and to some degree the elite media) makes it important to be observant. Actors, who previously have been a part of government, can be tempted to defend their former positions and actions, and vice versa. They can also be tempted to argue, quite uncritically, for their current employer.

A handful of think tanks in Washington, DC, is permanently focusing on—and in many ways promoting—transatlantic relations. ACUS is one of them, founded in 1961. It is one of the most influential think tanks regarding transatlantic issues in the world. Many of its experts have been or are in central positions in government.

A second think tank, permanently focusing on NATO issues, is the Center for Strategic and International Studies (CSIS), founded in 1962, and counted as one of the most influential think tanks in the world. The CSIS is, however, not only working with transatlantic relations. It has a global focus and deals with other issues than security as well, such as global health, technology, and trade.

A third influential Washington think tank regarding transatlantic relations is the Center for Transatlantic Relations (CTR), a center within the Paul H. Nitze School of Advanced International Studies (SAIS), at Johns Hopkins University.

Finally, the German Marshall Fund of the United States (GMF) shall be mentioned. It was founded in Washington, DC, by a German donation in 1972. GMF is dedicated to the promotion of greater understanding and common action between Europe and the US in a broad sense. It is one of the most influential independent American public policy and grant making institutions regarding transatlantic studies.[55]

With this in mind it is perhaps trivial to argue that this constant flow of people strengthens the impact of the think tanks in US politics, and makes

---

[55] Nicols Siegel, *The German Marshall Fund of the United States: A Brief History*, Washington, DC: GMF, 2012.

the think tanks important to study when trying to capture the US NATO debate. In a great, and too seldom mentioned, study, Kristina Klinkforth at the *Osteuropa-Institut der Freien Universität Berlin* has analyzed the United States think tank debate on NATO between 9/11 and 2004, dividing the think tanks into four political camps: libertarian, neo-conservative, conservative, and liberal. The focus of Klinkforth's study was the arguments of the think tank actors concerning NATO's role in US grand strategy, especially regarding burden-sharing and NATO enlargement: how the arguments were presented, what the line of the arguments were, and which strategies that were proposed.[56]

The result of Klinkforth's study was that neoconservatives, conservatives, and liberals—in contrast to libertarians—advocated the importance of the United States staying in Europe. However, she argues, the United States would probably "continue to make use of NATO selectively" and be cautious to use NATO as a multilateral institution: "U.S. policymakers and analysts mostly are not principled multilateralists, but instrumental multilateralists who see multilateralism in terms of a cost-benefit analysis rather than a primary principle guiding the conduct of policy."[57] Hallams subscribes to that, when she writes that "Obama views NATO's value to the US in typically functionalist, instrumental terms, as a "force multiplier" and a mechanism for advancing US interests."[58]

Klinkforth's predictions about the development of US NATO policy have been quite accurate, and that is also an important reason why the think tanks are one of the main parts of the policy arena for the US NATO debate in this book. The other main part is elite media.

The elite media—such as the *New York Times*, the *Wall Street Journal*, and the *Washington Post*—are contributing to shape elite opinion, and through it foreign and security policy. Matthew A. Baum, Harvard University, and Philip B. K. Potter, University of California (LA),

---

[56] Kristina Klinkforth, *NATO in US Policymaking and Debate—An Analysis: "Drawing the Map" of the US Think Tank Debate on NATO Since 9/11*, Berlin: Osteuropa-Institut der Freien Universität Berlin, 2006.

[57] Klinkforth, *NATO in US Policymaking and Debate*, pp. 71–72.

[58] Hallams, "Between Hope and Realism," p. 225.

argue that elite media "influences the thinking of leaders about foreign policy," and that decision makers "rely on these sources for factual information as well as informed opinion." Furthermore, they point at the fact that there are also a constant flow of people between elite media and government. This "cross-fertilization" is not as extensive and frequent as it is between think tanks and government, but it exists and is also impacting politics.[59]

In this book the *New York Times* and the *Washington Post* have been systematically studied, especially the articles from their editorial boards and columnists. In roughly 1,000 articles per year and per newspaper, NATO has been mentioned at least once. It can be argued that those newspapers, in particular their editorials, are representative for US elite media, not least since the *New York Times* is liberal ("democrat"), and the *Washington Post* conservative ("republican"). Since these papers have a quite international focus, they are, however, not representative for US media. US media in general have a domestic focus, and do not discuss US NATO policy systematically.

One should also bear in mind that the elite media, just as the actors at the political level, operate with shorter time lines than think tanks. They often have to publish, for example, editorials the same day or the day after something has happened. The think tank reports, policy briefs, etc., that this study is building on, are normally published days, weeks, or even months after something has happened, which gives the think tank actors more time to reflect upon, and analyze, the events more thoroughly. The think tank sources are therefore more similar to books and articles in the academic debate in some ways, but on the other hand they are almost always prescriptive in the same way as editorials and columns in the elite media.

The scholarly debate, lastly, is probably the most useful debate to analyze, when it comes to discovering analytical perspectives, complexity, and longer trends in US security policy. The problem with the scholarly debate is, however, that it is slowly developed, and since this book covers the US

---

[59] Matthew Baum and Philip B. K. Potter, "The Relationship Between Mass Media, Public Opinion, and Foreign Policy: Toward a Theoretical Synthesis," *Annual Review of Political Science*, Vol. 11 (2008), p. 53.

NATO debate since 2011, the scholarly debate on NATO after Libya is yet too premature to motivate its own sub-chapter. Instead, the scholarly debate will be woven into the text on the political debate and the policy debate to create context.

To summarize:

- The actors in the US NATO debate are members of Congress and the administration. They constitute the political debate arena. Representatives of think tanks and elite media are also actors in the US NATO debate. They constitute the policy debate arena.
- The sources of the political debate are mainly records and hearings from Congress, and speeches from the central actors in the administration. The sources of the policy debate are mainly reports, briefs, columns, and other written material from US think tank actors, and from the *New York Times* and the *Washington Post*.

The political and policy arenas of the US NATO debate, and the issues debated (vision, mission, and guidance), can thus be illustrated in Table 1.2:

Table 1.2 The US NATO debate

Issue/Arena	The Political Debate (Congress and the administration)	The Policy Debate (think tanks and elite media)
Vision	Military/political/cultural	Military/political/cultural
Mission	Interests/security/values	Interests/security/values
Guidance	Rational/authoritarian/ charismatic	Rational/authoritarian/ charismatic

Taken together, the political and policy debate, from the Libya War to the Ukraine Crisis, constitutes the empirical base of the book and represents the US NATO debate. The result of the analysis will be the answer to the main question proposed in the book: How is the importance of NATO in US long-term security policy manifested in the US NATO debate?

Limitations and the structure of the book

It is fair to say that there does not exist a permanent NATO debate in the United States (except for in the think tank world). For example, Secretary Panetta did not mention NATO once in his two last speeches in Washington, DC, in February 2013,[60] and when Secretary Clinton left office a month earlier, in January 2013, she made five interviews with the largest US broadcasting companies (ABC, NBC, NPR, FoxNews, and CNN) plus a "townterview" in Washington, DC, where she answered questions from people worldwide. NATO was mentioned only once.[61]

Rather, the US NATO debate is animated by events such as 9/11, its Summits, the Libya War, the Syria Conflict, and the Ukraine Crisis.[62] Through such events the US NATO debate can be captured and analyzed, and they will therefore create the main structure of the book. But since the debate about NATO in US security policy is not permanent, it is important to note that the debate that constitutes the empirical base of the book is not representative for the greater debate on the wider trends and tendencies in US security policy. Since the United States is a global actor with a global grand strategy and security policy, the NATO debate is just a part of that debate.[63]

Furthermore, the research design used in this book has two other important limitations that regard representativity: one internal and one

---

[60] Leon E. Panetta, "Farewell Ceremony," Speech February 8, 2013, http://www.defense.gov (homepage), date accessed February 11, 2013; Leon E. Panetta, "Pentagon Community Farewell Event," Speech February 12, 2013, http://www.defense.gov (homepage), date accessed February 11, 2013.

[61] ABC, "Interview with Cynthia McFadden of ABC," January 29, 2013, www.state.gov (homepage), date accessed January 29, 2013; NBC, "Interview with Andrea Mitchell of NBC," January 29, 2013, www.state.gov (homepage), date accessed January 29, 2013; NPR, "Interview with Michele Kelemen of NPR," January 29, 2013, www.state.gov (homepage), date accessed January 29, 2013; CNN, "Interview with Elise Labbot and Jill Dougherty of CNN," January 29, 2013, www.state.gov (homepage), date accessed January 29, 2013; FoxNews, "Interview with Greta Van Susteren of Fox News," January 29, 2013, www.state.gov (homepage), date accessed January 29, 2013; Hillary R. Clinton, "Secretary Clinton Holds a Global Townterview," January 29, 2013, www.state.gov (homepage), date accessed January 29, 2013.

[62] Research by Ellen Hallams demonstrates that point. See Hallams, *The United States and NATO Since 9/11*; Hallams and Schreer, "Towards a 'Post-American' alliance?," pp. 313–327; Hallams, *A Transatlantic Bargain for the 21ˢᵗ Century*; and Hallams, "Between Hope and Realism," pp. 217–238.

[63] The wider US debate on US security policy and grand strategy can be found in, for example, Barry Posen, *Restraint: A New Foundation for U.S. Grand Strategy*, New York: Cornell University Press, 2014.

external. The internal limitation is that the book does not cover the US NATO debate within the Obama administration, that is, different views between and within the White House, Pentagon, and State Department. In former Secretary of Defense Robert Gates's memoirs, for example, it was revealed that there was a division in the administration about the intervention in Libya in 2011; Secretary Gates was against and Secretary Clinton was for an intervention.[64] That means that statements made by individual actors, such as Gates, defending the policy of the administration, is not necessarily representative for him as a person. They are, however, representative for the administration.

The external limitation of representativity is perhaps more important to note, since it has to do with the potential difference between declaratory policy and operational policy. In security and strategic studies it has been shown that to get a comprehensive picture of a state's security policy or strategy, it is important to concentrate on both what policy makers say (declaratory policy), and what they actually do (operational policy). It has also been shown that there could be important differences between declaratory and operational policy.[65]

Since this book is a study on the US NATO debate, it is built solely on declaratory policy, which means that it is representative for the US NATO debate, but not necessarily representative for US NATO policy as a whole. What the actors in the Obama administration or in Congress say about the importance of NATO does not necessarily reflect what they do in terms of priorities, funding, etc., in relation to NATO; saying that NATO is very important in US security policy does not necessarily mean that it actually is very important in US security policy. This limitation will be considered and further discussed in the empirical chapters and in the concluding chapter.

---

[64] Robert Gates, *Duty: Memoirs of a Secretary at War*, London: WH Allen, 2014.

[65] See, for example, Paul H. Nitze, "Atoms, Strategy and Policy," *Foreign Affairs*, Vol. 34, No. 2 (January, 1956), pp. 187–198; David Alan Rosenberg, "The Origins of Overkill: Nuclear Weapons and American Strategy, 1945–1960," *International Security*, Vol. 7, No. 4 (Spring, 1983), pp. 3–71; David Alan Rosenberg, "Reality and Responsibility: Power and Process in the Making of United States Nuclear Strategy, 1945–68," *The Journal of Strategic Studies*, Vol. 9, No. 1 (1986), pp. 35–52; and Mats Berdal, *The United States, Norway and the Cold War, 1954–60*, Basingstoke: Macmillan, 1997.

In the next chapter, Chapter 2, the Libya War will be the main focus. When NATO is discussed in other contexts, such as in the budget hearings in Congress, in speeches by the central actors of the administration, or in different types of sources generated by the think tanks and elite media, the debate will also be analyzed. In Chapter 3, NATO's Chicago Summit and the Syria Conflict will be the main events that generate debate about NATO, and in Chapter 4 the Ukraine Crisis and NATO's Wales Summit will play the main role. It is important to acknowledge that the book is not about the events as such. It is not a historiography of the Libya War, the Syria Conflict, and the Ukraine Crisis. It is about the US NATO debate. The events create debate, but it is the debate, not the events, that is the focus of the book.

2

2011: The Libya War

NATO's Libya War dominated the US NATO debate during 2011. In the literature, the war has been described as a watershed. "The operation in Libya represented a real breakthrough from a transatlantic perspective, as it can be considered the first Western large-scale coercive military engagement not led by the United States," writes Phillippe Gros, Research Fellow at the *Foundation pour la Rechereche Strategique*, Paris, France.[1]

Before going in to the Libya War, it is, however, proper to say a few words about NATO's status before the War started. At that time, the alliance had just, at the Lisbon Summit in the end of November, 2010, agreed on a new strategic concept, "Active Engagement, Modern Defence," which has, together with the "Deterrence and Defence Posture Review" (DDPR), been a point of departure for the US NATO debate during the whole period 2011–2014. The reason is that the Strategic Concept can be seen as NATO's most important steering document (except for the North Atlantic Treaty itself), since it prescribes what NATO should be and do.[2]

NATO has developed three such concepts since the end of the Cold War: the 1991 concept, the 1999 concept, and the 2010 concept. According to Aybet at the University of Kent, UK, the first concept reflected "the extension of the Western security community's liberal norms to the post-communist

---

[1] Philippe Gros, "Libya and Mali Operations," GMF Foreign Policy Paper, July 2014, www.gmfus.org (homepage), date accessed August 2, 2014, p. 2.
[2] A description and critical analysis of the strategic concept is provided by Steve Marsh and Alan Dobson in "Fine Words, Few Answers: NATO's 'Not So New' New Strategic Concept," in *NATO Beyond 9/11: The Transformation of the Atlantic Alliance*, eds Ellen Hallams, Luca Ratti and Benjamin Zyla, Basingstoke: Palgrave Macmillan, 2013, pp. 155–177. An overview of NATO's DDFP can be found in Simon Lunn and Ian Kearns, "NATO's Deterrence and Defence Posture Review: A Status Report," European Leadership Network, NATO Policy Brief, February, 2012, www.europeanleadershipnetwork.org (homepage), date accessed August 3, 2014.

space in Central and Eastern Europe" and the second "the Western security community's leadership in championing an international system of collective security".[3]

NATO's 2010 Strategic Concept could be seen as a further step toward a global NATO with its three core tasks: collective defense, crisis management, and cooperative security. Jens Ringsmose and Sten Rynning, both at the University of Southern Denmark, Odense, have argued that it signalizes "a collective intention to push NATO further in the direction of global engagement."[4]

However, it should be underscored that all three concepts also attach great importance to homeland defense—at least on paper.[5] In the 1991 concept it was clearly stated that "[a]ny armed attack on the territory of the Allies, from whatever direction, would be covered by Articles 5 and 6 of the Washington Treaty," and that "[t]he primary role of Alliance military forces, to guarantee the security and territorial integrity of member states, remains unchanged."[6]

In the 1999 concept it was, in a similar way, stated that a "fundamental" security task is to "deter and defend against any threat of aggression against any NATO member state as provided for in Articles 5 and 6 of the Washington Treaty," that "[a]ny armed attack on the territory of the Allies, from whatever direction, would be covered by Articles 5 and 6 of the Washington Treaty," and that:

> [t]he primary role of Alliance military forces is to protect peace and to guarantee the territorial integrity, political independence and security of member states. The Alliance's forces must therefore be able to deter and

---

[3] Gülnur Aybet, "The NATO Strategy Concept Revisited: Grand Strategy and Emerging Issues," in *NATO: In Search for a Vision*, eds Gülnur Aybet and Rebecca Moore, Washington, DC: Georgetown University Press, 2010, p. 35.

[4] Jens Ringsmose and Sten Rynning, "Introduction. Taking Stock of NATO's New Strategic Concept," in *NATO's New Strategic Concept: A Comprehensive Assessment*, eds. Jens Ringsmose and Sten Rynning, Copenhagen: DIIS, 2011, p. 7.

[5] Magnus Petersson, "The Forgotten Dimension? NATO and the Security of the Member States," in *Pursuing Strategy: NATO Operations from the Gulf War to Gaddafi*, eds Håkan Edström and Dennis Gyllensporre, Basingstoke: Palgrave Macmillan, 2012.

[6] NATO, *The Alliance's New Strategic Concept*, NATO: Brussels, 1991, #12, and #40.

defend effectively, to maintain or restore the territorial integrity of Allied nations and—in case of conflict—to terminate war rapidly by making an aggressor reconsider his decision, cease his attack and withdraw.[7]

In the 2010 concept, finally, it was stated that "[t]he primary role of Alliance military forces is to protect peace and to guarantee the territorial integrity, political independence and security of member states," and that "[t]he greatest responsibility of the Alliance is to protect and defend our territory and our populations against attack, as set out in Article 5 of the Washington Treaty."[8]

Most of the US NATO debate during 2011 was, however, connected to the Libya War, a civil war between opponents to the Libyan dictator Muammar Gaddafi and his regime. The civil war escalated in February 2011, and on March 17, the United Nations Security Council passed Resolution 1973 (UNSCR 1973) that authorized UN member states to establish a no-fly zone over Libya to protect the civil population against Gaddafi's military forces. Two days later, on March 19, 2011, British, French, and US forces started to implement the resolution (*Operation Odyssey Dawn*), and from March 23, NATO gradually took command over the operation, named *Operation Unified Protector*. After six months of heavy NATO bombardment, a transitional government was recognized by the UN in September 2011. Gaddafi was eventually captured and killed on October 20, 2011, and NATO ended the operation on October 31, 2011.[9]

The Libya War caused a comprehensive discussion in the United States about both external and internal aspects of US security policy. The debate on the external aspects was a lot about the burden sharing in NATO between the United States and Europe, and especially who should take the lead in such an operation. The United States wanted NATO's European member states to take the lead, and the European NATO members and NATO's partners to do the job in their own region.

---

[7] NATO, *The Alliance's Strategic Concept*, NATO: Brussels, 1999, #10, #24, and #47.

[8] NATO, *Active Engagement, Modern Defence*, NATO: Brussels, 2010, #4, and #16.

[9] For an overview of the Libya War, see Kjell Engelbrekt, Marcus Mohlin, and Charlotte Wagnsson (eds.), *The NATO Intervention in Libya: Lessons Learned from the Campaign*, London: Routledge, 2013; and Jeffrey H. Michaels, "A Model Intervention? Reflections on NATO's Libya 'Success'," in *NATO Beyond 9/11*, pp. 198–214.

The internal US debate was to a large extent a constitutional debate, a debate about the power relations between Congress and the president. The War Powers Resolution of 1973—a federal law that forbids the president of using military force for more than sixty days without the consent of Congress—was widely discussed in connection to the Libya War, and NATO became, at times, a parameter in the discussion.

This chapter will focus on the external aspects of the debate, the burden sharing discussion, but it will also touch upon the internal aspects of the debate, when NATO is dragged into the discussion.

In Congress, the discussion about the vision of NATO was moderate to high (maximalist). NATO's role was described as a military, political, and cultural tool, and the emphasis was on NATO as a political and cultural organization rather than a military one. The same pattern can be found regarding NATO's mission. It was sometimes described as serving solely US interests, especially by republicans, but more often as serving collective security and promoting values. Regarding how NATO should be led, the debate was more polarized: either should NATO be led in a rational—minimalist—way, or it should be led in a charismatic—maximalist—way, argued the actors in Congress.

In the Obama administration, NATO was generally described in a moderate way, as a military and political tool, but seldom as a cultural one. Furthermore, NATO was supposed to promote collective security and to some degree values, but seldom pure US interests. The administration also made it clear, time and time again, that NATO was supposed to be guided in a rational way. The administration clearly differed from Congress in its view on NATO; its views were minimalist to moderate, rather than moderate to maximalist.

In the think tank and elite media environment, lastly, the debate was similar to the debate in Congress, but clearly more moderate than maximalist regarding the vision and mission of NATO. Most similar to the discussion in Congress was the think tank and media actors' arguments on how NATO should be led: either rational or charismatic, that is, a more polarized view of how NATO should be guided.

Taken together, the political debate and the policy debate indicate a moderate US view of NATO's importance in US long-term security policy, with the administration as more moderate than Congress and the policy debate arena. The alliance was on the whole not described in maximalist terms, which indicates its more limited role in US security policy compared to during the Cold War.

In the following sections, the importance of NATO in US long-term security policy as manifested in the US political and policy debate will be demonstrated in detail.

The political debate in Congress

In Congress, several members expressed skepticism to the Libya War, and saw it as a European issue to solve. Some of them did not even consider the United States as a NATO member. In a debate over the War in the House of Representatives June 21, 2011, Congressman Ted Poe (R, Texas), for example, argued that the Libya War was a war that was "sponsored by NATO." It is said, he continued, that the United States had to help NATO out: "Well, if NATO wants to continue this war, let them."[10]

More common, however, on the more "skeptical" side, was to picture the war in terms of unfair burden sharing between the United States and its European partners. In a hearing in the House of Representatives October 31, 2011, Mike Coffman (R, Colorado) also generalized the problem when he argued that:

> I think only 4 of our 28 NATO allies are spending the required 2 percent required under the NATO charter. In South Korea, they are spending 2.7 percent of their gross domestic product on defense. I believe we are at north of 3.6 percent. It seems like we care more about defending the South Koreans and the Europeans than the Europeans and the South Koreans. So I think that we need to strike a balance in that.[11]

---

[10] Congressional Record, House of Representatives (CRHR), June 21, 2011, "The Way It Is on American Involvement in Libya," p. H4354.

[11] US Congress, House of Representatives, Armed Services Committee (HASC), *The Future of National Defense and the United States Military Ten Years After 9/11: Perspectives of Secretary of Defense Leon Panetta and Chairman of the Joint Chiefs of Staff General Martin Dempsey*, October 13, 2011, No. 112–76, Washington, DC: USGPO, 2011, p. 47.

Since the Riga Summit in 2006, NATO has had a "two per cent guideline" for its member's defense spending.[12] Only a few of the members, however, meet that guideline—among them the United States—which is why the topic comes up in the US NATO debate from time to time, especially when burden sharing issues are discussed.

But overall, the NATO debate in Congress during 2011 indicates that NATO was viewed as something more than just a military alliance, that its existence was also politically and culturally motivated, and that it should be more than a military organization.

More specific, *the vision of NATO*, what NATO should be, was debated several times in Congress: before, during, and after the Libya War. In a budget hearing in the Senate on March 29, 2011, after the intervention in the Libya War, and when the United States had turned over the operation to NATO, Senator Joe Lieberman (I, Connecticut) was happy for the development. It was, according to Lieberman, "very important" to understand what NATO was:

> I'm glad NATO's involved, of course, because what's happening in Libya is not just a concern for America or a threat to America, it's a concern to most of the rest of the civilized world.[13]

In a hearing on May 18, 2011, about the administration's priorities for Europe, Senator Jeanne Shaheen (D, New Hampshire) argued in a similar way. It would be wrong, she said, "to underestimate the transatlantic influence in the international community:"

> NATO still represents the most successful, most capable military alliance in the history of the world. Europe and the United States still make up more than 54 percent of world GDP and over 90 percent of global foreign exchange holdings. And, as the most open, transparent, and democratic societies in the world today, the United States and Europe still represent a model for citizens everywhere who support the rule of law and want their voices heard and their legitimate needs met.[14]

---

[12] See, for example, Anders Fogh Rasmussen, *The Secretary General's Annual Report 2012*, Brussels: NATO, 2013, p. 11.

[13] SASC, *Department of Defense Authorization for Appropriations for Fiscal Year 2012 and the Future Years Defense Program*, Washington, DC: USGPO, 2011, p. 604.

[14] US Congress, Senate, Foreign Relations Committee (SFRC), *Administration Priorities for Europe in the 112th Congress*, May 18, 2011, No. 112–84, Washington, DC: USGPO, 2011, p. 4.

Such statements indicate that NATO is seen as something more than a military alliance, that the character of the alliance was viewed as political, and even cultural. And Shaheen went on reinforcing that impression when she said that the former Warsaw Pact countries and Soviet Republics, thanks to NATO, had made "impressive and rapid transitions to democratic rule since they first shed the authoritarian control of the former Soviet Union," and that this could be a good example in handling the ongoing upheavals in the Middle East and North Africa:[15]

The idea that the experiences of successful transition in Central and Eastern Europe, thanks to NATO, could be applicable also in Africa and the Middle East has been relatively common in the US NATO debate, as well as in Europe. In fact, it can be argued that NATO's whole partnership policy is designed to accomplish democratic reforms in totalitarian or authoritarian countries, and both the Mediterranean Dialogue (MD), initiated in 1994, and the Istanbul Cooperation Initiative (ICI), launched at NATO's Istanbul Summit in 2004, where specifically directed to those countries.[16]

Also Republican members of Congress argued along the same lines. In a remark in the House of Representatives regarding deployment of US forces in Libya June 3, 2011, Congressman Joseph J. Heck (R, Nevada) argued that "[t]he safety and security of our nation depends greatly on the cooperation and commitments of our allies," and that "[t]he NATO alliance is the centerpiece of our efforts to support and promote safety and stability throughout the world."[17]

Also in the "struggle" between Congress and the president about "war powers"—described above as the internal aspect of US security policy triggered by the Libya War—a wider role of NATO in US security policy was defended by members of Congress. On June 24, 2011, the House of Representatives debated a resolution that was supposed to limit US defense funds for supporting NATO's operation in Libya. Congressman Norman D. Dicks (D, Washington)

---

[15] US Congress, Senate, Foreign Relations Committee (SFRC), *Administration Priorities for Europe in the 112th Congress*, May 18, 2011, No. 112–84, Washington, DC: USGPO, 2011, p. 6.

[16] See, for example, Håkan Edström, Janne Haaland Matlary and Magnus Petersson: "Utility for NATO - Utility of NATO" in NATO: The Power of Partnerships, eds. Håkan Edström, Janne Haaland Matlary and Magnus Petersson, Houndmills, Palgrave Macmillan, 2011.

[17] Congressional Record, Extensions of Remarks (CRER), June 7, 2011, "Regarding Deployment of United States Armed Forces in Libya," p. E1060.

then argued that a limitation of funding for the operation "would be unwise," and that it could "materially harm our relationship with NATO allies from whom we will undoubtedly require support in the future."[18]

In the same debate, Congressman David A. Scott (D, Georgia) reminded the Congress that they were "the leaders of the free world," and that the US standing was on stake. The allies should be encouraged, he argued: "So it is very important that we defeat this amendment and make sure that we send the right message to our allies, that we will not pull the rug out from under them."[19]

In a debate over the defense budget two weeks later, on July 7, 2011, Congressman Steny Hamilton Hoyer (D, Maryland) reinforced that argument when he said that:

> Our allies have taken the leading role in Libya, but it is crucial that America continue to support them. It's crucial because the campaign against Gadhafi has made significant progress, which would be dramatically set back by a sudden withdrawal of American support; because that sudden withdrawal of support could endanger civilian lives and stall democratic movements across the Middle East; and because it would represent a failure to keep faith with our NATO allies. As I said the last time this issue came to the floor: either we are in an alliance, or we are not. And if we are, that means supporting our allies in their time and place of need, so that they will continue to do the same for us—a principle that is especially important when civilian lives are at stake.[20]

So to sum up the debate about the vision of NATO in Congress, it can be argued that during the Libya War, Congress interpreted NATO as something more than a purely military tool, that the organization also had a political and cultural character. In short, Congress had a relatively maximalist, a moderate to high, vision of NATO.

NATO's mission, what NATO should do, was also debated in Congress several times in connection with the Libya War, and also in this case the debate was more maximalist than minimalist. Congress representatives pointed at the institutional utility of the alliance that created security and defended values.

---

[18] CRHR, June 24, 2011, "Limiting Use of Funds for Armed Forces in Libya," p. H 4559.
[19] Ibid., p. H 4560.
[20] CRHR, July 7, 2011, "Department of Defense Appropriations Act, 2012," p. H4694.

In a hearing in the Senate on the defense budget on February 17, 2011, just a couple of weeks before the intervention in Libya, Senator Lieberman argued that NATO could not afford to fail in Afghanistan:

A failure in this first time at war, interestingly outside of the geographic area of NATO, would have terrible consequences for NATO's credibility, and NATO's credibility at this uncertain, dangerous time in the world is critically important to the stability and security of a lot of other places far from the United States, Europe, and Afghanistan.[21]

In a hearing in the House of Representatives on the US relations with Europe and Eurasia March 10, 2011, Congressman Eliot L. Engel (D, New York) in a similar way argued that NATO had an important role to play in creating security for the former Soviet republics of Estonia, Latvia, and Lithuania: "If we hadn't brought the Baltic countries, Lithuania, Latvia and Estonia into NATO when we did, does anyone think that we would have been able to bring them into NATO now? It would have been impossible."[22]

Furthermore, in an article in the *Washington Post* March 11, 2011, the future US Secretary of State, back then Senator (D, Massachusetts) John Kerry, even argued that US use of force in Libya could be dangerous and illegitimate if it was not carried out with the support of NATO and other institutions such as the Arab League and the African Union: "If the United Nations cannot approve a resolution for implementing a no-fly zone, then the United States and its allies in NATO and the Arab world must be prepared to prevent a massacre like the one that occurred in Srebrenica in 1995, when more than 8,000 men and boys were slaughtered."[23]

NATO's mission was, in other words, by Kerry and others described as to provide a legitimate framework for the "responsibility to protect" Libya's people from being killed by its own leader—a central value that had been

---

[21] US Congress, Senate, Armed Services Committee (SASC), *Department of Defense Authorization for Appropriations for Fiscal Year 2012 and the Future Years Defense Program*, February 17; March 1, 8, 17, 29, 31; April 5, 7, 12; May 19, 2011, No. 112–80, Pt. 1, p. 43.

[22] US Congress, House of Representatives, Foreign Affairs Committee (HFAC), *Overview of US Relations with Europe and Eurasia*, March 10, 2011, No. 112–20, Washington, DC: USGPO, 2011, p. 41.

[23] John Kerry, "Libya: An Iraq Redux?," *Washington Post*, March 11, 2011.

made a norm by the UN after the genocide in Rwanda in 1994—even in cases when the UN itself was paralyzed by great power rivalry.[24]

The analogy that Kerry made with NATO's operations in former Yugoslavia was a frequently used analogy in the US NATO debate, both in relation to the Libya War and—as will be shown in the next chapter—in relation to the Syria Conflict. The operations in Bosnia and Kosovo that had hindered mass murder, it was argued, and the frame of those operations, that is, that the United States operated within a NATO frame, was seen as a success story by many, both in the political sphere and in the policy sphere. It was, as Williams argues, "a turning point amongst liberals in Europe and America; a good war to stop crimes against humanity."[25]

On March 31, 2011, Congresswoman Allyson Schwartz (D, Pennsylvania) argued in a similar way in a hearing about Libya in the House of Representatives. NATO should do cost-effective, legitimate, military operations to protect central values:

> President Obama has emphasized the military mission in response to potential humanitarian crises be both limited and have the support of a broad international coalition, including the endorsement of the U.N. and the Arab League and the African Union. The President has upheld this pledge by successfully handing off command and control to the NATO lead coalition. The fact that the call to action by the broad international coalition is there has been absolutely critical. There is a clear regional and international agreement on the use of military force to protect civilian, and the coalition leadership helps ensure that we do not assume sole responsibilities for operations or costs.[26]

In the same hearing, Congressman Albio Sires (D, New Jersey) filled in with the same message, when he said that he wanted to "compliment" the president for his rapid action and "commend" him for working with the international community and the NATO community, "especially on protecting the lives of

[24] On the responsibility to protect, "R2P," see Jennifer Welsh, "The Responsibility to Protect: Dilemmas of a New Norm," *Current History*, November, 2012.

[25] Michael Williams, *The Good War: NATO and the Liberal Conscience in Afghanistan*, Basingstoke: Palgrave Macmillan, 2011, p. 49.

[26] HFAC, *Libya: Defining US National Security Interests*, March 31, 2011, No. 112–25, Washington, DC: USGPO, 2011, p. 14.

civilians in Libya."[27] Congressman Gregory W. Meeks (D, New York) also made the point clear that the United States was part of an alliance, that it was bound by the common good of the alliance, and that it should not be focusing solely on its own interests. The allies had joined the United States in Afghanistan and Iraq, he argued, and this time it was the United States turn to back up the allies in Libya. The United States could not say "it is my way or the highway:"

> So how dare we say it is just United States go on your own again, forget our allies, forget what they need, forget working with them, forget considering anything that they said; that is unilateralism. That would make the American people unsafe. That is exactly what the terrorists want; they want to be able to isolate us and to say that we are just doing whatever we want irrespective of everyone else. I am glad that this President has not done that and is working collectively with everyone else.[28]

In a hearing in the Senate on May 18, 2011, about the administration's priorities for Europe, Senator Shaheen argued in a similar way, when she said that NATO still remained "fundamentally critical to transatlantic security interests around the globe," and that it found itself engaged in military operations in Afghanistan and Libya, "as well as taking on new challenges like missile defense, cyber security, energy security, piracy, counterterrorism, and proliferation."[29]

There were, in short, many voices in Congress that argued that NATO's mission was to create collective security and defend values. There were, however, voices in Congress as well—especially Republican—that argued that NATO was of no use at all, and that it, if it should be doing something, should promote US interests. In addition, in the internal power struggle over "war powers" between Congress and the president, NATO was used as a bad example of how the president sidestepped Congress.

In a hearing about the constitutional aspects of the Libya War in the House of Representatives on May 25, 2011, Congressman Donald A. Manzullo (R, Illinois) argued that his "big concern" was that the president followed the

---

[27] HFAC, *Libya: Defining US National Security Interests*, March 31, 2011, No. 112–25, Washington, DC: USGPO, 2011, p. 17.

[28] Ibid., p. 41.

[29] SFRC, *Administration Priorities for Europe in the 112th Congress*, p. 5.

lead of NATO, the Arab Union, the Arab League, and the UN, and excluded Congress, "believing that if he can get the blessings of one or more of those organizations, he doesn't need the imprimatur of—or any input from the elected representatives of this country."[30]

Furthermore, in the middle of June, Senator Kay Bailey Hutchison (R, Texas) complained about the European NATO members' lack of willingness and ability to use military force on their own. According to her, the United States could not afford to pay for operations that were not of "vital security interest" for the United States.[31]

And in the debate about funding the Libya Operation in the House of Representatives on June 24, 2011, Congressman "Ron" Paul (R, Texas) expressed that he did not see much use of NATO, or other institutions for that matter, when he said that the United States was not supposed to "roll over for NATO and the United Nations," but "stand up" for the United States.[32] Congresswoman Candice S. Miller (R, Michigan) was, on her side, of the opinion that NATO was an "antiquated organization," and that instead of spending money on its defense, Congress should spend money on social programs and lower corporate taxes.[33]

Despite these voices, the general impression of the debate about NATO's mission in relation to the Libya war in Congress is that NATO should be working for collective security and Western values through institutional cooperation. On July 5, 2011, Senator Lindsey Graham (R, South Carolina) underscored that point, when she said that the United States should be involved with its NATO partners:

> Our NATO partners depend on Libya more than we do. They came to Afghanistan not because they were attacked but because we were attacked. They are our friends. They are our allies. They have been with us trying to make sure Afghanistan never goes back into the darkness, a place that attacked us or them again ... I just cannot tell you how upset I am with

---

[30] HFAC, *War Powers, United States Operations in Libya, and Related Legislation*, May 25, 2011, No. 112–38, Washington, DC: USGPO, 2011, p. 6.
[31] Congressional Record, Senate (CRS), June 15, 2011, "NATO," p. S3804.
[32] CRHR, June 24, 2011, "Limiting Use of Funds for Armed Forces in Libya," p. H 4561.
[33] Ibid.

policies coming from this administration that are sending the signal to our allies that we are not as reliable as we should be, and to our enemies that we do not have the same amount of will to protect our freedom as they do to take it away from us.[34]

On the whole, that indicates a moderate to high (maximalist) view of what NATO should be doing, and of the importance of NATO in US long-term security policy.

The debate about the guidance of NATO in Congress, lastly, was more polarized during the Libya Operation than the debates about the vision and mission of NATO in US security policy. On one hand it was argued that the United States should lead NATO as the primus inter pares, which according to the analytical frame of this book means in a "charismatic" way. On the other hand it was argued that the United States should let others lead when appropriate, which means in a "rational" way. Unlike the debate about NATO's mission, but similar to the debate about its vision, the party lines in Congress did not seem to matter much.

Congresswoman Lynn Woolsey (D, California) was arguing along the first line of argumentation in a hearing the House of Representatives on March 30, 2011. She was, she said, not "comforted" by the fact that NATO was leading the mission because the United States was "the dominant force within NATO." Therefore, she continued, the United States had an "enormous responsibility" for any NATO-led operation.[35]

Congressman Louise Buller "Louie" Gohmert (R, Texas) expressed a similar opinion in the House of Representatives on March 30, 2011, when he spoke about the Libya Operation. We are turning over command, he argued, "but our U.S. military is doing the lion's share of the fighting." It does not come as a "great comfort," he continued, "that we are turning over this great responsibility" when the United States constituted 65 percent of NATO:

> I know I look stupid sometimes, but, I mean, I can get that. If we are turning it over to a group that is 65 percent us, we really haven't turned it over. Unless

---

[34] CRS, July 5, 2011, "Shared Sacrifice in Resolving the Budget Deficit—Motion to Proceed," p. S4325.
[35] CRHR, March 30, "Is Two Wars in the Middle East Not Enough?," p. H2045.

we want to say, "Yeah, but we are not leading anymore. We are putting our military under the command of foreigners who have never taken an oath to support and defend the Constitution of this country."[36]

Senator John McCain (R, Arizona) went even further in a budget hearing in the Senate on April 5, 2011, when he said that "[r]ather than playing a supporting role within NATO, America should be leading."[37] Three days later, on April 8, 2011, he said that "America must lead. NATO is America. We need to be leading in a strong and sustained way, not sitting on the side lines or playing a supporting role."[38] Finally, on July 5, 2011, he said that "The United States of America leads, not NATO. We lead NATO. And when someone says NATO is leading on this conflict, I would remind my colleagues, of the 28 members of NATO, only 8 members are actually in the fight."[39]

There are several more examples from Congress that point in the same direction, and, as argued above, it is interesting that, in contrast to the perceptions regarding NATO's mission described above, the party lines do not seem to be decisive. On April 7, 2011, Senator John Cornyn (R, Texas) stated in a hearing that NATO "could not function as a fighting force without U.S. support,"[40] and on June 3, Congressman Jim Moran (D, Virginia) argued that "none of us should be so naive as to think that NATO can operate independent of United States leadership."[41]

The party lines do not seem to be decisive regarding the second line of argumentation—that is, that the United States should let other nations lead when proper—either. On June 15, 2011, Senator Huchison argued that the United States "should lead" when and where US capabilities are essential: "But others can lead where they have the capability to do so, and they need to do it

---

[36] CRHR, March 30, "What's So Special About Libya?," p. H2098. See also SASC, *Department of Defense Authorization for Appropriations for Fiscal Year 2012 and the Future Years Defense Program*, p. 604.

[37] SASC, *Department of Defense Authorization for Appropriations for Fiscal Year 2012 and the Future Years Defense Program*, p. 840.

[38] CRS, April 8, 2011, "Libya," pp. S2305–S2306.

[39] CRS, July 5, 2011, "Shared Sacrifice in Resolving the Budget Deficit—Motion to Proceed," pp. S4324–4325.

[40] SASC, *Department of Defense Authorization for Appropriations for Fiscal Year 2012 and the Future Years Defense Program*, pp. 882–883.

[41] CRHR, June 3, 2011, "Regarding Deployment of United States Armed Forces in Libya," p. H4007.

with personnel and with the appropriate level of funding." Smaller operations, she continued, such as Kosovo and Libya (potentially also Syria and Yemen), could be led by other NATO members, "so that when the big things happen— such as Afghanistan which will continue to require our commitment—those major efforts can be led by the United States with our unique capabilities and our commitment."[42]

On June 21, 2011, Senator Kerry argued along the same lines when he said that "here is the alliance leading. Here is the alliance doing what we have wanted them to do for years."[43] Three days later, in a debate about the funding of US forces in the Libya operation in the House of Representatives, Congressman Barnett Frank (D, Massachusetts) said that "America can no longer be asked to be the one that does everything, everywhere, every time. Our allies have to step up."[44] And in the same debate Congressman David Adam Smith (D, Washington) argued that "[f]or once, NATO is actually carrying the bulk of the mission."[45]

So, to summarize the views of how NATO should be guided in the US Congress during the Libya War, the picture is that there were two "camps": one that argued for a maximalist, charismatic US leadership, and another that argued for a minimalist, rational US leadership.

The results from the first part of the political debate, Congress, can thereby be summarized and visualized in terms of the following table (Table 2.1).

Table 2.1 Results from the US NATO debate over Libya in Congress

Vision	Political and cultural
Mission	Collective security and values
Guidance	Rational or charismatic

The view in Congress of NATO's importance in US long-term security policy was that NATO mainly was a political and cultural tool, that its mission of

---

[42] CRS, June 15, 2011, "NATO," p. S3805.

[43] CRS, June 21, 2011, "Libya," pp. S3945–3946. See also Kerry's statement in SFRC, *Libya and War Powers*, 28 June, No. 112–189, Washington, DC: USGPO, 2011, p. 3.

[44] CRHR, June 24, 2011, "Limiting Use of Funds for Armed Forces in Libya," p. H 4560.

[45] Ibid., p. H 4563.

NATO was to promote collective security and values, and that it should be led either in a rational or in a charismatic way. What that means, in sum, is that Congress had a moderate to high (maximalist) view of what NATO should be (vision), what NATO should do (mission), and how NATO should be led (guidance). In the next section, the Obama administration's view will be scrutinized.

The political debate in the administration

While Congress stood for a moderate to high (maximalist) view of NATO, the Obama administration rather stood for a moderate to low (minimalist) view. NATO was generally described as a military and political, rather than a cultural, tool, and its mission was seldom described as to promote values. The administration also made it clear that NATO should be led in a rational way, rather than a charismatic way.

It is a tradition that US Secretaries of Defense and/or Secretaries of State give a visionary talk focusing on transatlantic security at the Munich Security Conference, a conference that with a few exceptions has been held in Munich in February every year since the 1960s. The conference is a gathering of the Western security elite, and it has a huge impact on transatlantic relations.

In the beginning of February 2011, before the Libya War, Secretary Clinton held a talk at the conference, focusing almost entirely on NATO as a military organization. She talked about NATO's strategic concept, US force structure in Europe, and how the United States should be credible in the alliance in the future:

> We will maintain the necessary balance of forces and capabilities to meet our enduring commitment to Article Five. And we will maintain our ability to protect ourselves and our allies, not just against traditional threats, but also new ones such as cyber-attacks, terrorism, and weapons of mass destruction.[46]

---

[46] Hillary R. Clinton, "Munich Security Conference Plenary Session Remarks," February 5, 2011, www.state.gov (homepage), date accessed February 21, 2013.

In a hearing regarding the defense budget in Senate later in February 2011, Secretary Gates also emphasized NATO as a military organization rather than a political and cultural one.[47]

However, NATO's existence was also motivated in wider terms by the representatives of the administration. In a hearing in the House of Representatives on March 10, 2011, Philip H. Gordon, Assistant Secretary, Bureau of European and Eurasian Affairs, U.S. Department of State, underscored NATO's political and cultural importance:

> If you just take the countries in the part of Europe that are receiving our assistance in Central and Eastern Europe, they are contributing some 10,000 troops to Afghanistan because they are now more stable, democratic and capable allies who have joined the EU and NATO, and that investment is paying off.[48]

Daniel Rosenblum, Coordinator of U.S. Assistance to Europe and Eurasia, Bureau of Central and South Asian Affairs, U.S. Department of State, argued in a similar way in a hearing about the president's budget request on April 14, 2011, in the House of Representatives. Rosenblum said that the NATO enlargement in the 1990s and the early 2000s "played an absolutely critical role in getting them [the new NATO members] to where they are today," and that the support also generated "enormous goodwill in those countries so that today these are some of the most pro-American places on Earth."[49]

To describe NATO in such terms, as a cultural organization, was however not common within the Obama administration. The organization was rather described as military and political tool.

In Vice President Biden's speech at the Atlantic Council's 50th Anniversary Dinner on May 4, 2011, for example, NATO was first and foremost described as a military and a political alliance. America's partners across the Atlantic were described as the US "oldest friends," and "closest allies." It was hard

---

[47] SASC, *Department of Defense Authorization for Appropriations for Fiscal Year 2012 and the Future Years Defense Program*, pp. 104–105.

[48] HFAC, *Overview of US Relations with Europe and Eurasia*, p. 32. See also SFRC, *Administration Priorities for Europe in the 112th Congress*, pp. 8–9.

[49] HFAC, *Budget Oversight: Examining the President's 2012 Budget Request for Europe and Eurasia*, April 14, 2011, No. 112–143, Washington, DC: USGPO, 2011, p. 9.

to imagine, Biden said, "a single threat or opportunity" that they could not address more effectively together:

> President Obama and I firmly believe that there must be no distinction between old and new members of NATO. So to adapt, we began to move, and all of us moved together, on making sure that the Article 5 commitments extended to every nation in NATO not implicitly, explicitly. An attack on one is an attack on all, because all NATO members deserve the same protection.[50]

And when President Obama himself gave a speech in the British Parliament on May 25, 2011, he also emphasized NATO's military and political character:

> At its core, NATO is rooted in the simple concept of Article Five: that no NATO nation will have to fend on its own; that allies will stand by one another, always. And for six decades, NATO has been the most successful alliance in human history.[51]

Obama also said that "a revitalized NATO will continue to hew to that original vision of its founders, allowing us to rally collective action for the defense of our people."[52] It could hardly have been said clearer. His vision of NATO was military and political, rather than cultural.

Furthermore, in Gates's "farewell speech" in Brussels on June 10, 2011, he argued that NATO was "the main instrument" for protecting Europe's security. He also took the opportunity to criticize the burden sharing within NATO in a quite frank way. He argued that "true friends" had to speak bluntly sometimes "for the sake of those greater interests and values that bind us together":

> In the past, I've worried openly about NATO turning into a two-tiered alliance: Between members who specialize in "soft" humanitarian, development, peacekeeping, and talking tasks, and those conducting the "hard" combat missions. Between those willing and able to pay the price and bear the burdens of alliance commitments, and those who enjoy the benefits

---

[50] Joe Biden, "Remarks by the Vice President at the Atlantic Council's 50th Anniversary Dinner," Speech May 4, 2011, www.whitehouse.gov (homepage), date accessed February 17, 2013.

[51] Barack Obama, "Remarks by the President to Parliament in London, United Kingdom," Speech May 25, 2011, www.whitehouse.gov (homepage), date accessed February 20, 2013.

[52] Ibid.

of NATO membership—be they security guarantees or headquarters billets—but don't want to share the risks and the costs. This is no longer a hypothetical worry. We are there today. And it is unacceptable.[53]

The description of NATO as a military and a political alliance was, in other words, a distinct feature in the Obama administration's vision of NATO before, during, and after the Libya conflict. But the picture is not unequivocal. In the new Secretary of Defense Leon Panetta's first long speech on NATO, at Carnegie Europe in Brussels in October 2011, which was also the first visit to Europe by him as a Secretary of Defense, he—as child of immigrants coming to the United States in the 1930s—underscored "the shared bonds of culture, and values and history that tie our continents together and form the foundation of the Atlantic Alliance."[54]

But, as argued, NATO's character as a military and political organization was almost consequently emphasized by the Obama administration, and when his National Security Adviser, Tom Donilon, wrote an article in the *Washington Post* on October 28, 2011, summing up the Libya War, he argued that the United States had been "revitalizing" NATO through the operation: The operation had been organized with great speed and effectiveness, two Arab partner countries—the United Arab Emirates and Qatar—were full partners of the operation, the United States played a supporting role after the initial attacks, the costs of the operation was no more for the United States than a week of operations in Afghanistan or Iraq, and last—but not least—it had identified how the alliance could be more effective in the future. The European allies faced several shortages in military assets and needed to make great investments, especially in precision munitions and unmanned systems that were "critical on today's battlefields."[55]

Even though Donilon finished his article with a few words on NATO's role in promoting US prosperity and values, the message was quite clear. NATO's existence was motivated first and foremost from a military and a political

---

[53] Robert M. Gates, "The Security and Defense Agenda (Future of NATO)," Speech June 10, 2011, http://www.defense.gov (homepage), date accessed September 18, 2011.

[54] Leon E. Panetta, "Carnegie Europe (NATO)," Speech October 5, 2011, http://www.defense.gov (homepage), date accessed January 24, 2013.

[55] Tom Donilon, "The Continuing Need for a Strong NATO," *Washington Post*, October 28, 2011.

perspective, a moderate to low (minimalist) view of NATO's importance in US long-term security policy.

Also *regarding NATO's mission*, the actors in the Obama administration stood for a more moderate view than Congress. NATO should focus on collective security, rather than promoting solely US interests, or to promote values. Before the Libya War started, in a hearing in the Senate on February 17, Gates argued that the Department of Defense would "continue to work with America's Allies through the NATO Defense Planning Process to determine the correct mix of forces and capabilities needed to maintain and develop our individual and collective capacity to resist armed attack, and to maintain the security of the North Atlantic area."[56] The United States, he continued, "is committed to a defense posture in Europe that meets its enduring commitment to NATO's Article 5, ensures a credible deterrent against all forms of aggression, and maintains a robust capacity to build Allied and partner capacity for coalition operations."[57]

When the Libya War was getting closer, on February 23, 2011, the president himself declared that the United States intended to work collectively, through institutions. He had his administration to prepare the full range of options, which included "those we will coordinate with our allies and partners, or those that we'll carry out through multilateral institutions."[58] During the whole war, Obama continued to underscore collectiveness and the utility of institutional cooperation that was characterizing the war efforts. On March 19, 2011, he said that he had authorized the US Armed Forces to begin a limited military action in Libya, that the United States was acting within "a broad coalition" that was supported by the UNSCR 1973, and that the

---

[56] SASC, *Department of Defense Authorization for Appropriations for Fiscal Year 2012 and the Future Years Defense Program*, p. 104.

[57] Ibid., pp. 104–105.

[58] Barack Obama, "Remarks by the President on Libya," Speech February 23, 2011, www.whitehouse .gov (homepage), date accessed February 17, 2013. Regarding collective missile defense, see also HASC, *The Status of United States Strategic Forces*, March 2, 2011, No. 112–12, Washington, DC: USGPO, 2011, p. 7; SFRC, *Administration Priorities for Europe in the 112th Congress*, pp. 9, 13, and 14; and HASC, *The Current Status and Future Direction for US Nuclear Weapons and Policy and Posture*, November 2, 2011, No. 112–188, Washington, DC: USGPO, 2011, p. 8. Regarding the "in together, out together" principle in Afghanistan, which is an additional example of collective thinking, see Robert M. Gates, "Statement to NATO Defense Ministers," Speech March 11, 2011, http://www.defense.gov (homepage), date accessed January 24, 2013. See also Gates, "The Security and Defense Agenda (Future of NATO)."

coalition brought together many European and Arab partners.[59] The next day he reiterated that the United States had not acted alone. "In just one month," he argued, "the United States has worked with our international partners to mobilize a broad coalition, secure an international mandate to protect civilians, stop an advancing army, prevent a massacre, and establish a no-fly zone with our allies and partners."[60]

Promoting US interests and collective security was also central to Secretary Gates on March 31, 2011, when he, in the House of Representatives, underscored that it was a national interest for the United States "as part of a multilateral coalition with broad international support" to prevent a humanitarian crisis that could have destabilized the entire region.[61]

Furthermore, in Vice President Biden's speech at the Atlantic Council's 50th Anniversary Dinner on May 4, 2011, the value of collectiveness and working through institutions was emphasized: "We obviously don't agree on everything," he said: "But we agree on this, we need each other. We're stronger with each other. And we can do more for the world with each other."[62] "Can the transatlantic relationship be sustained?" he asked himself rhetorically:

> Well, ladies and gentlemen, the truth is the relationship remains as central to our interests—our mutual interests in my view—as it ever has. And this alliance continues to serve the interest of its members.[63]

And in his October speech at Carnegie Europe in Brussels, 2011, Panetta characterized NATO's transformation after the Cold War as "moving from an alliance that was built around safeguarding our collective territorial defense of Europe to one built on safeguarding our shared interests around the world." NATO continued to do its job, he continued, which was demonstrated by the Libya operation: "In support of a UN mandate, NATO

[59] Barack Obama, "Remarks by the President on Libya," Speech March 19, 2011, www.whitehouse.gov (homepage), date accessed February 17, 2013.

[60] Barack Obama, "Remarks by the President in Address to the Nation on Libya," Speech March 28, 2011, www.whitehouse.gov (homepage), date accessed February 17, 2013.

[61] Robert M. Gates, "Statement on Libya—House Armed Service Committee," Speech March 31, 2011, http://www.defense.gov (homepage), date accessed January 24, 2013. See also HFAC, *Libya: Defining US National Security Interests*, p. 17, and the statements by James B. Steinberg, Deputy Secretary, U.S. Department of State, p. 42.

[62] Biden, "Remarks by the Vice President at the Atlantic Council's 50th Anniversary Dinner."

[63] Ibid.

led an international effort to save innocent civilian lives from a dictator
who threatened to inflict great harm upon his own people." Panetta also
took the opportunity to underscore the importance of NATO partners
around the world:

> A look at the composition of NATO's ongoing operations—in Libya,
> Afghanistan, off the coast of Somalia—makes it clear that non-NATO
> partners will be increasingly central to NATO's future activities, particularly
> as we all strive to more broadly share the burden of defending our common
> interests.[64]

"Security," Panetta said, "will not be achieved by each nation marching to its
own drummer." "It can only," he continued, "be achieved by a willingness to
fight together to defend our common security interests."[65]

Panetta reiterated his message when he visited Canada in November 2011,
and said that "[i]t will be even more essential, as we confront new and more
complex security challenges in the years ahead, to be able to build strong
alliances and strong partnerships, from terrorism to nuclear proliferation,
from cyber-attacks to the threats we face often." All of these challenges, he
argued, did not recognize national boundaries and could not be "addressed
effectively by any one nation alone."[66]

He also said that the US alliance system remained "the bedrock" of
its approach to security across the globe, and that the United States would
maintain its excellence, and its leadership:

> But in the effort to maintain our excellence and our leadership, we also
> have to meet our security commitments around the world. And in doing
> that, we must, and we will, sharpen the application of our resources,
> better—better deploy our forces in the world, and share our burdens more
> and more effectively with our partners. And frankly, all of our allies need
> to do the same.[67]

---

[64] Panetta, "Carnegie Europe (NATO)."
[65] Ibid.
[66] Leon E. Panetta, "Halifax International Security Forum," Speech November 18, 2011, http://www
.defense.gov (homepage), date accessed January 24, 2013.
[67] Ibid.

Last but not least, Secretary Clinton was quite representative for the administration when she, on December 15, 2011, said that NATO was "the premier military alliance in all of history," and that there were no indications that it would be less needed in the future. "There will be new challenges and threats," she argued, "but the environment is certainly not one yet that we would like to see, where the collective defense that we've all pledged to under NATO will never be needed again."[68]

It could hardly be said clearer; NATO's mission, from the Obama administration's perspective, was first and foremost argued to promote collective security; a moderate view of NATO in US security policy. The "in together, out together" principle of the Afghanistan Operation is an additional example of how the US administration viewed NATO's mission during this time and after. When Gates talked to NATO's defense ministers in Brussels on March 11, 2011, he underscored that principle. Security was built together, through NATO and its partners.[69]

Regarding how NATO should be led, The Obama administration was much clearer than Congress in connection to the Libya War. The United States did not intend—at least not always—to lead NATO in a "charismatic" or "authoritarian" way, but rather in a "rational" way, they argued. And there are lots of examples of this minimalist view of US leadership. On March 18, 2011, Obama said in a speech about the situation in Libya that "American leadership is essential, but that does not mean acting alone— it means shaping the conditions for the international community to act together." The United States should, according to the president, "provide the unique capabilities," and that was, according to him, precisely how the international community should work, "as more nations bear both the responsibility and the cost of enforcing international law."[70]

---

[68] Hillary R. Clinton, "Remarks with Danish Foreign Minister Villy Sovndal After Their Meeting," December 15, 2011, www.state.gov (homepage), date accessed March 4, 2013.

[69] Gates, "Statement to NATO Defense Ministers." See also Gates, "The Security and Defense Agenda (Future of NATO)."

[70] Barack Obama, "Remarks by the President on the Situation in Libya," Speech March 18, 2011, www .whitehouse.gov (homepage), date accessed February 17, 2013.

Three days later, on March 21, 2011, Secretary Gates said that the United States would continue to support the coalition, continue to be a member of the coalition, continue to have a military role in the coalition, "but we will not have the preeminent role."[71] And the same day, President Obama declared that the United States' most effective alliance, NATO, had taken command of the enforcement of the arms embargo and the no-fly zone, and that the United States from then would play "a supporting role."[72]

James B. Steinberg, Deputy Secretary, U.S. Department of State, perhaps gave the most thorough explanation of the administration's minimalistic view of how NATO should be led in a hearing on Libya in the House of Representatives on March 31, 2011:

> First, in some ways from our perspective the transition to NATO command gives us the best of both worlds, which is that we are able now to step back, to leave the principal responsibility for enforcing the no fly zone and the protection of civilians to other forces, both NATO and the associated forces that are working under NATO command and control. And we will focus on support activities like intelligence and reconnaissance, and the like. So, we are definitely playing a less front line role in terms of the operation of military activities. At the same time, we get the benefit of the well established, well oiled machine that can conduct effective military activities. And even for the limited role we can be assured that our forces are under American command because ultimately all the forces are under Admiral Stavridis who is American Admiral. So, we have an opportunity for us to play less of an operational role, but still have the benefits of a well established and disciplined NATO command and control.[73]

[71] Peter Finn and Greg Jaffe, "U.S. Jets Strike Gaddafi's Ground Forces," *Washington Post*, March 21, 2011.

[72] Obama, "Remarks by the President in Address to the Nation on Libya." See also Hillary R. Clinton, "Remarks After the International Conference on the Libyan Crisis," March 29, 2011, www.state.gov (homepage), date accessed February 21, 2013; Gates, "Statement on Libya—House Armed Service Committee," p. 17; Hillary R. Clinton, "Remarks with British Foreign Secretary William Hague," May 23, 2011, www.state.gov (homepage), date accessed February 21, 2013; and HASC, *The Current Status and Future Direction for US Nuclear Weapons and Policy and Posture*, p. 11.

[73] HFAC, *Libya: Defining US National Security Interests*, p. 48.

Secretary Clinton was also arguing along the same lines when she spoke in Paris on September 1, 2011, on Libya. The United States and its international partners were proud of their effort, she said. The United States had sought, and won, "local, regional, and international support, including the backing of the UN and the Arab League," and after deploying its unique military capabilities at the outset, the United States "played a key role in a genuinely shared effort as our allies stepped up."[74] And in the UN, on September 20, President Obama said that the United States "was proud" to play a decisive role in the early days of the operation, and then in a supporting capacity:

> It was the world's most effective alliance, NATO, that's led a military coalition of nearly 20 nations. It's our European allies—especially the United Kingdom and France and Denmark and Norway—that conducted the vast majority of air strikes protecting rebels on the ground. It was Arab states who joined the coalition, as equal partners.[75]

Furthermore, in Brussels in October 2011, Secretary Panetta praised the European leadership in the Libya operation, when he said that "this was a mission where we saw greater leadership from our European allies." France and the United Kingdom engaged on a large scale, he continued, "flying one third of the overall sorties and attacking forty percent of the targets... They also exercised leadership roles politically and diplomatically."[76] A couple of days later in Washington, he said that the United States had "helped" NATO achieve its mission in Libya.[77]

It could not possibly be said clearer, that the United States had "helped" their own alliance to achieve its mission in Libya. The Obama administration's arguments of how NATO should be led during the Libya operation were

---

[74] Hillary R. Clinton, "Press Availability on Libya," September 1, 2011, www.state.gov (homepage), date accessed March 4, 2013.

[75] Barack Obama, "Remarks by President Obama at High-Level Meeting on Libya," Speech September 20, 2011, www.whitehouse.gov (homepage), date accessed February 20, 2013.

[76] Panetta, "Carnegie Europe (NATO)."

[77] Panetta, "Lee H. Hamilton Lecture," Speech October 11, 2011, http://www.defense.gov (homepage), date accessed January 24, 2013.

definitely minimalist in character. The United States should not lead NATO in a charismatic or authoritarian way; it should decrease its role as a leader as much as possible when proper.

Obama summed up this message when he spoke in France on November 4, 2011:

> The United States was proud to play a decisive role, especially in the early days, taking out Libyan air defenses and conducting precision strikes that stopped the regime in its tracks. But at the same time, this mission showed us why NATO remains the world's most effective alliance. We acted quickly, in days—the fastest mobilization in NATO history... And in a historic first, our NATO allies, including France, and especially the extraordinary leadership of President Sarkozy, helped us to conduct 90 percent of our strike missions—90 percent. So that showed more nations bearing the burdens and costs of peace and security. And that's how our alliance must work in the 21st century.[78]

So to summarize, the US administration was perceiving NATO as first and foremost a military and political tool, NATO's role as promoting collective security, and wanted to lead NATO in a rational way. These views can be visualized in Table 2.2.

Table 2.2 Results from the US NATO debate over Libya in the administration

Vision	Military and political
Mission	Collective security
Guidance	Rational

What that means, in sum, is that the Obama administration had a moderate to low (minimalist) view of what NATO should be (vision), what NATO should do (mission), and how NATO should be led (guidance). NATO should primarily be a military and political organization; NATO should

[78] Barack Obama, "Remarks by President Obama in Honoring the Alliance Between the United States and France," Speech November 4, 2011, www.whitehouse.gov (homepage), date accessed February 20, 2013.

primarily create collective security; and NATO should be led in rational way. In the next section the think tank debate and the debate in the elite media will be scrutinized.

The policy debate in the think tank and elite media environment

The views of NATO in US security policy in the policy debate was moderate to high. All views were, however, represented: NATO as a military, political, and cultural tool; and NATO as a promoter of US interests, collective security, and universal values. What is similar to the debate in Congress is that the discussion about NATO's guidance was polarized; the actors either wanted the United States to lead in a maximalist way ("charismatic leadership") or in a minimalist way ("rational leadership").

Regarding the *vision* of NATO the editorial board in the *Washington Post* was, in an editorial on April 17, 2011, of the opinion that NATO was a bearer of Western culture that could help democratize North Africa and the Middle East, and that it was rightful to intervene in Libya: "We believed that Mr. Obama was right to support NATO's intervention in Libya not only because of the risk that Mr. Gaddafi would carry out massacres but because defeating the dictator is crucial to the larger cause of democratic change in the Middle East."[79]

Such an argument could be recognized from the political debate in Congress (Senator Shaheen, for example), and, as mentioned, it was not unusual in the US NATO debate to allude to the success stories of Central and Eastern Europe when approaching the "Arab Spring" and handle the countries in North Africa and the Middle East. NATO was seen as a vehicle for spreading Western culture such as democracy, rule of law, human rights, and free markets.

In another context, in a Hearing in the House of Representatives about the security issues in Europe and Eurasia on May 5, 2011, Sally McNamara,

---

[79] "The Libya Stalemate," Editorial, *Washington Post*, April 17, 2011.

Senior Policy Analyst at the Heritage Foundation, argued in a similar way, that NATO was a great vehicle to foster former not-so-well working countries. "What we have found," she said, "is that countries, who have got into NATO ... generally do very well inside the alliance, because they pick up best practices; they liaise with their colleagues."[80]

The same argument was used by Kurt Volker, former US NATO Ambassador, now with CTR, in hearing about the situation in the Balkans on November 15, 2011:

> For the past 15 years, U.S. policy has been based on the premise that bringing the countries of the region [the Balkans] into the EU and NATO—so, integration in European institutions—provides such a powerful incentive for reform that it is going to drive change in the region, and they will overcome their differences, much as Western Europe successfully did at the end of World War II, getting beyond the wars of the 20th century.[81]

But even though Volker pointed at NATO as a political and cultural organization, he also underscored its military value. In an ACUS brief in June 2011, he argued that if NATO should appeal to public opinion, it had to restore credibility "by achieving success in its missions."[82] And in another brief from ACUS the same month, Harlan Ullman, Chairman of the Killoween Group, argued in a similar way, that the US European Command (EUCOM) was the key to a strong NATO, when the European members decreased their defense spending. The EUCOM, he wrote:

> ... will have to sustain and in some cases strengthen direct military-to-military relations at various levels of command and especially at the highest echelons. It is through these relations that the viability of NATO can be enhanced even as force levels decline.[83]

---

[80] HFAC, *Overview of Security Issues in Europe and Eurasia*, May 5, 2011, No. 112–144, Washington, DC: USGPO, 2011, p. 73.

[81] HFAC, *The State of Affairs in the Balkans*, November 15, 2011, No. 112–112, Washington, DC: USGPO, 2011, p. 38.

[82] Kurt Volker, "Increasing Outreach, Public Understanding and Support for NATO across the Transatlantic Community," Atlantic Council Issue Brief, June 2011, http://www.atlanticcouncil.org (homepage), date accessed January 29, 2014, p. 4.

[83] Harlan Ullman, "U.S. European Command and NATO's Strategic Concept: Post Afghanistan and Beyond," Atlantic Council Issue Brief, June 2011, http://www.atlanticcouncil.org (homepage), date

An editorial article in the *New York Times* on June 29, 2011, was also focusing on NATO as a military organization and the editorial board warned that the unfair burden sharing between the United States and NATO's European allies was dangerous. During the Libya War it had been clear, they argued, that "years of military underinvestment" by most European members had forced them to "turn to Washington for bombs and other basic support." European NATO's "inability to master a minor challenge like Libya" should frighten European governments, they continued, and the European leaders had to find "some broader vision of their own quickly, or Europeans—and their American allies—could pay a huge price."[84]

Another editorial in the *New York Times* on August 30, 2011, also pointed out the military shortcomings of the European NATO allies. The Libya operation had been successful and the allies should be proud, the editorial team argued, but it would be a "mistake to deny the serious problems revealed by the six-month campaign." The European military ability was too low "even for such a limited fight." There was shortage of "specialized aircraft, bombs and targeting specialists," and most European militaries had "failed to keep up with technological advances in battlefield management and communications." For "decades" the European NATO members had "counted on a free-spending Pentagon to provide the needed capabilities they failed to provide themselves." It was time for them to ask themselves: "If it was this hard taking on a ragtag army like Qaddafi's, what would it be like to have to fight a real enemy?"[85]

---

accessed February 3, 2014, p. 1. In a third ACUS breefing from June, 2011, Kori Schake, Associate Professor of International Security at the US Military Academy, argued along the same lines. Kori Schake, "EUCOM's Future Force Structure," Atlantic Council Issue Brief, June 2011, http://www .atlanticcouncil.org (homepage), date accessed February 3, 2014, p. 5.

[84] "Leaderless in Europe: The List of Crises Is Frightening, So Is the Lack of Vision," Editorial, *New York Times*, June 29, 2011. On the lack of military ability and political will to use force for political purposes among NATO's European NATO members is well known in the policy and scholarly literature. See, for example, National Intelligence Council, *Global Trends 2030: Alternative Worlds*, Washington, DC: National Intelligence Council, 2012, p. 66; and Janne Haaland Matlary and Magnus Petersson (eds.), *NATO's European Allies: Military Capability and Political Will*, Basingstoke: Palgrave Macmillan, 2013.

[85] "Teachable Moment: The Alliance Helped Topple Quaddafi—But Had to Struggle to Keep Up the Campaign," Editorial, *New York Times*, August 30, 2011. See also Steven Erlanger, "Libya's Dark Lesson for NATO," *New York Times*, September 4, 2011. That argument has also been discussed in the scholarly literature. See, for example, Michaels, "A Model Intervention? Reflections on NATO's Libya 'Success.'"

And in an ACUS issue brief from December 2011, Volker and the retired Vice Admiral Kevin P. Green, US Navy, were characterizing NATO as a military and political organization, when they argued that "[w]ithout a common understanding of what it is that threatens NATO nations, it will be extremely difficult to agree on common actions to address those threats." Even assuming common threat perceptions, they continued, "there is no credibility to the notion of Alliance action if most Allies actually lack meaningful capabilities to contribute to NATO missions."[86]

So in sum, the policy debate about the vision of NATO in connection to the Libya War was pluralistic; the organization was described as military, political, and cultural. Such a pluralistic vision supports the view that the importance of NATO in US long-term security policy was moderate to high (maximalist).

That is also the case regarding the view of *NATO's mission*. Here the focus was on collective security and universal values in the policy debate, rather than on US interests. On March 22, 2011, Max Boot, Senior Fellow at the Council on Foreign Relations, argued in an article in the *New York Times* that it was time to plan for the post-Qaddafi Libya, and in connection to that NATO had an important role to play together with the UN and the Arab League. He thought the Libya War was "worthwhile" for both strategic and humanitarian reasons.[87] And that is a relatively comprehensive view of NATO's mission, that NATO had a role as stabilizer in a post-conflict situation, similar to the role of NATO in Bosnia, Kosovo, and Afghanistan.

Meghan O'Sullivan, Professor of the Practice of International Affairs at Harvard University's Kennedy School of Government, argued in a similar way in the *Washington Post* on April 3, that it served US interests to use NATO's framework and NATO partners in military operations to create legitimate, collectively based security: "[t]he political benefits of a coalition (particularly one involving Arab countries) are enormous in an intervention such as the one in Libya."[88]

---

[86] Kurt Volker and Kevin P. Green, "NATO Reform: Key Principles," *Atlantic Council Issue Brief*, December 2011, www.atlanticcouncil.org (homepage), date accessed 29 January 2014, p. 2.

[87] Max Boot, "Planning for a Post-Quaddafi Libya," *New York Times*, March 22, 2011.

[88] Meghan O'Sullivan, "Will Libya Become Obama's Iraq?," *Washington Post*, April 3, 2011.

Daniel Serwer, Senior Fellow at SAIS, also held a similar view in an article in the *Washington Post* on August 23, 2011. If a UN–EU effort failed to ensure stability in Libya, "the United States should be prepared to mobilize and support a NATO-led effort," he argued. Only NATO had the military capacity required, according to Serwer, and a unilateral US intervention "would entail risks without commensurate gains to vital national security interests."[89]

Also Damon M. Wilson, Executive Vice President of ACUS, wrote about the usefulness of NATO for the United States in an ACUS brief in September 2011:

> Libya underscores how relevant NATO remains. At the start of this crisis, no one was anticipating the Alliance would play a leading role. Yet as leaders scrambled to determine how best to organize a military campaign, NATO was the only viable instrument. The European Union was never a credible possibility. Furthermore, the default option—a coalition of the willing led by France or the UK—didn't sit well with others willing to join the fight, but unwilling to do so under the leadership of one European nation. No entity is better suited than NATO to integrate multinational contributions into an effective operational force.[90]

According to Wilson, France had learned, as the United States before them, that working through NATO "delivers greater political legitimacy than working around it."[91]

There were also other views of NATO's mission in the US policy environment. George Will, Columnist in the *Washington Post*, was of the totally opposite opinion compared to Wilson, when he wrote in June 19, 2011, that NATO did not serve US interests, and that the Libya War had "revealed" NATO as an "increasingly fictitious military organization." According to Will, NATO was "a Potemkin alliance." "It provides," he argued, "a patina of multilateralism to U.S. military interventions on which Europe is essentially a

---

[89] Daniel Serwer, "Once Gaddafi Is Gone … ," *Washington Post*, August 23, 2011.

[90] Damon M. Wilson, "Learning from Libya: The Right Lessons for NATO," *Atlantic Council Issue Brief*, September 2011, http://www.atlanticcouncil.org (homepage), date accessed January 29, 2014, p. 2.

[91] Ibid., p. 2. See also Klaus-Dieter Frankenberger, "The Atlantic Imperative in an Era of a Global Power Shift," Transatlantic Academy Paper Series, April 2011, http://www.gmfus.org (homepage), date accessed February 21, 2014, p. 3

free rider." When the "Libyan misadventure" was over, he went on, "America should debate whether NATO also should be finished."[92]

The same day Richard N. Haass, President of the Council on Foreign Relations, wrote in the *Washington Post* that NATO had no huge role to play in US security thinking, but that it could do some good anyway:

> The alliance still includes members whose forces help police parts of Europe and who could contribute to stability in the Middle East. But it is no less true that the era in which Europe and transatlantic relations dominated U.S. foreign policy is over. The answer for Americans is not to browbeat Europeans for this, but to accept it and adjust to it.[93]

But in sum the policy debate about NATO's mission was, just as in the administration, focused on the view that NATO should serve collective security, and institutional cooperation.

More similar to the debate in Congress was the debate about NATO's *guidance* within the think tank and elite media environment. Just as in Congress, the debate about how NATO should be led was polarized between the actors. Some of them wanted the United States to lead in a "rational," minimalist way, and others wanted the United States to lead in a "charismatic," maximalist way.

In an editorial article in the *New York Times* in March 24, 2011, the editorial board was arguing that other NATO members' leadership best served American interests:

> The United States took the lead in knocking out Libyan air defenses. That made sense because it alone has the cruise missiles for the job. Now the Obama administration rightly wants to hand off military leadership to its NATO partners.[94]

Eugene Robinson, Opinion Writer in the *Washington Post*, was on the other side of the debate the day after when he refused to believe that the United States would not lead the Libya operation. Without US diplomatic leadership

---

[92] George F. Will, "Lawless war," *Washington Post*, June 19, 2011.
[93] Richard N. Haass, "Continental Drift," *Washington Post*, June 19, 2011.
[94] "Discord Among Allies," Editorial, *New York Times*, March 24, 2011.

it would not have been a UN Security Council Resolution, he argued, and without US military leadership, it would not have been a coordinated attack against Libya:

> On Thursday, after days of bickering, we heard a grand announcement that NATO will take command of at least part of the operation. Don't believe it. The United States will be functionally in charge, and thus on the hook, until this ends.[95]

Charles Krauthammer, also Opinion Writer in the *Washington Post*, argued along the same lines in March 25, 2011, at the same time as he was complaining about Obama's lack of leadership:

> Obama seems equally obsessed with handing off the lead role ... America should be merely "one of the partners among many," he said Monday. No primus inter pares for him. Even the Clinton administration spoke of America as the indispensable nation. And it remains so. Yet at a time when the world is hungry for America to lead—no one has anything near our capabilities, experience and resources—America is led by a man determined that it should not.[96]

Steven Biddle, Senior Fellow at the Council on Foreign Relations, saw a pattern in Obama's security policy, "the Obama doctrine," in an article in the *Washington Post* in March 26, 2011: "First, humanitarian interests warrant U.S. military action. Second, such military action should be strictly limited—especially, there should be no ground forces committed. Third, military action must be multilateral, with others sharing the burden and taking the lead whenever possible."[97] That was also something that Jim Hoagland, PostOpinions Contributor in the *Washington Post*, subscribed to in an article on March 30, 2011. "By allowing flexibility in NATO command arrangements," he argued, "Obama opens the door for greater sharing of the real burdens and internal change in the world's most important military alliance."[98]

---

[95] Eugene Robinson, "Lost in a Libyan Fog," *Washington Post*, March 25, 2011. See also Ross Douthat, "A War by Any Name," *New York Times*, March 28, 2011.

[96] Charles Krauthammer, "The Professor's War," *Washington Post*, March 25, 2011.

[97] Steven Biddle, "What Bombs Can't Do in Libya," *Washington Post*, March 26, 2011.

[98] Jim Hoagland, "A Burden Worth Bearing," *Washington Post*, March 30, 2011. See also "Keeping Ahead of Quaddafi," Editorial, *New York Times*, April 8, 2011.

Anne Applebaum, Opinion Writer in the *Washington Post*, did not, however, subscribe to that. She was disappointed in Obama's lack of willingness to lead, in an article on April 12. It had been "odd," she wrote, "to hear American officials refer to 'NATO' the past few days as if it were something alien and foreign," in other words as if the United States was not a part of it. According to her, that was "extraordinary, given that, until last week, most people assumed NATO was an American-led alliance."[99]

The editorial team in the *Washington Post* seems to share that view. They argued that President Obama was more interested in "proving an ideological point," that the United States must not always lead, than creating success for the coalition forces in Libya:

> Yet having reluctantly joined the fight—and accepted the goal of Mr. Gaddafi's ouster—Mr. Obama seems determined to limit the American role even if it makes success impossible. If the president is very lucky, Mr. Gaddafi will be betrayed and overthrown by his followers or somehow induced to step down voluntarily. We can only hope that the NATO alliance does not collapse between now and then.[100]

Also James M. Dubik, Senior Fellow at the Institute for the Study of War, argued along the same lines in the *New York Times* on April 26, 2011:

> In war, leadership is not exercised from the rear by those who seek to risk as little as possible. Washington must stop pretending that we've passed the leadership for the Libyan operation on to NATO. We did so in Bosnia, claiming Europe would take the lead, only to have the 1995 Srebrenica genocide jolt us back to reality. Like it or not, America's leadership has been crucial to most of NATO's successes. The same will be true in Libya.[101]

And Klaus-Dieter Frankenberger, Fellow at the Transatlantic Academy, argued that the United States must lead, even if it did not want to, in a paper from April 2011:

---

[99] Anne Applebaum, "NATO's Last Mission?" *Washington Post*, April 12, 2011.

[100] "The Libya Stalemate," Editorial, *Washington Post*, April 17, 2011. See also "Saving Lives in Libya," Editorial, *Washington Post*, 28 April; and "At Odds over Libya," Editorial, *Washington Post*, May 26, 2011.

[101] James M. Dubik, "Finish the Job," *New York Times*, April 26, 2011.

… Europe does not have global ambitions, even though its economic and financial interests certainly have a global reach. When it comes to global order or geopolitics in Asia, its presence is hardly felt, perhaps with climate change policies being a notable exception. Sometimes it is not engaged at all. This will not change any time soon, however welcome a change in European outlook would be, not the least from an American perspective. But Europe is shrinking. No matter how much the United States wants to redistribute the burdens of maintaining global stability, it cannot defer leadership to others.[102]

The editorial board in the *Washington Post* continued to attack President Obama's policy during the spring and summer of 2011, and the criticism was getting more and more intense, when the discussion on the president's war powers was added. In an editorial on May 1, they called Obama's policy "a strategy of slowness." The president's aides portrayed slowness as "a considered policy," it was argued, and called it a "leading from behind." "Could it be that American passivity is a virtue, worthy of elevation into doctrine?" it was rhetorically asked:

That is an unprecedented yielding of U.S. global leadership on matters of human rights and democracy. It is more likely to increase than lessen anti-Americanism in the Arab world. In both practical and moral terms, "leading from behind" is a mistake.[103]

On May 20, the editorial team wrote that the president's arguments, that it was NATO, and not the United States, that led the Libya War and that he therefore did not need congressional approval, was quite problematic from a legal perspective. "We sympathize," they wrote, "with his dilemma, but ignoring the law of the land is not an acceptable way out."[104]

David Ignatius, a columnist in the *Washington Post*, took a more philosophical position on June 12, 2011, when he wrote that the "genuinely multilateralist" Obama administration, "eager to break with the unilateral

---

[102] Frankenberger, "The Atlantic Imperative in an Era of a Global Power Shift," p. 7.

[103] "A Strategy of Slowness," Editorial, *Washington Post*, May 1, 2011. See also Bruce Ackerman and Oona Hathaway, "Libya's Looming Deadline," *Washington Post*, May 18, 2011; and George F. Will, "Obama's Illegal War," *Washington Post*, May 29, 2011.

[104] "A Deadline on Libya," Editorial, *Washington Post*, May 20, 2011.

policymaking of George W. Bush," had trouble finding reliable partners. This was a world, he continued "that resents American domination but is also wary of sharing the burden," where the allies did not want to be followers, "but they don't want to share leadership, either."[105]

After Secretary Gates's speech in Brussels on June 10, 2011, when he "accused" the European NATO members for not taking their fair share of the burden and responsibility for the alliance, the *Washington Post's* editorial board noted that the secretary's "sermon" was "well-justified," but also ironic, since the United States stood before huge defense cuts itself. It was hard, they argued:

> … to see Europeans responding to appeals like that of Mr. Gates at a time when the United States is reducing its military capabilities, scaling back its objectives and insisting on taking a back seat during a war. It may be that NATO has a dim future, but if so it's not only because its smaller members are shirking their responsibilities. It's also because its dominant member leader is eschewing its indispensable role of leadership.[106]

And the criticism of the lack of leadership went on. In an editorial on June 18, the War Powers Resolution became a vehicle for the criticism. At the same time as Obama undermined NATO's operation with halfhearted US engagement, he also violated the US legislation, they argued.[107] Furthermore, on June 27, Fred Hiatt, Editorial Page Editor at the *Washington Post*, wrote that the president had "undermined NATO" by refusing to let US forces play a full part, "putting caveats" on US forces, comparable to those set by the allies in Afghanistan to great US irritation, and creating "a collection of shifting coalitions of the willing" instead of strengthening the alliance.[108]

Volker was also critical to the concept of leading from behind. In an article in the *Christian Science Monitor* on July 28, 2011, he argued that the United States could not "abdicate NATO leadership," and "take a back seat:"

---

[105] David Ignatius, "Where are the Allies?," *Washington Post*, June 12, 2011.

[106] "Mr. Gate's Sermon," Editorial, *Washington Post*, June 14, 2011.

[107] "War by Any Other Name," Editorial, *Washington Post*, June 18, 2011. See also Ross Douthat, "The Diminished President," *New York Times*, August 1, 2011.

[108] Fred Hiatt, "Choosing Decline," *Washington Post*, June 27, 2011. See also Jim Hoagland, "An Uncertain Alliance," *Washington Post*, July 17, 2011.

It is understandable that Americans would be frustrated that Europe does not pull more of the load. But an America that "leads from behind" is not leading at all. We must lead, and bring others with us. By rejecting this role in Libya, the US is allowing NATO to appear a paper tiger. That serves no one's interests.[109]

Applebaum was slightly more positive in the *Washington Post* of August 24, 2011, when she summarized a war that was about to come to an end. The "absence" of US and Western leadership in Libya had been "a disaster for the NATO alliance," she wrote, and NATO's weaknesses had been on "full display," when European troops ran out of arms and ammunition. But, according to Applebaum, "leading from behind" was merely the only option, and the best option:

> This was their [Libya's] revolution, not ours. Now it is poised to become their transition, not ours. We can help and advice. We can point to the experience of others—in Iraq, Chile, Poland—who have also attempted the transition from dictatorship to democracy and who can offer lessons in what to do and what to avoid. We can keep expectations low and promises minimal.[110]

Hoagland was also relatively positive to the US leadership in an article in the *Washington Post* of August 25, 2011, when he wrote that "leading from behind" should bring a sound "redistribution of responsibility and authority within NATO." "We must not," he argued, "rush past this opportunity to recognize success, even as it revealed shortcomings, and to encourage Europe to take on more responsibility (and burden-sharing) in an alliance the United States still needs."[111]

Even more positive was Robert Kagan, Senior Fellow at the Brookings Institution, and famously known for coining the concept "Europeans are from Venus and Americans are from Mars," in an article in the *Washington Post* of August 28. "This was a major triumph for the Atlantic alliance," he declared. It had "disproved" the common view "that the world's great democracies are

---

[109] Kurt Volker, "Afghanistan and Libya Point NATO to Five Lessons," *The Christian Science Monitor*, July 28, 2011.
[110] Anne Applebaum, "Let Libya Take Charge of Its Revolution," *Washington Post*, August 24, 2011.
[111] Jim Hoagland, "What We've Learned in Libya," *Washington Post*, August 25, 2011.

in terminal decline," and showed that they were "still powerful and capable of acting together when their interests and ideals are threatened." Furthermore, the United States had not at all led from behind, according to him:

> ... only the United States had the weaponry to open a safe path for the air and ground war against Gaddafi's forces ... The president and the secretary of state also carried out an adept diplomacy, garnering not only European but also, remarkably, Arab support, which in turn forced Russia and China to acquiesce ... Only the United States could have pulled this off. In an allegedly "post-American" world, it is remarkable how indispensable the United States remains.[112]

Ignatius was also relatively positive in an article in the *Washington Post* on September 4, 2011, when he summarized his impressions. The danger of taking "a back seat" on Libya, he argued, was that without "decisive American leadership," the Libya campaign could have fell apart. But Obama and his NATO allies proved, he continued, "steadier and more patient" which eventually led to success:

> For an administration that came into office believing that allies needed to do more of the fighting and pay more of the costs, Libya has been a validation ... But for a world used to an America out front, the quiet and secondary U.S. role—however realistic—seems strange. It certainly isn't making America any more beloved by the Arabs ... Obviously, it will take a while to accept that quiet American leadership is still leadership.[113]

Ignatius was even more positive in an article in the *Washington Post* on October 21, when he argued that Obama's "cautious, back-seat approach to Libya" denied Gaddafi the final, apocalyptic confrontation with the US:

> Indeed, the denouement in Libya has been a good argument for halfway measures (or at least, half-visible ones). This was an instance when Mr. Cool had it pretty much right ... Obama deliberately kept the United States in the background even when critics began howling for a show of American "leadership." And most important, he was patient through the

---

[112] Robert Kagan, "An Imperfect Triumph in Libya," *Washington Post*, August 28, 2011.
[113] David Ignatius, "A Foreign Policy That Works," *Washington Post*, September 4, 2011.

summer, rejecting the counsel of those who argued that he must escalate U.S. military intervention to break the stalemate or, alternatively, bail out.[114]

Positive was also Harvard Professor Stephen M. Walt, in an article in the *National Interest*, published by the think tank "The Center for the National Interest," in Washington, DC, in the end of 2011:

> Forcing NATO's European members to take the lead in the recent Libyan war was a good first step, because the United States will never get its continental allies to bear more of the burden if it insists on doing most of the work itself. Indeed, by playing hard to get on occasion, Washington would encourage others to do more to win our support, instead of resenting or rebelling against the self-appointed "indispensable nation."[115]

So in sum, similar to the debate about how NATO should be guided in Congress, the policy debate shows that there were two relatively strong groups of actors that either supported a "rational," minimalist US way of leading NATO, or wanted the United States to lead in a "charismatic," maximalist way.

In sum, the policy debate during the Libya War can be visualized in Table 2.3.

Table 2.3 Results from the US NATO debate over Libya in think tanks and elite media

Vision	Military, political, and cultural
Mission	Collective security and values
Guidance	Rational or charismatic

Similar to the case of the US Congress, the actors within the think tank and elite media environment did have a moderate to high (maximalist) view of NATO's importance in US long-term security policy. The vision of NATO was

---

[114] David Ignatius, "A Moment to Savor," *Washington Post*, October 21, 2011. See also Clark, A. Murdock and Becca Smith, "The Libyan Intervention: A Study in U.S. Grand Strategy," in *Global Forecast 2011: International Security in a Time of Uncertainty*, eds Craig Cohen and Josiane Gabel, Washington, DC: CSIS, 2011, p. 62.

[115] Stephen M. Walt, "The End of the American Era," *The National Interest*, November/December 2011, p. 14.

described as a military, political, and cultural tool, NATO's mission was to promote collective security and values, and NATO should be led either in a rational or in a charismatic way.

It is now time to summarize the first empirical chapter on the US NATO debate that was going on before, during, and after the Libya War, and make some reflections.

Summary and reflections

As has been demonstrated in this chapter, US Congress, think tanks, and elite media expressed a similar view of NATO's importance in US long-term security policy—a moderate to high importance. The Obama administration had a more minimalistic view—a moderate to low importance. The results of the empirical investigation are summarized in Table 2.4.

Table 2.4 The US NATO debate during the Libya War

Issue/Arena	The Political Debate		The Policy Debate
	Congress	*Administration*	*Think tanks and elite media*
Vision	Political, and cultural	Military and political	Military, political, and cultural
Mission	Collective security and values	Collective security	Collective security and values
Guidance	Rational or charismatic	Rational	Rational or charismatic
Importance	Moderate to high	Moderate to low	Moderate to high

As the table shows, the debate taken together indicates a moderate role for NATO in US security policy during the Libya War. The administration expressed the most minimalist view of NATO, while Congress and the policy actors expressed a more maximalist view. The administration neither emphasized NATO as a cultural tool (maximalist vision), nor argued for a charismatic US leadership of NATO (maximalist guidance). In Congress, think tanks, and elite media both maximalist and minimalist views of the vision of NATO and the guidance of NATO were expressed.

The moderate importance of NATO in US long-term security policy manifested in the US NATO debate during 2011, before, during, and after the Libya War thus supports the arguments made in scholarly literature on NATO, that the alliance is on its way to be—or already is—a post-American alliance with a lower level of US engagement and leadership.

3

2012–2013: The Chicago Summit and the Syria Conflict

In May 20–21, 2012, NATO held a summit in President Obama's hometown, Chicago. It was the first time a NATO Summit had been held in the United States outside Washington, DC. The three issues discussed most frequently at the summit were NATO's exit from Afghanistan, "smart defense" (including missile defense), and NATO's partnership policy.

The Syria Conflict, an ongoing civil war between opponents to the Syrian dictator Bashar al-Assad and his regime, started around the same time as the Libya War, escalated in November 2011, and has, since then, been one of the bloodiest conflicts in the world since the Cold War ended. Around 200,000 people have been killed, and more than three million Syrians had fled the country, one of the largest forced migrations since World War II. In late August 2013, al-Assad launched an attack with chemical weapons (sarin) at the opposition-controlled suburbs of Damascus, killing hundreds of innocent civilians. The attack was condemned by the UN, but the Security Council could not agree on a military intervention, because of Chinese and Russian resistance. Britain, France, and the United States made preparations to strike without a UN mandate, but they could not get enough domestic support for it.[1]

The Syria Conflict, especially after the gas attacks, animated the US NATO debate because it was a case where the United States did not want to act unilaterally. NATO was by many actors seen as a vehicle to create legitimacy

---

[1] For an overview of the Syria Conflict, see Brian Michael Jenkins, *The Dynamics of Syria's Civil War*, RAND Corporation, Perspective, RAND: Santa Monica, CA, 2014, www.rand.org (homepage), date accessed July 5, 2014.

for military action against al-Assad's regime. The Syria Conflict was once again actualized in the US NATO debate during the summer and autumn of 2014, when the "Islamic State" (IS or ISIL) became a major actor in the region, then animating US and coalition military strikes in Iraq and Syria to protect allied personnel, and civilians threatened by IS (this will be analyzed in the next chapter).[2]

This chapter will focus on the US NATO debate during 2012–2013, especially around the Chicago Summit and in connection to the Syria Conflict. The picture of the importance of NATO in US long-term security policy as manifested in the US NATO debate is similar to the chapter on the Libya War.

In Congress, the discussion about the vision of NATO was still moderate to high (maximalist). NATO's role was described as a military, political, and cultural tool, and the emphasis was on NATO as a political and cultural organization rather than a military one. NATO's mission was most often described as serving collective security and promoting values. And the view of the guidance of NATO was still polarized: either should NATO be led in a rational—minimalist—way, or it should be led in a charismatic—maximalist—way.

In the Obama administration, NATO's importance continued to be described as moderate to low (minimalist). The alliance was first and foremost described as a military and political tool, but seldom as a cultural tool. Furthermore, NATO's main mission was still described as promoting collective security and to some degree values. The administration also continued to underscore that NATO was supposed to be guided in a rational way.

In the think tank and elite media environment, lastly, the debate was also similar to the previous period. The actors within the policy arena were still arguing for a moderate to high (maximalist) view of the vision and mission of NATO, but the arguments on how NATO should be led were less polarized

---

[2] See, for example, Barack Obama, "Statement by the President," August 28 , 2014, www.whitehouse .gov (homepage), date accessed September 6, 2014; Barack Obama, "Statement by the President on Airstrikes in Syria," September 23, 2014, www.whitehouse.gov (homepage), date accessed January 6, 2015.

during 2012–2013 than during 2011. The focus was on rational (minimalist) leadership rather than either rational or charismatic leadership, which indicates a slightly lower importance of NATO in US long-term security policy.

Taken together, the results reinforce the conclusion from the preceding chapter, that is, a moderate US view of NATO's importance in US long-term security policy.

In the following sections, the importance of NATO in US long-term security policy as manifested in the US political and policy debate will be demonstrated in detail.

The political debate in Congress

The same pattern that was found in Congress regarding the *vision* of NATO before, during, and after the Libya War in 2011 can be found during the period 2012–2013. NATO was not seen as solely a military organization—it also had political and cultural relevance. And the party lines did not seem to matter much during this period either.

The arguments were also similar; NATO was seen as a collective force for good, creating stability and security, and spreading Western culture. In the House of Representatives on January 25, 2012, Congressman John Mondy Shimkus (R, Illinois), talked about "the values that underpin NATO: freedom, democracy, fundamental human rights, and the rule of law."[3] NATO's military character was sometimes mentioned, but the focus was on its political and cultural sides. The alliance was seen as political tool, but not least as a tool for spreading democracy and Western culture, through its "open door" policy and ability to facilitate valuable reforms.

Before the Chicago Summit was held several Congress members touched upon such issues.[4] Senator Shaheen, for example, said in a budget hearing on March 1, 2012, that she hoped that NATO's "open door" policy should be addressed at NATO's Chicago Summit, and—perhaps most important

---

[3]   CRHR, January 25, 2012, "High-Level Nuclear Waste," p. H172.
[4]   SFRC, *National Security and Foreign Policy Priorities in the FY 2013 International Affairs Budget*, February 28, No. 112–599, Washington, DC: USGPO, 2012, pp. 133, 137.

of all—"to find a way to introduce the organization to the next generation of citizens and leaders who are not yet familiar with this alliance's many past successes and its future potential." A NATO that was relevant for the twenty-first century was, according to her, "flexible, adaptable, and able to transform itself."[5]

Another example is Senator Benjamin L. Cardin (D, Maryland), who in a hearing about NATO on May 10, 2012, was disappointed that the summit was not going to be "an enlargement summit," because enlargement was driving cultural change, according to him:

> It has been that ability or desire to join either the European Union or NATO that has been a motivating factor to accelerate democratic reforms in many countries of Europe. And we have seen that work very successfully. I think there must be some disappointment that the summit [in Chicago] will not be an enlargement summit.[6]

Cardin wanted the administration to continue to "keep the momentum moving toward democratic reform and ultimate membership in NATO in countries that we have been very actively engaged."[7]

In a hearing about the situation in Kosovo and Serbia in the House of Representatives on April 24, 2013, Congressman Engel argued along the same lines, when he said that Kosovo's pathway toward NATO was very important. According to him, a membership in NATO would "cement" Kosovo's "Western outlook." He looked forward to the day when Kosovo's military forces would stand "side by side with American soldiers in the fight against international terrorism and other global ills."[8]

Besides that it was also a lot of appreciation of NATO because of its great political importance for US, transatlantic, and global security. Senator Carl Levin (D, Michigan) argued in a hearing in Senate on February 28, 2012,

---

[5]   SASC, *Department of Defense Authorization for Appropriations for Fiscal Year 2013 and the Future Years Defense Program*, Pt. 1, Washington, DC: USGPO, 2012, pp. 371–372.

[6]   SFRC, *NATO: Chicago and Beyond*, May 10, No. 112–601, Washington, DC: USGPO, 2012, p. 19.

[7]   Ibid., p. 19. See also SASC, *Department of Defense Authorization for Appropriations for Fiscal Year 2013 and the Future Years Defense Program*, Pt. 1, pp. 343–344.

[8]   HFAC, *Kosovo and Serbia: A Pathway to Peace*, No. 113–23, Washington, DC: USGPO, 2013, pp. 7–8.

that the strategic guidance that the Department of Defense recently had issued "reaffirmed that Europe is our principal partner in seeking global and economic security for now and for the foreseeable future," and that it also stressed the central role NATO served "for the security of Europe and beyond."[9] The next day, Senator Shaheen was talking about the coming Chicago Summit, and that it was "a unique and timely opportunity to reiterate that the NATO alliance continues to wield unprecedented influence in our world and remains a critical element of U.S. and European security." According to her, NATO still represented "the most capable military alliance the world has ever seen."[10] And in another hearing, on May 10, 2012, she said that NATO was a "dominant force for good in the world," and that the United States and NATO continued to wield "unprecedented influence."[11]

During the rest of the year 2013, the pattern was the same; NATO's political and cultural character was highlighted in Congress. On March 13, 2013, Congressman John P. Sarbanes (D, Maryland) said in the House of Representatives that NATO's Partnership for Peace program brought "peace and stability to conflict regions."[12] In a hearing in the House of Representatives March 15, 2013, Congresswoman Loretta Sanchez (D, California) said that the military integration that was an effect of NATO had created interoperability and mission readiness that was a good thing "for stability around the world."[13]

In sum, the focus in Congress regarding the vision of NATO was the same as in 2011, moderate to high (maximalist); NATO was described as a military organization, but its political and cultural character was much more in focus in the discussion than its military character.

---

[9] SASC, *Department of Defense Authorization for Appropriations for Fiscal Year 2013 and the Future Yars Defense Program*, February 14, 28; March 1, 6, 8, 13, 15, 20, 27, No. 112–590, Pt. 1, Washington, DC: USGPO, 2012, p. 266.

[10] Ibid., p. 371.

[11] SFRC, *NATO: Chicago and Beyond*, pp. 32–33.

[12] CRER, March 13, 2013, "The Nagorno Karabakh," p. E 280. See also Congressional Record, Extensions of Remarks (CRER), June 11, 2013, "Regarding American Leadership in the Balkans," p. E 837, where Congressman Robert E. Andrews (D, New Jersey), makes a similar argument.

[13] HASC, *The Posture of the U.S. European Command and U.S. Africa Command*, March 15, No. 113–119, Washington, DC: USGPO, 2013, p. 4.

Regarding NATO's mission, the pattern was also similar to that in 2011; NATO's mission was to serve US interests, but the focus in the discussion in Congress was on its mission as a promoter of collective security and values.

A good example of when two of NATO's functions—promoting US interests and creating collective security—melted together was the development of NATO's ballistic missile defense (BMD) system directed against Iran and other potentially hostile countries that had the ability to threaten NATO's territory with nuclear weapons or other types of missiles. Such a system had been discussed for long in NATO, but at the NATO Summit in Lisbon in 2010, the NATO members decided to develop such a system.[14]

In a budget hearing on March 1, 2012, the question of NATO's BMD came up, and Senator Levin said that the BMD system protected US deployed forces, US allies, and US partners. In addition, it could intensify cooperation with Russia, which would send "a powerful signal to Iran of world unity against their developing long-range missiles or their having nuclear weapons."[15] Senator McCain was in the same hearing underscoring the value of NATO, including the BMD system, when it came to collective action to handle the present security challenges:

> Our European allies remain our preeminent security partners. Today, the US European Command (EUCOM) and NATO are being called upon to bear an ever greater responsibility for diverse international security challenges, from Afghanistan and Libya, to cyber threats and transnational terrorism, to BMD and the strategic balance of forces on the continent. We must be mindful of the enduring value and impact of our European alliances as we evaluate change to our force posture.[16]

---

[14] See, for example, Tom Sauer and Bob van der Swaan, "US Tactical Nuclear Weapons After NATO's Lisbon Summit: Why Their Withdrawal Is Desirable and Feasible," *International Relations*, Vol. 26, No. 1 (2012), pp. 78–100.

[15] SASC, *Department of Defense Authorization for Appropriations for Fiscal Year 2013 and the Future Years Defense Program*, Pt. 1, p. 267. A similar argument of how US interests and collective security could reinforce each other was made by Senator Marco Rubio (R, Florida) in a Senate hearing about the US "rebalancing" toward Asia. See SFRC, *Rebalance to Asia II: Security and Defence; Cooperation and Challenges*, No. 113–138, Washington, DC: USGPO, p. 17.

[16] SASC, *Department of Defense Authorization for Appropriations for Fiscal Year 2013 and the Future Years Defense Program*, p. 271.

In the same hearing, Senator Lieberman also took up the Syria Conflict, where he wanted the US and NATO to act. Just like Senator Kerry the year before, in connection with the Libya War, he used the experiences from NATO's operations in the former Yugoslavia, Bosnia, and Kosovo in the 1990s, to underpin his argument: "In both of those cases, when we got involved, we were able to stop it—NATO, our coalition of the willing—and brought about a much better situation than existed before. I hope before long we will be able to do that there [in Syria] as well."[17] NATO should, in other words, be used to create collective security and promote human rights, according to several members of Congress.

In the end of March 2012, the Senate also approved a Resolution before the NATO summit in Chicago, where it expressed strong support for NATO for promoting collective security. The Senate stated that NATO for more than sixty years had "served to ensure peace, security, and stability in Europe and throughout the world," it reaffirmed that NATO was "oriented for the changing international security environment and the challenges of the future," and urged NATO members to utilize the NATO summit to "address current NATO operations, future capabilities and burden-sharing issues, and the relationship between NATO and partners around the world."[18]

Similar to the previous period, there were critical voices as well, especially from republicans. Congressman Coffman, for example, said in the House of Representatives on May 10, 2012, that the two US Army Brigades that the Department of Defense had announced to be withdrawn from Europe was not enough:

> The current proposal is only a step in the right direction. We should retain only the headquarters and support infrastructure necessary for expeditionary capabilities, and we should withdraw all four combat brigades from Europe. In order for the U.S. military to modernize and move forward towards a more agile strategy, we must close bases

[17] SASC, *Department of Defense Authorization for Appropriations for Fiscal Year 2013 and the Future Years Defense Program*, pp. 343–344.
[18] CRS, March 29, 2012, "Expressing Sense of Senate in Support of NATO and NATO Summit Being Held May 20 Through 21, 2012," p. S2280.

in Europe. There is no longer a strategic reason to maintain nearly 80,000 troops in Europe.[19]

Two longer discussions on NATO and NATO's mission were held in the Senate in January 2013, in the hearings about the nominations of Senator Kerry to be Secretary of State, and of Chuck Hagel to be Secretary of Defense. Both Kerry's and Hagel's statements in the hearings belong to the political debate, but it is difficult to decide if they belong to the debate in Congress or to the debate in the administration. Formally they were not part of the Obama administration during the hearings. On the other hand it can be argued that they both wanted to represent the Obama administration more than anything else.

Anyway, on January 24, 2013, when Senator Kerry's hearing was carried out in the Foreign Relations Committee, he was asked by Senator Rubio about Libya, and Kerry replied that the engagement through NATO in the Libya War had been in the US interests, that he supported it, and that it had resulted in "exactly" what the United States wanted to achieve.[20] Almost all of Kerry's responses about NATO's mission were supportive of the organization in general, and of NATO's ability to promote collective security and universal values in particular.

On a question from Senator "Bob" Corker (R, Tennessee), for example, about the New START Treaty, he answered that it was "critical" that the United States continued to "consult" with its NATO allies, who had said that they looked forward to develop "transparency and confidence-building ideas with Russia."[21] On a question from Senator "Bob" Menendez (D, New Jersey) about his attitude to supporting the former Yugoslav Republic of Macedonia's future NATO membership, he answered that he would "fully support" that once the dispute with Greece over Macedonia's name has been resolved. According to Kerry, it was "in the interest of Euro-Atlantic integration, economic prosperity, peace, and security in the region," to solve the name dispute as soon as possible so that Macedonia could be a NATO member.[22]

---

[19] CRHR, May 10, 2012, "Reducing America's Military Footprint and Spending in Europe," p. H 2572.
[20] SFRC, *Nomination of John F. Kerry to Be Secretary of State*, January 24, No. 113–163, Washington, DC: USGPO, 2013, p. 32.
[21] Ibid., p. 67.
[22] Ibid., p. 104.

On another question from Senator Corker about if he was prepared to "press all NATO members to increase their defense expenditures," he replied:

I will continue to urge allied commitments to sustain and build critical capabilities, as part of an effort to invest in a NATO Force for 2020 that is fully trained and equipped to respond to any threat and defend our common interests. Adequate levels of spending are crucial to that goal … Among our ongoing top priorities is ensuring the alliance has the assets and capabilities it needs to carry out current and future operations.[23]

On another question from Senator James E. Risch (R, Idaho) he also said that he would "continue the United States unwavering support" for NATO's "open door" policy:

The enlargement process has, and will, continue to serve as a vehicle for promoting democratic institutions and civilian control of the military within the countries of the Euro-Atlantic region. Through NATO's open door, the United States has made great strides in realizing the goal of a Europe whole, free, and at peace.[24]

Through all those answers, Senator Kerry, in sum, confirmed the relatively maximalist view of NATO's mission that was a pattern in Congress during in 2011, and during 2012–2013: NATO should serve US interests, but not least promote collective security and universal values.

So did Hagel in his hearing before the Senate's Armed Services Committee on January 31, 2013. Hagel said that the United States was working with its allies "to achieve a peaceful and orderly political transition in Syria."[25] Hagel also said that US and NATO operations in Libya were a success:

Both operations had limited and clear objectives for the unique capabilities the U.S. military could provide, avoided U.S. boots-on-the-ground, integrated allies and partners, minimized collateral damage and civilian casualties to a historically unprecedented extent, and enjoyed the legitimacy

---

[23] SFRC, *Nomination of John F. Kerry to Be Secretary of State*, January 24, No. 113–163, Washington, DC: USGPO, 2013, p. 118.

[24] Ibid., p. 141.

[25] SASC, *Nominations Before the Senate Armed Service Committee, First Session, 113ᵗʰ Congress*, January 31; February 12, 14, 28; April 11; July 18, 25, 30; September 19; October 10, No. 113–270, Washington DC: USGPO, 2013, p. 176.

of U.N. Security Council authorization. This was all achieved at a fraction of the cost of recent interventions in the Balkans, Iraq, or Afghanistan.[26]

And on a question from Senator Levin, about if it was in the US interest to participate in NATO, Hagel answered that the transatlantic relationship was of "critical importance" to US security interests, that NATO had been "the cornerstone of European security and an integral part of U.S. foreign policy for more than 60 years," and that the alliance had "been vital to stability and has moved us closer to the goal of a Europe whole, free, and at peace." NATO "must remain the central Alliance" in US global strategy, he said, and it had to adapt to meet the new threats, such as cyber-attacks, terrorism, proliferation of WMD, and regional conflicts.[27] Hagel also supported NATO enlargement, and that the United States worked through NATO to reduce the amount of non-strategic nuclear weapons.[28] Regardless of the US rebalance to the Asia-Pacific, NATO was "crucial," according to Hagel.[29]

The focus on collective security and values continued during 2013. In a hearing on March 21, 2013, Tom Marino (R, Pennsylvania) wanted to make cyber warfare "top priority" for NATO.[30] And at the time when the debate about the Syria Conflict peaked in the United States, on September 4, 2013, Congressman Meeks warned against using force unilaterally in a hearing in the House of Representatives. If force should be used, it should be used within a multilateral framework, that is, through NATO, according to him:

> I believe that the use of chemical weapons by the Assad regime is indeed a flagrant violation of international norms against the use of such weapons, and this and other repugnant acts by Syrian forces are indeed against U.S. interests. But it is not only against U.S. interests; it is also against the international interests. So if we act in a unilateral way, I have huge concerns; that if there is a violation, we should act, especially militarily, in a multilateral way. We have regional countries—and I have been listening to the testimony

---

[26] SASC, *Nominations Before the Senate Armed Service Committee, First Session, 113th Congress*, January 31; February 12, 14, 28; April 11; July 18, 25, 30; September 19; October 10, No. 113–270, Washington DC: USGPO, 2013, p. 176.

[27] Ibid., p. 180.

[28] Ibid., p. 181.

[29] Ibid., p. 260.

[30] HFAC, *Cyber Attacks: An Unprecedented Threat to U.S. National Security*, No. 113–118, Washington, DC: USGPO, 2013, p. 17.

here, but I don't know where NATO is. At least I have heard NATO, who basically said they have condemned it, but I don't hear them saying that they will step up with us militarily.[31]

To sum up, the discussion about NATO's mission in Congress during 2012–2013 was quite similar to the debate in 2011, that is, a moderate to high (maximalist) view. The Congressmen and Congresswomen acknowledged that NATO should promote US interests, but the emphasis was on promoting collective security and universal values.

Regarding how NATO should be led, lastly, it was also the same pattern in Congress as before, under, and after the Libya War in 2011; some argued that the United States should lead in a "rational way," that it was a good thing the allies took the lead when proper (the minimalist view), and others argued that the United States should lead in a "charismatic way," that the United States should lead as NATO's primus inter pares (the maximalist view).[32]

The results from the first part of the political debate, the debate in Congress, can thereby be summarized in Table 3.1.

Table 3.1 Results from the US NATO debate over Syria in Congress

Vision	Political and cultural
Mission	Collective security and values
Guidance	Rational or charismatic

The US Congressmen and Congresswomen continued to argue for a moderate to high importance of NATO in US long-term security policy, which also is a sign of continuity over time. Still, Congress was expressing ambivalence to the question of NATO's guidance; the representatives were either arguing for rational leadership or arguing for charismatic leadership.

---

[31] HFAC, *Syria: Weighing the Obama Administration's Response*, September 4, No. 113–113, Washington, DC: USGPO, 2013, pp. 28–29.

[32] See, for example, SFRC, *National Security and Foreign Policy Priorities in the FY 2013 International Affairs Budget*, p. 140; SASC, *Department of Defense Authorization for Appropriations for Fiscal Year 2013 and the Future Years Defense Program*, Pt. 1, p. 267.

The political debate in the administration

The views of the Obama administration on NATO's importance in US long-term security policy during 2012–2013 were also characterized by continuity rather than change. The administration continued to put most emphasis on the vision of NATO as a military and political tool. The cultural side of the alliance was, similar to the period before, mentioned now and then, but that was not a common description.

That the Obama administration seldom argued for a cultural vision of NATO can be explained by the arguments made by Thomas Carothers, at the Carnegie Endowment for International Peace, in a recent book chapter. Carothers argues that "stability," rather than "democracy promotion," has been the focus of the Obama administration, that "the administration has not yet made democracy promotion a truly central concern in any major region that is in the heart of American geostrategic agenda."[33]

In his "Munich Speech" on February 4, 2012, Secretary Panetta underscored that, despite financial problems, the alliance remained "rooted in the strong bonds of transatlantic security cooperation and collective defense." Panetta also talked about the buildup of a missile defense system in Europe and shared intelligence capabilities "that will ensure NATO remains the strongest and most capable military alliance on earth."[34]

Secretary Clinton was also underscoring NATO's military and political character in her speech, but she also mentioned the alliance's cultural character. The Munich Conference, she said, "founded at the height of the Cold War," had become "an important symbol of our commitment to stand together as a transatlantic community:"

> ... we come to Munich each year, not only to advance our shared values, our shared security, and our shared prosperity, but to take stock of where we stand in the efforts to forge that union between us, and also to lift up our heads and look around the world at the global security situation. That

---

[33] Thomas Carothers, "Barack Obama," in *US Foreign Policy and Democracy Promotion: From Theodore Roosevelt to Barack Obama*, eds Michael Cox, Timothy J. Lynch, and Nicholas Bouchet, London: Routledge, 2013, p. 211.

[34] Leon E. Panetta, "Munich Security Conference," Speech February 4, 2012, http://www.defense.gov (homepage), date accessed January 23, 2013.

calling is no less powerful today than it was 50 years ago … our commitment to European defense is just as deep and durable as our diplomacy … So when President Obama says that "Europe remains the cornerstone of our engagement with the world," those aren't just reassuring words. That is the reality.[35]

In a budget hearing in the Senate in the end of February 2012, she was almost entirely focusing on NATO as a military tool. On a question from Senator Lugar, regarding the agenda of the administration for the Chicago Summit, she replied that the NATO allies had to develop and maintain "critical alliance capabilities to ensure that NATO is able to perform a variety of roles and missions in the evolving security environment." This included, according to her, completion of NATO's "Deterrence and Defense Posture Review" (DDPR), as well as meeting the capabilities requirements agreed upon at the Lisbon Summit in 2010. And when she talked about NATO's "open door" policy she was not focusing on political and cultural aspects but military aspects. The important thing was operational effectiveness:

> The United States works bilaterally and through NATO to support aspirants' efforts to meet NATO standards and encourage them to take the steps required to become interoperable with NATO. We offer joint training opportunities, in addition to encouraging and supporting partner contributions to NATO's worldwide operations in order to increase interoperability and build an atmosphere of cooperation and trust at all levels of planning and operations.[36]

Secretary Panetta was also focused on defense and security when he defended his budget in a Senate hearing on February 28, 2012. NATO, he said, was a "net provider of global security," and it was "the most capable alliance in history:"

[35] Hillary R. Clinton, "Remarks at Euro-Atlantic Security Community Initiative and Keynote Session Q&A," February 4, 2012, www.state.gov (homepage), date accessed March 11, 2013. See also Hillary R. Clinton, "Press Availability Following Ministerial Meetings at NATO Headquarters," December 5, 2012, www.state.gov (homepage), date accessed March 16, 2013.

[36] SFRC, *National Security and Foreign Policy Priorities in the FY 2013 International Affairs Budget*, p. 102. See also p. 134, regarding "smart defense."

Our NATO allies are our most reliable and capable partners for advancing our shared international security objectives. The transatlantic relationship is critical to confronting the challenges of a complex, dangerous, and fast-changing world. The President, Secretary Clinton, and I have been emphasizing this to allies since we announced our new Defense Strategic Guidance in January and will continue to do so during the NATO summit in Chicago.[37]

In a speech on April 3, Secretary Clinton carried on with her military focus. The vision of NATO that had been laid out in Lisbon 2010 "commits us to ensuring that NATO can deter and defend against any threat" she said.[38] Other actors representing the Obama administration were also promoting a mainly military and political vision of NATO. Jim Townsend, Deputy Assistant Secretary of Defense for European and NATO Policy, Department of Defense, was for example describing NATO in such a way in a Senate hearing on May 10, 2012. Even after the Cold War, he said, the Article V commitment remained "the core" of the alliance: "NATO serves as the organizing framework to ensure that we have allies willing and able to fight alongside us in conflict and provides an integrated military structure that puts the military teeth behind alliance political decisions to take action."[39]

In the same hearing, Assistant Secretary Gordon argued that NATO enlargement had been good for Europe; that it had "contributed to democracy in Europe and stability."[40] But his focus was also founded on NATO as a military and political organization. Its capacity to deter and respond to security challenges would only be as successful if its forces were "able, effective, interoperable, and modern," he argued.[41]

When the president himself talked at the NATO Summit in Chicago on May 20, 2012, he also underscored NATO's military and political character. The alliance had been a "bedrock of our common security," Obama said,

---

[37] SASC, *Department of Defense Authorization for Appropriations for Fiscal Year 2013 and the Future Years Defense Program*, Pt. 1, p. 128.
[38] Hillary R. Clinton, "Remarks to the World Affairs Council 2012 NATO Conference," April 3, 2012, www.state.gov (homepage), date accessed February 22, 2013.
[39] SFRC, *NATO: Chicago and Beyond*, pp. 10–11.
[40] Ibid., p. 20.
[41] Ibid., p. 4.

"of freedom and of prosperity" in more than sixty years. The "bold plan of action" to revitalize the alliance and ensure that it had the tools required "to confront a changing and uncertain strategic landscape, that were agreed upon in Lisbon in 2010, was implemented in Chicago." According to him:

> NATO is a force multiplier, and the initiatives we will endorse today will allow each of our nations to accomplish what none of us could achieve alone. We can all be proud that in Lisbon we committed, and now in Chicago we are delivering.[42]

The trend in the Obama administration to describe NATO as first and foremost a military and political tool, not a cultural tool, in US security policy went on during 2013. In a speech at King's College, London, on January 18, 2013, Secretary Panetta's last "NATO speech," he said that NATO must work more cost-effectively together to be able to meet "the most relevant security challenges that we face today and tomorrow:"

> NATO can no longer be an alliance focused on a single type of mission, whether deterring the aggression of another superpower or conducting stability operations in Afghanistan. To be prepared to quickly respond to a wide range of threats in an era of fiscal constraint, we have got to build an innovative, flexible, and rotational model for forward-developed presence and training.[43]

According to Panetta, NATO has been "the most effective and capable and enduring multilateral security alliance the world has ever seen," and "the bedrock of America's global network of alliances and partnerships."[44]

In Vice President Biden's talk in Munich on February 2, 2013, he was mainly describing NATO as a political organization. He also seemed to play down the US "rebalancing" toward Asia Pacific, when he argued that the United States would "remain both a Pacific power and an Atlantic power," and that the US strategy shift was in the interest of Europe: "we all have an important and

---

[42] Barack Obama, "Remarks by President Obama at Opening NAC Meeting," Speech May 20, 2012, www.whitehouse.gov (homepage), date accessed February 21, 2013.

[43] Leon E. Panetta, "King's College London," Speech January 18, 2013, http://www.defense.gov (homepage), date accessed January 22, 2013.

[44] Ibid.

specific interest in an Asia-Pacific region that is peaceful and growing ... So we ought to intensify our cooperation in advance of those interests, moving forward together."[45]

Also in a speech on July 19, 2013, at the George Washington University in Washington, DC, Biden played down the US "rebalancing," when he said that "we're not leaving Europe," and that "[w]e're not going anywhere." Biden was convinced that the combination of new transatlantic economic agreements and the Trans-Pacific Partnership "reinforce one another." "Folks," he said "that's what big powers do. To use the vernacular, we can walk and chew gum at the same time. That's what big powers do."[46]

The trend to present NATO as first and foremost a military and political tool continued during the year. On April 11, 2013, the new Secretary of Defense, Chuck Hagel, said in a hearing in the House of Representatives, that the United States would fully support NATO, and were committed to "the entire framework, the objective, the purpose of NATO." He did not believe that there had existed a collective security arrangement in the world like it, ever.[47]

And after a meeting with the Polish foreign minister on June 3, 2013, in Washington, DC, Secretary Kerry said that "we are both focused on European security," and "of course, our commitment to Article 5 of NATO is ironclad."[48] Finally, when he spoke in Brussels on December 3, 2013, he said that "we have to take every single opportunity in order to renew our commitment to the transatlantic relationship and to cement NATO's role as the transatlantic core of a global security community."[49]

So, to sum up, the view of the vision of NATO within the Obama administration did not change much during 2012–2013 compared to 2011.

[45] Joe Biden, "Remarks by the Vice President to the Munich Security Conference," Speech February 2, 2013, www.whitehouse.gov (homepage), date accessed July 1, 2014.
[46] Joe Biden, "Remarks by the Vice President Joe Biden on Asia-Pacific Policy," Speech July 19, 2013, www.whitehouse.gov (homepage), date accessed July 1, 2014.
[47] HASC, April 11, 2013, *Budget Request from the Department of Defense*, No. 113–125, Washington, DC: USGPO, 2013, pp. 33–34.
[48] John Kerry, "Remarks with Polish Foreign Minister Radoslaw Sikorski After Their Meeting," June 3, 2013, www.state.gov (homepage), date accessed June 6, 2013.
[49] John Kerry, "Solo Press Availability at NATO," December 3, 2013, www.state.gov (homepage), date accessed December 4, 2013.

NATO was occasionally described as a cultural organization, but normally and frequently as a military and political organization, and that represents a moderate to low (minimalist) vision of NATO in US security policy.

Regarding NATO's mission, the administration went on emphasizing collective security and to some degree universal values, rather than US interests. When Panetta presented the new US defense strategy in January 2012, he talked about the function of NATO. He said that the United States would "continue to strengthen its key alliances, to build partnerships and to develop innovative ways to sustain U.S. presence elsewhere in the world," and that the close political and military cooperation with the European NATO allies and partners was "critical" in that case: "We will invest in the shared capabilities and responsibilities of NATO, our most effective military alliance." In addition, it was not solely US interests that were at stake:

> We are committed to sustaining a presence that will meet our Article 5 commitments, deter aggression, and the U.S. military will work closely with our allies to allow for the kinds of coalition operations that NATO has undertaken in Libya and Afghanistan.[50]

Later in January 2012, Secretary Clinton held a speech in which she said that she looked forward to the Chicago Summit. The United States, she said, was "fully committed to maintaining a force posture in Europe that meets our enduring commitment to European security and our collective defense obligations to our NATO allies." She also said that the transatlantic partnership was "absolutely indispensable to our own security and well-being."[51]

Secretary Panetta also underscored that NATO's main mission was promoting collective security, but he mentioned universal values as well in his Munich speech on February 4, 2012. Panetta said that the United States should remain a larger military footprint in Europe than in any other place in the world: "That's not only because the peace and prosperity of Europe

---

[50] Leon E Panetta, "Statement on Defense Strategic Guidance," Speech January 5, 2012, http://www .defense.gov (homepage), date accessed January 23, 2013.
[51] Hillary R. Clinton, "Remarks with German Foreign Minister Guido Westerwelle," January 20, 2012, www.state.gov (homepage), date accessed March 11, 2013.

is critically important to the United States, but because Europe remains our security partner, our security partner of choice for military operations and diplomacy around the world."[52] We must, continued Panetta, "meet the great and necessary tests of the 21st century together. And we must draw strength from our common values, our common interests and our common purpose to forge a better and a safer world and to give our children a better life."[53]

In Clinton's speech the same day in Munich, she also related to values, although promoting collective security was described as the main mission for NATO. She said that "Europe is and remains America's partner of first resort," and that "[t]he breadth and depth of our cooperation is remarkable."[54] "We also need to build our capacity to work with partners," she continued, and it would be the focus of NATO's Chicago Summit "to ensure that NATO remains the hub of a global security network with a group of willing and able nations working side-by-side with us."[55] The shared values were "the bedrock of our community," according to Clinton:

> We need to vigorously promote these together around the world, especially in this time of transformational political change. In the Middle East we have a profound shared stake in promoting successful transitions to stable democracies... We have to help consolidate democratic gains in places like Cote d'Ivoire and Kyrgyzstan, and support democratic openings in Burma, and wherever people lack their rights and freedom... And wherever tyrants deny the legitimate demands of their own people, we need to work together to send a clear message: You cannot hold back the future at the point of a gun.[56]

In a budget hearing in the Senate on February 28, 2012, Clinton continued to highlight collective security. The United States was, she said, "able to fulfill its Article Five commitments" and would remain so:

> We are committed to maintaining a robust and visible military presence in Europe capable of deterring and defending against aggression... The United

[52] Panetta, "Munich Security Conference."
[53] Ibid.
[54] Clinton, "Remarks at Euro-Atlantic Security Community Initiative and Keynote Session Q&A."
[55] Ibid.
[56] Ibid.

States is modernizing its presence in Europe at the same time our NATO allies, and NATO itself, are engaged in similar steps… We are determined to adapt NATO forces to make them more deployable, sustainable, and interoperable, and thus more effective. We continue to encourage allies to meet their defense spending commitments and to contribute politically, financially, and operationally to the strength and security of the alliance, even in these austere economic times.[57]

On a question from Senator Shaheen in the same hearing, regarding the agenda of the Obama administration at the Chicago Summit, Clinton replied:

> Looking ahead, in this period of budget austerity, NATO allies need to agree on how to develop and maintain critical alliance capabilities to ensure that NATO is able to perform a variety of roles and missions in the evolving security environment. NATO's Deterrence and Defense Posture Review will outline what allies envision as the appropriate mix of nuclear, conventional, and missile defense forces to meet new security challenges… NATO's partnerships with non-NATO members have been key to the success of our recent operations. Therefore, we would also like to use the summit as an opportunity to highlight the value of some of our key partners' contributions to NATO's operations and broader strategic goals and to ensure we have means in place to work with them when combat operations in Afghanistan have ended.[58]

In a speech on April 3, 2012, Clinton touched upon all aspects of NATO's mission—US interests, collective security, and promotion of universal values—when she said that after the Cold War, "NATO's mission evolved to reforming and integrating Central and Eastern Europe," and that since the NATO Summit in Lisbon, in 2010, had been to adopt "a strategic concept that takes on the security threats of the 21st century from terrorism to cyber-attacks to nuclear proliferation:"

> So as we look at the future before us, as complex and unpredictable as it is, we need to be guided by our own very clear-eyed view of what is in

---

[57] SFRC, *National Security and Foreign Policy Priorities in the FY 2013 International Affairs Budget*, p. 103.
[58] Ibid.

America's interests, and then to chart a path along with our partners in
NATO and other nations who share the values that we believe represent the
best hope for humanity—freedom and democracy, respecting the dignity
and human rights of every person.[59]

In a Senate hearing on February 14, 2012, Panetta was also emphasizing
NATO's role in promoting collective security when he said that the United
States, "even in a resource-constrained era," remained committed to the
security of its allies and partners across Europe:

> We will maintain a military presence that meets our enduring NATO Article
> 5 security commitment, deters aggression, and promotes enhanced capacity
> and interoperability. The real measure of U.S. commitment to Europe is
> the ability and will to work together to promote shared regional and global
> interests, and to build and employ collective capabilities as an alliance, as we
> did in Libya.[60]

Also other representatives of the Obama administration underscored
NATO's ability to create security through collective solutions. In a
Senate hearing, Madelyn R. Creedon, Assistant Secretary of Defense for
Global Strategic Affairs, and Andrew C. Weber, Assistant Secretary of
Defense for Nuclear, Chemical, and Biological Defense Programs, said
that NATO's strategic concept, adopted in Lisbon in 2010, "made real
progress... through NATO's adoption of territorial missile defense as an
Alliance mission."[61] They also said that the administration continued to
believe that "cooperation with Russia on missile defense, both bilaterally
and through NATO, can enhance the security of the United States, our
allies and partners in Europe, and Russia."[62]

Occasionally, the representatives of the Obama administration also
promoted universal values as a part of NATO's mission. In a hearing in the
Senate about the Chicago Summit on May 10, 2012, Assistant Secretary

---

[59] Clinton, "Remarks to the World Affairs Council 2012 NATO Conference."
[60] SASC, *Department of Defense Authorization for Appropriations for Fiscal Year 2013 and the Future Years Defense Program*, Pt. 1, pp. 128–129.
[61] Ibid., p. 181.
[62] Ibid., p. 217.

Gordon, for example, argued that his "overall message" was that it was "simply in the national security interests of the United States" to strengthen its relations with its "key allies" in NATO: "Whatever the drawbacks and deficiencies in defense spending or different points of view we may have on some international questions, it is clearly in our interest to face the daunting challenges we face around the world with a standing alliance of countries who broadly share our values and interests."[63]

Gordon also said that "NATO is a hub for building security," and "a forum for dialogue and for bringing countries together for collective action."[64] And Deputy Assistant Secretary Townsend reinforced that view of NATO's mission as promoting collective security when he said that NATO served "as the organizing framework to ensure that we have allies willing and able to fight alongside us in conflict and provides an integrated military structure that puts the military teeth behind alliance political decisions to take action." In addition, Townsend continued, NATO ensured the interoperability of the US allies and NATO served "as a hub and an integrator of a network of global security partners."[65] NATO was simply the framework for US action, according to him:

> … we have with NATO an organizing entity to help us quickly come together just on a political basis at 28 around a table and try to sort out what do we need to do. We are able to go to the U.N. with these nations with us and get U.N. assistance. The U.N. Security Council takes on these issues. And then when politically we all decide on a course of action, you have at NATO on the military side the integrated military structure that actually helps us to organize ourselves militarily and take action pretty quickly.[66]

The administration's attitude to what NATO should do, to promote collective security and to some extent values, is also captured to a large extent in Panetta's King's College speech on January 18, 2013. He said that the partnership approach of US policy "is not to build a global NATO, but rather to help other regions

---

[63] SFRC, *NATO: Chicago and Beyond*, p. 25.
[64] Ibid., pp. 8–9.
[65] Ibid., pp. 10–11.
[66] Ibid., p. 26.

do more to provide for their own security and in the process become more capable every day of partnering with us to be more effectively equipped to meet global challenges." That type of partnerships had, according to Panetta, "added credibility and capability to the alliance in the latest operations and laid the groundwork for continued cooperation in the future."[67]

Panetta also said that it was in the interests of both the United States and Europe "for the NATO alliance to become more outwardly focused and engaged in helping to strengthen security institutions in Asia." "We need to help," Panetta argued, "all nations in the region contribute more to regional security and regional prosperity. As members of the historic alliance, it is our responsibility to demonstrate global leadership and to advance those ideals." Europe should not fear the US rebalancing to Asia, he argued; Europe should join it.[68]

Vice President Biden's talk in Munich on February 2, 2013, was in many ways representative for the administration's view of NATO's mission, collective security, and to some extent promotion of universal values. Initially, he was underlining the basic friendship between the United States and Europe. "President Obama and I," he said, "continue to believe that Europe is the cornerstone of our engagement with the rest of the world and is the catalyst for our global cooperation. It's that basic. Nothing has changed." Biden continued:

> Time and again, when it comes to a search for partners in this extremely complex world, Europe and America still look to each other before they look anywhere else. Our soldiers, diplomats, security personnel, and citizens continue to stand shoulder-to-shoulder … European partnership remains an indispensable force in advancing democracy and universal rights. We've joined forces in response to the unprecedented promise and unresolved turmoil of the Arab Spring. From Tunis to Tripoli, Cairo to Sana'a, our collaboration could not be closer. And it's going to be required to continue. We also know there is unfinished business in our common project of a Europe whole and free. Georgia and the states of the Balkans have unfulfilled aspirations for Euro-Atlantic integration. The pace of these

---

[67] Panetta, "King's College London."
[68] Ibid.

integration efforts will be determined by the aspirants themselves. But we too share a responsibility for helping them achieve their rightful place in Europe and the Transatlantic Alliance.[69]

The Obama administration continued to underline the collectiveness in NATO's mission during the rest of 2013. On March 21, in a hearing in the House of Representatives, Christopher Painter, Coordinator, Office of the Coordinator for Cyber Issues, US Department of State, said that it was a "key consideration" that NATO made cyber defense a part of its strategic concept adopted in Lisbon in 2010, that it was a "foundational thing."[70] And on April 23, Secretary Kerry said that NATO was "a vibrant and critical institution for ensuring the security not just of our region but all across the globe."[71]

NATO as a global security provider was also mentioned in a hearing in Senate on April 25, 2013, about the US rebalancing to Asia, when Senator Rubio asked David F. Helvey, Deputy Assistant Secretary for East Asia, Office of Security and Defense, US Department of Defense, what role he saw for NATO in the US rebalance to Asia.[72] Helvey answered that the administration had some very initial discussions with NATO partners about the Asia-Pacific, not with NATO as an institution, and he also went into the promotion of values:

> We have had some discussions with our European partners outside of the context of NATO where we find that we have shared values and principles as we look toward the Asia-Pacific, and we are identifying areas where we can work together to either engage in China or to cooperate with other countries in the Asia-Pacific region to support common goals.[73]

---

[69] Biden, "Remarks by the Vice President to the Munich Security Conference." This argumentation correspond well with what Ellen Hallams has concluded elsewhere, that "US foreign policy is not a zero-sum game: a 'pivot' to Asia Pacific does not mean a turning away from Europe, nor does the current focus on a rising China mean that Europe is somehow marginalized." See Ellen Hallams, 'Between Hope and Realism: The United States, NATO and a Transatlantic Bargain for the 21st Century,' in *NATO Beyond 9/11: The Transformation of the Atlantic Alliance*, eds. Ellen Hallams, Luca Ratti and Benjamin Zyla, Basingstoke: Palgrave Macmillan, 2013, pp. 231–232.

[70] HFAC, *Cyber Attacks*, March 21, No. 113–118, p. 19.

[71] John Kerry, "Press Availability After NATO Ministerial," April 23, 2013, www.state.gov (homepage), date accessed May 2, 2013.

[72] SFRC, *Rebalance to Asia II*, p. 20.

[73] Ibid.

On May 8, 2013, Creedon, Assistant Secretary of Defense, in a hearing on Missile Defense in the House of Representatives, said that the United States was working "in close collaboration with our NATO Allies" to develop a BMD to protect NATO territory. The administration had, according to her, made BMD protection of Europe "a central feature of transatlantic security policy."[74] In a hearing in the Senate the next day, she also said that the United States was exploring "opportunities for missile defense cooperation in a multilateral setting via the NATO-Russia Council," to reassure Russia that the BMD was not a threat to Russia's security.[75]

On May 31, 2013, after a meeting with NATO's Secretary General, Anders Fogh Rasmussen, President Obama said that the Libya War had been a success, and that NATO had a role to play in the Libyan transition process.[76] And when he spoke in Berlin on June 19, 2013, he said that "Europe remains the cornerstone of our freedom and our security; that Europe is our partner in almost everything that we do; and that although the nature of the challenges we face have changed, the strength of our relationships, the enduring bonds based on common values and common ideals very much remains."[77]

Finally, in Brussels on December 3, 2013, Secretary Kerry spoke about the importance of NATO when it came to supporting local security forces, "particularly as a means of stabilizing post-conflict situations," and how the alliance could "energize existing partnership frameworks" in the Mediterranean and the Gulf region. He also made a quite clear statement of what NATO should not do, in relation to the crisis in Ukraine:

> I think NATO has done what it has done today, which is make a statement about it, but I don't think NATO has a role. NATO is a defense alliance. It's a national—it's a security alliance. And NATO has spoken out, out of

---

[74] HASC, *Budget Request for Missile Defense Programs*, May 8, No. 113–144, Washington, DC: USGPO, 2013, pp. 34–35.

[75] SASC, *Department of Defense Authorization for Appropriations for Fiscal Year 2014 and the Future Yars Defense Program*, No. 113–108, Pt. 7, Washington, DC: USGPO, 2013, p. 306.

[76] Barack Obama, "Remarks by President Obama and NATO Secretary General Anders Rasmussen After Bilateral Meeting," Speech May 31, 2013, www.whitehouse.gov (homepage), date accessed July 1, 2014.

[77] Barack Obama, "Remarks by President Obama and German Chancellor Merkel in Joint Press Conference," Speech June 19, 2013, www.whitehouse.gov (homepage), date accessed July 1, 2014.

its concern, but it does not have a role, does not play a role, and is not contemplating a role. This is really something that the people of the Ukraine need to work out with their leadership, and the leadership needs to listen to the people and work out with the people. Clearly, there is a very powerful evidence of people who would like to be associated with Europe and who had high hopes for their aspirations to be fulfilled through that association. And we stand with the vast majority of the Ukrainians who want to see this future for their country, and we commend the EU for keeping the door open to that. But that is not a NATO piece of business, beyond the statement that it has issued today.[78]

To summarize, the Obama administration did not change its view of NATO's mission much during 2012 and 2013, compared to the view during 2011. The focus was consequently to underscore NATO's mission as promoting collective security and multilateral cooperation, and only to some extent universal values, which means that the administration's view of NATO's mission was moderate.

Regarding the guidance of NATO, lastly, the administration withheld that NATO should be led in a rational way, and that the allies had to take more responsibility for the leadership of the alliance, a minimalist view of how NATO should be guided.

Secretary Panetta, for example, said in Munich on February 4, 2012, that NATO had proven that it could handle the security challenges of the twenty-first century, and moved closer to the vision for the Atlantic community that was articulated by President John F. Kennedy already in 1962, namely that the United States and Europe should cooperate on a basis of "full equality."[79] That was clearly a continuation of the Obama administration's attitude toward how NATO should be led that characterized the period around the Libya War. And it should continue that way.

In a budget hearing in the Senate on February 28, 2012, Secretary Clinton said that the modernization of US and NATO forces was "an opportunity for our European allies to take on greater responsibility."[80] But the actual

---

[78] Kerry, "Solo Press Availability at NATO."
[79] Panetta, "Munich Security Conference."
[80] SFRC, *National Security and Foreign Policy Priorities in the FY 2013 International Affairs Budget*, p. 103.

rate of defense spending was not the only criteria when the United States valued its allies, according to Clinton:

> The value of allied and partner contributions has been clear for more than a decade in Afghanistan and more recently was seen in the case of Operation Unified Protector in Libya, where the United States was able to provide operational support while other allies and partners took the lead in combat efforts. Such nations achieve greater influence for themselves in the alliance by leading through example. We seek to encourage these nations by recognizing the contributions they have made and rewarding their efforts.[81]

Assistant Secretary Gordon was of the same opinion when he, in a Senate hearing on May 10, 2012, said that NATO could maintain a strong defense despite the fiscal austerity:

> This is a clear opportunity—you might even say necessity—for our European allies to take on greater responsibilities. The United States continues to strongly urge those allies to meet the 2-percent benchmark for defense spending and to contribute politically, financially, and operationally to the strength of the alliance. In addition to the total level of defense spending, we should also focus on how these limited resources are allocated and for what priorities.[82]

Secretary Panetta delivered a similar message in a speech on June 28, 2012, at the United States Institute for Peace (USIP), that the United States should strengthen NATO's capabilities, meet its Article 5 commitments, and ensure that it could conduct expeditionary operations with NATO's European allies: "And we must ensure that they can assume a greater burden of the responsibility when we do engage." The United States must, he said, remain the strongest military power on the face of the earth, but "more than ever" the US strength depended on "our ability to govern and to lead," and on "capable allies and partners willing to help shoulder the burden of global security."[83]

---

[81] SFRC, *National Security and Foreign Policy Priorities in the FY 2013 International Affairs Budget*, p. 135.

[82] SFRC, *NATO: Chicago and Beyond*, p. 4.

[83] Leon E. Panetta, "Building Partnership in the 21st Century," Speech June 28, 2012, http://www .defense.gov (homepage), date accessed January 23, 2013. See also HASC, *Framework for Building Partnership Capacity Programs and Authorities to Meet 21st Century Challenges*, No. 113–115, Washington, DC: USGPO, 2013, p. 47.

The focus on a rational, minimalist leadership of NATO was also demonstrated several times during 2013, not least in connection to the "Mali Crisis," which animated debate about NATO in the United States. The background of the Mali Crisis was that Western forces and African partners tried to expel al-Qaeda in Islamic Maghreb (AQIM) from the north of Mali in 2012. The main effort came from the forces of Economic Community of West African States (ECOWAS) countries, with the support of the European Union Training mission in Mali (EUTM). The AQIM offensive came in January 2013, and was surprising. The government in Mali asked the French government for help. French president François Hollande then made a unilateral decision to launch *Operation Serval* on January 11. French military, without allied support, eventually broke down the AQIM offensive, and by April the operation had liberated the northern part of the country. The United States supported the French operation with strategic airlifting, air-to-air refueling, and intelligence.[84]

In the United States, *Operation Serval* was seen as another example of how the United States could "lead from behind," and play an enabling or supportive role. In Paris on February 27, 2013, Secretary Kerry talked about the crisis, and he wanted to thank France for its leadership:

> I want to say very clearly that we are extremely grateful for the leadership that France has shown here because things were really coming apart in a very dangerous way. And France stepped in understanding that danger, and it has made a huge difference. We continue—we are cooperating and helping in support of those efforts, providing lift for troops. We've been providing intelligence and some of the other needs that the French have expressed.[85]

Finally, Secretary Hagel was talking about US leadership in Washington, DC, on February 27, and he said that he had always believed that the US role in

---

[84] Gros, "Libya and Mali Operations," pp. 7–8.
[85] John Kerry, "Remarks with French Foreign Minister Laurent Fabius," Speech February 27, 2013, www.state.gov (homepage), date accessed March 2, 2013. See also John Kerry, "Remarks with Italian Foreign Minister Emma Bonino Before Their Meeting," May 9, 2013, www.state.gov (homepage), date accessed May 10, 2013.

the world had been to engage. "We can't dictate to the world," he said, "but we must engage in the world":

> We must lead with our allies. Allies are—as everyone in this room knows—particularly important. No nation—as great as America is—can do any of this alone. And we need to continue to build on the strong relationships that we have built ... We renew old alliances. We reach out and find new alliances based on the common interests of people ... The world looks to America for leadership.[86]

Even if Hagel argues for US leadership, it is a leadership that can be characterized as rational, leading with the allies. So, in sum, the same pattern appears as in the previous period, that is, that the administration continued to argue for a moderate to minimalist view of US guidance of NATO.

So to sum up the view of the Obama administration on the importance of NATO in US long-term security policy, as manifested in the US NATO debate during the period 2012–2013, it remained moderate to low (minimalist). The results are summarized in Table 3.2.

Table 3.2 Results from the US NATO debate 2012–2013 in the administration

Vision	Military and political
Mission	Collective security
Guidance	Rational

What that means is that the Obama administration continued to have a moderate to low (minimalist) view of what NATO should be (vision), what NATO should do (mission), and how NATO should be led (guidance). NATO should primarily be a military and political organization; NATO should primarily promote collective security; and NATO should be led in rational way. In the next section the think tank debate and the debate in the elite media will be scrutinized.

---

[86] Chuck Hagel, "Pentagon All-Hands Meeting," Speech February 27, 2013, http://www.defense.gov (homepage), date accessed March 2, 2013.

The policy debate in the think tank and elite media environment

In the think tank and elite press environment the vision of NATO was also expressed in a similar ways as during the Libya War: a pluralistic mix of military, political, and cultural characterization, which indicate a moderate to high (maximalist) level of NATO's importance in US security policy. In a column in the *Washington Post* on February 10, 2012, Harold Meyerson underlined NATO's military character when he wrote that "Western Europe was our staunch ally in blocking the spread of Soviet communism and today joins us in such joint ventures as the overthrow of Libya's Moammar Gaddafi."[87]

Examples that suggest that NATO was perceived as a military organization is also found in an ACUS issue brief from February 2012, written by Jason Healy from ACUS, and Leendert van Bochoven, Leader for NATO and European Defense at IBM, about cyber capabilities: "Since NATO is a military organization, it seems natural to consider if it should have offensive capabilities," they argued.[88] And in an ACUS Report from May 2012, Nicholas Burns, former US Ambassador to NATO and Board Member of ACUS, Damon Wilson, and Jeff Lightfoot, Vice Director of the Security Program at ACUS, argued in a similar way when they wrote that NATO was a "force-multiplier" for the United States worldwide.[89]

NATO's political character was articulated in an article by Volker published in the *Christian Science Monitor* on May 21, 2012, where he argued for the "a renewed emphasis on planning and exercises for our

---

[87] Harold Meyerson, "The GOP Misses Its Bogeyman," *Washington Post*, February 10, 2012.

[88] Jason Healy and Leendert van Bochoven, "NATO's Cyber Capabilities: Yesterday, Today, and Tomorrow," Atlantic Council Issue Brief, February 2012, http://www.atlanticcouncil.org (homepage), date accessed January 5, 2014, p. 6. See also Jame Stravidis, "The Dark Side of Globalization," *Washington Post*, June 2, 2013.

[89] Nicholas Burns, Damon Wilson and Jeff Lightfoot, "Anchoring the Alliance," Atlantic Council Report, May 2012, http://www.atlanticcouncil.org (homepage), date accessed January 15, 2014, p. 2. See also Jolyon Howorth, *CSDP and NATO Post-Libya: Towards the Rubicon*, Brussels: Egmont, 2012; John R. Deni, "The American Role in European Defence Reform," *Orbis*, Fall (2012), pp. 530–546; and Charles Barry and Hans Binnendijk, "Widening Gaps in U.S. and European Defense Capabilities and Cooperation," *Transatlantic Current*, No. 6, July 2012, http://www.ndu.edu (homepage), date accessed February 10, 2014.

collective defense—the core mission of NATO as summed up in Article 5 of its treaty."[90] And in an ACUS Brief from June 2012, Barry Pavel, Director of the Security Program at ACUS, and Lightfoot argued that NATO's Article V is the bottom line of the alliance: "This fundamental element of the bargain will not change, for when Europe's vital interests are threatened from within Europe or beyond, so too are those of the United States."[91]

Examples of how NATO was perceived as a cultural organization was also common within the think tank and elite press environment. In an Issue Brief from May 2012, published by the Atlantic Council, Vice President at IBM, Nancy DeViney, and former Assistant Secretary General of NATO, Edgar Buckley, argued for a more distinct cultural role for NATO:

> Culturally, NATO's default behavior patterns no longer match its vocation and mission. The fundamental cultural problem is that it has not adapted its political approach and military means to match its modern role as an international security organization with responsibilities going beyond simple defense.[92]

NATO should revisit its core values to determine if they are still relevant, they argued:

> A set of values that are explicitly understood and embraced by all members should provide the cultural foundation that will enable NATO to adapt and execute new strategies in an every changing world, while remaining true to its mission and identity. Values can help to unify a diverse set of members and constituents, providing a basis and lens for decision-making, actions and behaviors.[93]

And in the ACUS Report from May 2012, Burns, Wilson, and Lightfoot argued that NATO was the "essential bridge uniting the United States, Canada, and

---

[90] Kurt Volker, "Beyond Afghanistan, a Weakened NATO Can Still Write Its Own Future," *The Christian Science Monitor*, May 21, 2012.

[91] Barry Pavel and Jeff Lightfoot, "The Transatlantic Bargain After "the Pivot"," Atlantic Council Issue Brief, June 2012, http://www.atlanticcouncil.org (homepage), date accessed February 5, 2014, p. 3.

[92] Nancy DeViney and Edgar Buckley, "Change Management and Cultural Transformation in NATO: Lessons from the Public and Private Sectors," Atlantic Council Issue Brief, May 2012, http://www.atlanticcouncil.org (homepage), date accessed January 5, 2014, p. 2.

[93] DeViney and Buckley, "Change Management and Cultural Transformation in NATO," p. 4.

twenty-six European nations in the world's most democratic and powerful alliance."[94] They also argued that the United States:

> …should never forget the power of allies stepping forward in solidarity in the aftermath of the 9/11 attacks to invoke Article 5 of the Washington Treaty declaring the attack on the United States as an attack on all allies. Nations like China and Russia, and other emerging powers, do not have genuine allies today.[95]

Furthermore, in *Policy Review*, April/May 2012, published by the Hoover Institution, Charles Kupchan, Professor at Georgetown University and Senior Fellow at the Council on Foreign Relations, argued that common values and interests had kept the alliance together, despite the changing balance of power in the world.[96]

The *New York Times* editorial team also saw NATO as something more than a military organization. In an editorial about the situation in Georgia on September 30, 2012, it was argued that President Mikheil Saakashvili "jeopardizes his legacy and his ability to lead Georgia into NATO if he fails to keep the country moving forward toward democracy and human rights."[97]

During 2013 the same pattern appeared; a pluralistic mix of military, political, and cultural characterizations of NATO. In an Issue Brief published by the ACUS in February 2013, former US Ambassador to the EU, C. Boyden Gray, even suggested an "Economic NATO" to solve the economic crisis and keep the West prosperous.[98]

In a GMF Policy Brief from May 2013, Robert Ross, Professor of Political Science at Boston College, characterized NATO as a military and political organization when he argued that the European NATO states had to

---

[94] Burns, Wilson and Lightfoot, "Anchoring the Alliance," p. v.

[95] Ibid., p. 12.

[96] Charles Kupchan, "A Still-Strong Alliance," *Policy Review*, April & May (2012), p. 60.

[97] "Democracy in the Former Soviet Republics," Editorial, *New York Times*, September 30, 2012. See also "Georgia Speaks Its Mind," Editorial, *New York Times*, October 2, 2012.

[98] C. Boyden Gray, "An Economic NATO: A New Alliance for a New Global Order," Atlantic Council Issue Brief, February 2013, http://www.atlanticcouncil.org (homepage), date accessed January 5, 2014.

"compensate for the U.S. preoccupation with Asia with a greater contribution to common vital U.S.-European security interests in Europe and on the European periphery" if they still wanted to be relevant for the United States, and "make a vital contribution to transatlantic cooperation."[99]

And in another GMF Foreign Policy paper, Mark Simakovsky at GMF pointed at NATO's political and cultural sides when he argued that NATO enlargement was still in the West's interest, since it could help "modernize the strategic partnership between the United States and Europe by making the EU and NATO work closer together in Europe, and ensuring the United States remains invested in the success of Europe's periphery, just as it had helped transform Europe's west during the Cold War and Europe's east after:"[100]

> The success of the Western community and strength of the United States rested first and foremost on the strength of the Transatlantic alliance. Locking in peace and security in Europe on its strategic flank can help the United States promote its interests around the globe and pivot more effectively to Asia. A weak Europe and stagnation on Europe's periphery would run counter to this effort. President Obama's political legacy could . benefit greatly from one enlargement round, insulating the administration from accusations of ignoring and pivoting the United States away from Europe.[101]

In an ACUS Issue Brief from September 2013, Karl Heinz Kamp, Research Director at the NATO Defense College in Rome, pointed at NATO's military and political character when he argued that "NATO's standing as a cost-effective and mutually advantageous instrument of protection, deterrence, and defense is undeniable, regardless of whether it is actually running military assignments at any given time."[102] And in an GMF Policy Brief from

---

[99] Robert S. Ross, "What the Pivot Means for Transatlantic Relations: Separate Course or New Opportunity for Engagement?," *GMF Policy Brief*, May 2013, http://www.gmfus.org (homepage), date accessed March 12, 2014, p. 3.

[100] Mark Simakovsky, "Flexible Expansion: NATO Enlargement in an Era of Austerity and Uncertainty," GMF Foreign Policy Papers, 2013, http://www.gmfus.org (homepage), date accessed March 12, 2014.

[101] Simakovsky, "Flexible Expansion: NATO Enlargement in an Era of Austerity and Uncertainty," p. 24.

[102] Karl-Heinz Kamp, "Is NATO Set to Go on Standby?" *Atlantic Council Issue Brief*, September 2013, http://www.atlanticcouncil.org (homepage), date accessed January 5, 2014, p. 3.

November 2013, Nora Bensahel and Jacob Stokes, both at the Center for a New American Security (CNAS), argued that the European NATO members must improve their military capabilities to "ensure that the alliance remains relevant and effective" in three main ways: Preserve the interoperability gained in Afghanistan through a robust exercise program, encourage role specialization, especially within regional clusters, and expand the 2-percent metric to include more qualitative assessments of contributions.[103]

So the picture is relatively clear of the vision of NATO in the policy debate. It contained a pluralistic mix of military, political, and cultural characterizations, which indicates a moderate to high (maximalist) view of NATO in US security policy during the period.

Regarding NATO's mission, the think tanks and the elite media continued to focus on collective security and, to some degree, also universal values. NATO was seen as a force for good and as an instrument for the United States to create collective security. In an article in the *Washington Post* on January 3, 2012, Opinion Writer Richard Cohen argued that the United States remained "a mighty nation, capable of doing good in the world":

> The intervention in Libya, a NATO operation but an American enterprise, succeeded. So did the ones in Bosnia and Kosovo. The Libyan bombings will not bring democracy to that country, but they knocked out Moammar Gaddafi, and that ain't a bad day's work.[104]

In another article in the *New York Times* on February 3, 2012, Robert A. Pape, Professor at the University of Chicago, wondered why the West did not intervene in Syria as it did in Libya in 2011, and he underscored NATO's role as defending universal values:

> Not only was Libya's dictator, Col. Muammar el-Qaddafi, ousted with relatively few Western casualties, but the NATO campaign also set a

---

[103] Nora Bensahel and Jacob Stokes, "The U.S. Defense Budget and the Future of Alliance Burden Sharing," *GMF Policy Brief*, November 2013, http://www.gmfus.org (homepage), date accessed February 21, 2014, p. 3. See also Daniel Keohane, "Europeans Less Able, Americans Less Willing?," *GMF Policy Brief*, November 2013, http://www.gmfus.org (homepage), date accessed February 21, 2014, p. 3.

[104] Richard Cohen, "Paul's Amoral Policy," *Washington Post*, January 3, 2012.

precedent for successful humanitarian intervention. A new standard for humanitarian intervention is needed … The recent war in Libya was a case in point.[105]

In an ACUS Report from March 2012, Franklin D. Kramer (Distinguished Fellow, ACUS) argued that NATO's mission was to create collective security and spread values when he wrote that NATO should engage more in the Middle East and in North Africa. A Strategic Consultative Group within NATO, focusing on issues in the Greater Middle East, should be created, he argued, that could "recommend a full spectrum of approaches—political, diplomatic, economic, intelligence, information, and military." And in North Africa "[a] set of initiatives regarding the role of the military in a democracy could be a valuable contribution to the success of the North African countries," according to Kramer[106]

The ongoing Syria Conflict came up in the policy debate several times during 2012, and the solution was argued to be that if military force should be used, it should be used within a multilateral NATO frame. In an editorial in the *Washington Post* on April 10, 2012, for example, it was expressed that:

> The inescapable reality is that Mr. Assad will go on killing unless and until he is faced with a more formidable military opposition. That is why the shortest way to the end of the Syrian crisis is the one Mr. Obama is resisting: military support for the opposition and, if necessary, intervention by NATO.[107]

Three weeks later, on April 30, 2012, Jackson Diehl of the *Washington Post*, argued in a similar way, and criticized the Obama administration for "passivity:"

> They say that—and then they speculate about when and whether the Obama administration might decide to abandon its passivity. The United States, after all, is more than capable of creating and defending a humanitarian zone in Syria, with help from Turkey and NATO.[108]

---

[105] Robert A. Pape, "Why We Shouldn't Attack Syria (Yet)," *New York Times*, February 3, 2012.

[106] Franklin D. Kramer, "Transatlantic Nations and Global Security: Pivoting and Partnerships," Atlantic Council Report, March 2012, http://www.atlanticcouncil.org (homepage), date accessed January 5, 2014, pp. 5–6. See also Pavel and Lightfoot, "The Transatlantic Bargain After 'the Pivot,'" p. 3.

[107] "Facing Failure in Syria," Editorial, *Washington Post*, April 10, 2012.

[108] Jackson Diehl, "Who Needs the US?" *Washington Post*, April 30, 2012.

Furthermore, in an editorial in the *Washington Post* on May 22, 2012, Syria again came up and NATO was presented as the solution:

> NATO's "victory" in Libya, senior U.S. officials recently wrote, was a "model intervention," a "teachable moment." ... And yet, at the summit of NATO leaders in Chicago, no leader raised the subject of Syria, [the US NATO Ambassador] Mr. [Ivo] Daalder said. "We are very much concerned about the situation of Syria," NATO Secretary General Anders Fogh Rasmussen explained, but the alliance has "no intention whatsoever to intervene." Why not? What happened to the "teachable moment," just one year old? ... This is mystifying not just because the humanitarian stakes are as great in Syria as in Libya. As with Libya, NATO could support the Syrian opposition without putting its own troops at risk. And the alternative to NATO action in Syria is not just a slower democratic victory, nor even a return to Assad-regime stability. Instead, as we've written before, Syria's conflict, already increasingly violent, might well degenerate into full-blown sectarian warfare; this war could jump into Turkey, Lebanon and Iraq, and al-Qaeda would profit murderously from this opportunity ... As Syria burns, the Libya "victory" rings increasingly hollow.[109]

A month later, July 15, 2012, Charles Dunne, David J. Kramer, and William H. Taft IV—all at Freedom House—wrote in the *Washington Post* about Syria, and NATO was again argued to be the solution:

> The White House should publicly consider enforcing humanitarian corridors ("no drive" zones) as well as no-fly zones to counter the regime's increasing use of helicopter gunships. It should launch formal discussions of such measures with NATO allies. Merely planning for serious military options would have an important psychological effect on the regime and its military forces, possibly prodding more defections.[110]

And on July 29, the editorial team in the *Washington Post* wrote that the United States and its NATO allies "could begin contingency planning for a

---

[109] "NATO's Blind Spot," Editorial, *Washington Post*, May 22, 2012.
[110] Charles Dunne, David J. Kramer, and William H. Taft IV, "Our Role in Saving Syria," *Washington Post*, July 15, 2012.

no-fly zone, now that Mr. Assad is deploying aircraft against the opposition."[111] Furthermore, Kenneth M. Pollack at the Brookings Institution wrote in the *Washington Post* on August 12, 2012, that the United States and its NATO allies "could begin to provide military training for Syrian fighters." More competent opposition forces could better meet and defeat government troops, it was argued. According to Pollack, such a program "was crucial both to military victory in the Bosnian civil war and to fostering stability after the fighting."[112]

On August 14, 2012, lastly, the editorial board at the *Washington Post* started to argue even stronger for an intervention in Syria:

> At the moment, planes are flying over Syria and dropping bombs. Unfortunately, they are Syrian military aircraft bombing their own people. This could be stopped. The United States, NATO and others under the rubric of Friends of Syria have the capacity to implement a no-fly zone—and to do it fast. Grounding Syria's air force and helicopter gunships would not only aid the opposition but also send a strong message to the regime and its supporters that their days are numbered.[113]

All these examples show that the think tank and elite media environment perceived NATO's role as facilitating common security and universal values, a moderate to high (maximalist) view of NATO's mission. And there are more examples.

Before the NATO Summit in Chicago, April 19, 2012, an editorial in the *New York Times* criticized the unfair burden sharing between the United States and NATO's European members, but NATO was still described as the principal tool for using military force:

> Military force is not always the best answer. But, when it is, Europe must be able to provide its share. With all European governments committed to arbitrary and unrealistic deficit reduction targets, military spending is again being slighted. But by continuing to shortchange overdue military

---

[111] "Bracing in Aleppo," Editorial, *Washington Post*, July 29, 2012. See also Zalmay Khalilsad, "Five Things the U.S. Can Do in Syria," *Washington Post*, August 8, 2012; and "Syria's Hard Core," Editorial, *Washington Post*, August 9, 2012.

[112] Kenneth M. Pollack, "How. When. Whether. Stopping Syria's War," *Washington Post*, August 12, 2012.

[113] "On Syria's sidelines," Editorial, *Washington Post*, August 14, 2012.

investments, Europe is undermining the alliance on which its security depends. We are encouraged that earlier this year, NATO decided to acquire a new air-to-ground surveillance system and to expand member countries' aerial refueling fleets. That's a good start. But it won't be enough. Next month's NATO summit meeting in Chicago will likely feature speeches celebrating the alliance's past glories. It must be accompanied by hard private bargaining about better burden-sharing and addressing the yawning gaps exposed in Libya. NATO's credibility is on the line. And that is a serious problem for Europe and for the United States.[114]

Volker was of the same opinion that the European allies were needed, in an article in *Policy Review* (April/May, 2012): "A great power should not 'pivot' from wars in the Middle East and Asia, or from old allies in Europe, to new frontiers in the Pacific," he wrote. Rather, the United States needed to see an "integrated whole, where old allies are relevant even for new challenges, and where wars of necessity demand the most integrated global coalitions ever."[115]

And in a GMF Policy Brief from May 2012, Dhruva Jaishankar of the GMF argued that NATO should defend the "global commons," that is, the space, cyber, and maritime domains. Defending the commons is, he wrote, "a concept very much in line with the values of the Atlantic Charter," and may be "the only way for NATO to remain a credible player in international security in the 21st century."[116]

There were also voices in the policy debate that argued that NATO should promote only US interests. In an ACUS Issue Brief from June 2012, for example, Pavel and Lightfoot argued that "the days when the United States provided the preponderance of the assets of all types for operations that do not involve Article 5 are over." In the future, they argued, the United States "will support such European-led NATO operations when it deems it in its interests

---

[114] "NATO After Libya," Editorial, *New York Times*, April 19, 2012.

[115] Kurt Volker, "Reaffirming Transatlantic Unity," *Policy Review*, April & May (2012), p. 118.

[116] Dhruva Jaishankar, "Engaging Rising Powers in the Maritime, Space, and Cyber Domains," GMF Policy Brief, May 2012, http://www.gmfus.org (homepage), date accessed February 21, 2014, p. 8. The scholarly debate on NATO's handling of new challenges, such as cyber threats and energy security is discussed in, for example, Magnus Petersson, "Just an 'Internal Exercise'?: NATO and the 'New' Security Challenges," in Hallams, Ratti and Zyla, *Beyond 9/11*.

to do so and when such assets are available, but this support will no longer be automatic nor comprehensive."[117]

But such statements were relatively rare in the policy debate. Normally NATO was described as an organization that promoted collective security and universal values.[118] The same pattern continued during 2013. In an editorial about Hungary in the *Washington Post* on March 14, 2013, it was argued that "the European Union and NATO should not tolerate a member government that violates fundamental democratic principles." The country "should be asked to change constitutional provisions that are found by the Council of Europe to violate democratic norms," and if it refused "it should be subject to sanctions."[119]

In an ACUS Report from May 2013, Robert A. Manning, Senior Fellow at ACUS, argued that "NATO has demonstrated its enduring utility as a global security institution. Even if scaled back, it will remain an important actor, particularly with respect to the Middle East and North Africa, and on functional issues such as counterterrorism, maritime piracy, and cybersecurity."[120] And in June 2013, Heather Conley, Senior Fellow and Director for the Europe Program at the CSIS, and Maren Leed, also at CSIS, argued that NATO was a "crucial provider of stability and security, not only within Europe but globally."[121]

When the debate about the Syria Crisis peaked in the United States in August and September 2013, when it looked like the administration actually was prepared to use force against Syria, NATO continued to be described as the solution in the policy debate. Already on January 22, 2013, Richard Cohen wrote in the *Washington Post* that "[a] little muscle from NATO, which is to say the United States, could have put an end to this [the Syria Crisis] thing

---

[117] Pavel and Lightfoot, "The Transatlantic Bargain After 'the Pivot,' " p. 3.

[118] See, for example, "Libya's Achievement," Editorial, *Washington Post*, July 10, 2012.

[119] "A Hungarian Power Grab," Editorial, *Washington Post*, March 14, 2013.

[120] Robert A. Manning, "Global Trends 2030: Challenges and Opportunities for Europe," Atlantic Council Report, May 2013, http://www.atlanticcouncil.org (homepage), date accessed February 5, 2014, p. 8.

[121] Heather Conley and Maren Leed, "NATO in the Land of Pretend," CSIS Commentary, June 26, 2013, http://www.csis.org (homepage), date accessed February 6, 2014. See also Michel Foucher, "For a New Transatlantic Strategic Sequence: In, Near, and Beyond Europe," *GMF Policy Brief*, May 2013, http://www.gmfus.org (homepage), date accessed February 21, 2014 pp. 5–6.

early on. The imposition of a no-fly zone, as was done in Libya, would not only have grounded Syrian airplanes and helicopters but also have convinced the military and intelligence services early on that Assad was doomed and the outcome was not in doubt."[122] And on February 12 he again wrote that the United States and NATO "could have instituted a no-fly zone, keeping Bashar al-Assad's helicopters and warplanes on the ground." This could, he argued, have made a "major difference."[123]

Also the *New York Times* editorial team was arguing for a possible intervention, but not without NATO and other institutional support: "Without broad international backing, a military strike by the United States; France and Britain, two former colonial powers; and Turkey could well give Mr. Assad a propaganda advantage," they wrote on August 29.[124] And on August 31, 2013, they reiterated the argument:

> Not only is Mr. Obama lacking the Security Council's support, he has not obtained the backing of other organizations that could provide international legitimacy, such as NATO. In Libya in 2011, the Arab League supported the NATO air campaign, but it has not requested American military action in Syria, even though it publicly blamed Mr. Assad for the attack and called for accountability... Even in the best of circumstances, military action could go wrong in so many ways; the lack of strong domestic and international support will make it even more difficult.[125]

Former NATO Supreme Allied Commander Europe (SACEUR), Admiral James G. Stravidis, went further on September 3, 2013, in the *New York Times*, when he argued that NATO "must be part of an international effort to respond to the crisis in Syria, beginning immediately with punitive strikes following the highly probable use of chemical weapons by President Bashar Al-Assad's regime." The Obama administration should, he argued, secure NATO action:

---

[122] Richard Cohen, "Our share of Syria's Misery," *Washington Post*, January 20, 2013.
[123] Richard Cohen, "Looking the Other Way," *Washington Post*, February 12, 2013.
[124] "Moore Answers Needed on Syria," Editorial, *New York Times*, August 29, 2013.
[125] "Absent on Syria," Editorial, *New York Times*, August 31, 2013.

A consensus on NATO action is possible even without the Security Council, where Russia and China, which have veto power, have declined to support action against Syria ... NATO should be part of an international effort to sharply punish the Assad regime, which poses a clear and present danger to the alliance —and the United States should lead NATO in doing so.[126]

So to sum up, the think tank and elite media argued that NATO's mission was to promote collective security and to some extent universal values during 2012–2013 as well. That represents a moderate to high (maximalist) view in the policy debate of the importance of NATO in US long-term security policy.

Regarding the guidance of NATO during 2012–2013, lastly, the think tank and elite media environment more often than during 2011 argued for a "rational" (minimalist) US leadership. There were exceptions though, such as the editorial team in the *New York Times*, that on February 19, 2012, argued that the United States should lead NATO in an almost "authoritarian" way:

Afghanistan will not be able to foot the bill for even a smaller force, and Washington will very likely bear most of the cost for years to come. It should not have to do that alone. The Obama administration should use the NATO summit meeting in Chicago in May to press allies to make concrete commitments now. And then hold them to it.[127]

Burns, Wilson, and Lightfoot in their ACUS Report from May 2012, argued in a similar way. They state that the United States is the only country "capable of providing effective leadership," and that it therefore had to remain "at the forefront of leading NATO." The United States "cannot" lead from behind, they argued.[128]

But such statements were rare during this period, compared to the previous period, and the general impression of the views in the policy debate is that the United States should lead NATO in a "rational" way. In Pavel and Lightfoot's ACUS Issue Brief from June 2012, they argued that:

---

[126] James G. Stravidis, "NATO Must Help Obama on Syria," *New York Times*, September 3, 2013.

[127] "Beginning of the End," Editorial, *New York Times*, February 19, 2012.

[128] Burns, Wilson and Lightfoot, "Anchoring the Alliance," pp. 1–2. See also James Goldgeier, "Don't Forget NATO," *New York Times*, October 17, 2012.

… Washington will look to its European allies to take a leading role in managing certain crises and contingency operations on their own periphery. This does not mean that the United States will not come to the defense of its European allies when the chips are really down. If Article 5 beckons, the United States should and will be there. But if the types of discretionary operations that have characterized NATO's post-Cold War history—Bosnia, Kosovo, counter-piracy, etc.—continue to arise, then Europe should expect a relatively reduced US role, and a relatively greater role for its own forces. With Europe at peace and likely to remain so, it must tend to its neighborhood with greater care and call in the reinforcements of the United States only when absolutely needed. In this way, NATO's Libya operation indeed may be the model for humanitarian interventions along Europe's periphery. The United States will do what it must—playing roles and providing surge capabilities that only it can provide—and Europe will bear the rest of the burden for operations that are more in its own interests than those of the United States.[129]

Another example is John R. Deni at the US Army War College, who, in an ACUS Expert Analysis from January 2013, argues that the United States engagement in Mali is, and should be, characterized by leading from behind, and that the Libyan example should "comprise a workable model for future crises and operations." The United States, he continues, "can best support its allies as well as its own security interests by playing just this kind of supporting role in places like Mali—where their interests are vital and US interests are less so":

> … having as reliable, capable, and willing a partner as the United States can counter insularity among our European allies and encourage them to maintain full-spectrum, expeditionary military capabilities, thereby helping to share the burden of safeguarding Western interests well beyond North American or European shores. Far from a sign of weakness, Washington's emphasis today on "leading from behind" as one of its closest allies engages in combat operations in Mali represents a prudent policy choice and the best mean of promoting American interests.[130]

---

[129] Pavel and Lightfoot, "The Transatlantic Bargain After 'the Pivot,'" p. 2.

[130] John R. Deni, "Mali: Another Chance to Lead from Behind," January 14, 2013, http://www.acus.org (homepage), date accessed January 17, 2013.

But there were also experts in the policy debate who warned for too much leading from behind. Conley at the CSIS, for example, argued that Washington's pivot toward Asia and its frustration over Europe's mishandling of its debt crisis have left European nations wondering if this means they now get the cold shoulder. "The risk" many predicted, she argued, was that the United States "could take its greatest strategic and ideational partner for granted, waking up one day in the not-too-distant future to find a Europe unwilling or unable to take political or security risks in support of U.S. objectives." According to Conley, the United States had to be "much more engaged" in European affairs, and "not simply advising."[131].

Arguments for a rational guidance of NATO were, however, dominating the policy debate. In a byline in the *New York Times* on September 27, 2012, Michael Doran, Brookings Institution, and Boot, CFR, argued for intervention in Syria led from behind by the United States, similar to the interventions in Kosovo and Libya:

> To prevent Mr. Assad from staging a devastating response, the American-backed alliance would have to create a countrywide no-fly zone, which would first require taking apart Syrian air defenses. Mr. Assad has been using jets and helicopters to fight the rebels; a no-fly zone would quickly ground his entire air force. The zone could then be extended to provide the kind of close air support that NATO warplanes provided to rebel fighters in Kosovo and Libya. While our allies could take the lead in maintaining the no-fly zone, it is necessary in Syria, as in Libya, for America to take the lead in establishing it; only our Air Force and Navy have the weaponry needed to dismantle Syria's Russian-designed air defenses with little risk. A "lead from behind" approach can work in Syria. President Obama need only apply it.[132]

Furthermore, in the *New York Times* on March 25, 2013, Hans Binnendijk, CTR, argued for a new US strategy in line with a rational leadership model.

---

[131] Heather Conley, *Beware the Backburner: The Risk of a Neglected Europe*, Washington, DC: CSIS, 2012, www.csis.org (homepage), date accessed February 6, 2014, p. 1. See also Jim Hoagland, "America the Hesitant," *Washington Post*, January 20, 2013; and Anne Applebaum, "A New Cop on the Beat?" *Washington Post*, January 25, 2013.

[132] Michael Doran and Max Boot, "Five Reasons to Intervene in Syria Now," *New York Times*, September 27, 2012.

Obama's war strategy on Libya had derisively been called "leading from behind," but it worked, according to Binnendijk, who suggested a "forward-partnering" approach. "Developed at the National Defense University," he wrote, "the approach would continue to stress U.S. forward-force deployments but with a new purpose: to enable America's global partners to operate together with U.S. forces and to encourage partners to take the lead in their own neighborhoods."[133]

And in a GMF Policy Brief from May 2013, Michel Foucher, Institute of Higher National Defense Studies (IHEDN) in Paris, France, argued that the United States was ready to accept a larger degree of European leadership: "It means that the United States is ready to accept a European responsibility on its own, beyond a benevolent leadership. It means also that Europeans are ready to act in a more independent way."[134]

In another GMF Policy Brief from the same month, Ross argued in a similar way: "European countries will have to develop the resolve to assume leadership in security affairs," he argued, and "[g]iven the realities of U.S. interests in East Asia and its limited capabilities and Europe's unrealized capabilities, the prospects for transatlantic cooperation will depend on Europe's contribution to its own security."[135]

Finally, in November 2013, Daniel Keohane at the Foundation for International Relations and Foreign Dialogue (FRIDE) argued that the United States would not lead European security as before in a GMF Policy Brief:

> More broadly, Washington's rebalancing of its military forces toward the Asia-Pacific does imply that the still-relatively rich Europeans should take much more responsibility for most of their immediate neighborhood. Considering the U.S. non-responses to the 2006 Lebanese-Israeli and 2008 Georgia-Russia wars, initial reluctance to intervene in Libya in 2011, and a minor supporting role in Mali in 2013, Washington would probably be happy to leave most future Eastern and Southern neighborhood crises to the Europeans (east of Suez is a

[133] Hans Binnendijk, "Rethinking U.S. Security Strategy," *New York Times*, March 25, 2013.
[134] Foucher, "For a New Transatlantic Strategic Sequence," p. 6.
[135] Ross, "What the Pivot Means for Transatlantic Relations," p. 3.

different matter). The key point for European defense policies is that Europeans may have to increasingly act alone in the future.[136]

For budgetary, political, and geo-strategic reasons, the United States "may reduce its global military presence in the future," he wrote, and continue to "lead from behind" by increasing its reliance on others—including Europeans—"to assume some of its current military roles, such as protection of the global commons."[137]

So, in sum, it is quite clear that the policy actors wanted the United States to "lead from behind" in a rational (minimalist) way during 2012–2013. The polarization of the debate during 2011, when there were as many actors arguing for a charismatic US leadership of NATO as actors arguing for a rational leadership of NATO, was not present during 2012 and 2013. That, in turn, indicates that the level of importance of NATO in US long-term security policy was described as lower (minimalist) during this period compared to the former.

The results of the analysis of the US policy debate on NATO during 2012 and 2013 are summarized in Table 3.3.

Table 3.3 Results from the US NATO debate 2012–2013 in the think tanks and elite media

Vision	Military, political, and cultural
Mission	Collective security
Guidance	Rational

Similar to the case of the US Congress and to the previous period (2011) the actors within the think tank and elite media environment did have a moderate to high (maximalist) view of NATO's importance in US long-term security policy. The vision of NATO was described as a military, political, and cultural tool, and NATO's mission was to promote collective security and values. However, regarding NATO's guidance, it was much more clearly argued that

---

[136] Keohane, "Europeans Less Able, Americans Less Willing?" p. 3.
[137] Ibid., p. 3.

NATO should be led in a rational way during this period than during the previous period. That indicates a slightly lower importance of NATO in US long-term security policy as manifested in the US NATO policy debate.

Summary and reflections

As has been demonstrated in this chapter, US Congress, think tanks, and elite media continued to expressed a similar view of NATO's importance in US long-term security policy—a moderate to high importance. The Obama administration continued to have a more minimalistic view—moderate to low importance. The results of the empirical investigation are summarized in Table 3.4.

Table 3.4 The US NATO debate during 2012–2013

Issue/Arena	The Political Debate		The Policy Debate
	Congress	*Administration*	*Think tanks and elite media*
Vision	Political, and cultural	Military and political	Military, political, and cultural
Mission	Collective security and values	Collective security	Collective security and values
Guidance	Rational or charismatic	Rational	Rational
Importance	Moderate to high	Moderate to low	Moderate to high

As the table shows, the debate taken together still indicates a moderate role for NATO in US security policy during the Chicago Summit and the Syria Conflict. The administration expressed the most minimalist view of NATO, while Congress and the policy actors expressed a more maximalist view. The administration neither emphasized NATO as a cultural tool (maximalist vision), nor argued for a charismatic US leadership of NATO (maximalist guidance). In Congress, both maximalist and minimalist views of the vision of NATO and the guidance of NATO were expressed. In think tanks and elite media the arguments for a rational (minimalist) guidance of NATO were more clearly expressed than during the Libya War.

The moderate importance of NATO in US long-term security policy manifested in the US NATO debate during 2012 and 2013, strengthens the results from the previous period and the arguments made in scholarly literature on NATO, that the importance of the alliance in US long-term security policy is decreasing.

4

2014: The Ukraine Crisis and the Wales Summit

The Ukraine Crisis, Russia's annexation of the Crimean Peninsula and the international crisis that followed, started in February 2014, when Ukraine's President Viktor Yanukovych fled the country after a revolution. Russian Special Forces, without insignia, then started to occupy the peninsula, and after a "referendum," the Crimean "parliament" declared Crimea's independence from Ukraine and soon after that, on March 18, 2014, Crimea was incorporated in the Russian Federation. The crisis then spread to the eastern parts of Ukraine, where Russian-supported separatists tried to take control over areas that were populated by pro-Russian population, and Russia built up large amounts of troops on the Russian side of the border, which also have engaged in the conflict.

The crisis aggravated when the separatists, probably by mistake but with Russian support, shot down a civilian aircraft—Malaysian Airlines flight MH-17 on its way from Amsterdam, the Netherlands, to Kuala Lumpur, Malaysia—on July 17, 2014, and killed 298 people. Since the Ukraine Crisis started, economic and political sanctions have been imposed on Russia by the West, and NATO has reinforced its military readiness in general, and in the Baltic States, Poland, and Romania in particular.

NATO's Secretary General Fogh Rasmussen said in a speech at the Brookings Institution in Washington, DC, on March 19, 2014, that the Ukraine Crisis was a "wake-up call" for the transatlantic community,[1] and the crisis animated a US NATO debate because it was a case where the US vital interests and reliability as the leader of NATO was at stake. It became

---

[1] Anders Fogh Rasmussen, "The Future of the Alliance: Revitalizing NATO for a Changing World," Speech at the Brookings Institution, March 19, 2014, www.brookings.edu (homepage), date accessed July 31, 2014.

important for the United States to show that NATO's Article V was applicable to all NATO members. How that materialized in the debate will be the focus in this chapter.

NATO's Wales Summit is the other event that will be in the focus of the chapter. It was held in Newport, Wales, UK, September 4–5, 2014. The summit must be seen in connection to, and was dominated by, NATO's reaction to the Ukraine Crisis. However, during the weeks before, and during the Wales Summit, the issue of how to handle the Islamic State (IS, ISIL or ISIS) also came up on the US agenda, an issue that indirectly had an impact on the US NATO debate, since the coalition that were created by the United States to counter IS contained several NATO members and partners. The IS issue was also discussed in connection to—but not in the frame of—NATO's Wales Summit.

This chapter will show that the Ukraine Crisis did lead to an increased, but not highly increased, importance of NATO in US long-term security policy as manifested in the US NATO debate.

In Congress, the discussion about the vision of NATO was still similar to previous periods—moderate to high (maximalist). The role of the alliance was described as a military, political, and cultural tool, and the emphasis was on NATO as a political and cultural tool rather than a military one. The same pattern can be found regarding NATO's mission. It was sometimes described as serving solely US interests, but more often as serving collective security and promoting values. Regarding how NATO should be led, however, the debate was clearly more focused on charismatic—maximalist—US guidance of NATO than before.

In the Obama administration, the description of NATO's importance increased, but not dramatically. The vision of NATO was more often described also as cultural. Furthermore, regarding NATO's mission, "values" was underscored more often than before. Regarding guidance, however, NATO was still argued to be guided in a rational way. But expressions such as "leading from behind" was no longer used by the administration. So in many ways, the view of the administration of NATO's importance, as expressed in the debate, got closer to the view of Congress and the policy environment. The administration was for the first time arguing for a moderate to maximalist, rather than a moderate to minimalist, view of NATO's importance.

In the think tank and elite media environment, lastly, the debate was similar to the debate in Congress, and similar to previous periods. The think tank and elite media actors were arguing for a moderate to maximalist view of the vision and mission of NATO. During this period, however, the policy environment switched from supporting a rational (minimalist) US guidance of NATO to supporting a charismatic (maximalist) leadership.

Taken together, the political debate and the policy debate indicate a moderate to high, rather than a moderate, US view of NATO's importance in US long-term security policy during 2014.

In the following sections, the importance of NATO in US long-term security policy as manifested in the US political and policy debate will be demonstrated in detail.

The political debate in Congress

As mentioned, the crisis in Ukraine was described as a "wake-up call" by Secretary General Rasmussen in March 2014, and the expression has become a metaphor for Western politicians. It has, since then, been used plenty of times by Secretary Kerry, President Obama, and other state leaders.[2]

In Congress, the Ukraine Crisis did not change the description of the vision of NATO. The organization was still described as a military, political, and cultural tool, with a focus on the political and cultural sides. The tone in the debate was, however, louder. In the Senate, March 27, 2014, John McCain described NATO as first and foremost a military organization that could help Ukraine defend itself:

---

[2] Barack Obama, "Statement by the President on Ukraine," Speech July 18, 2014, www.whitehouse .gov (homepage), date accessed July 31, 2014; John Kerry, "Interview with Chris Wallace of Fox News Sunday," July 20, 2014, www.state.gov (homepage), date accessed July 29, 2014; John Kerry, "Interview with George Stephanopoulos of ABC's This Week," July 20, 2014, www.state.gov (homepage), date accessed July 29, 2014; John Kerry, "Interview with David Gregory of NBC's Meet the Press," July 20, 2014, www.state.gov (homepage), date accessed July 29, 2014; and John Kerry, "Interview with Bob Schieffer of CBS's Face the Nation," July 20, 2014, www.state.gov (homepage), date accessed July 29, 2014.

We have to expand sanctions under the Magnitsky Act, increase sanctions against Putin's sources of power, especially for corruption, target corrupt people, push for an arms embargo against Russia, prevent defense technology transfers, use the upcoming NATO summit to enlarge the alliance, move the process for Georgia into a membership action plan, expand NATO cooperation with Ukraine, conduct significant contingency plans within NATO to deter aggression, defend alliance members, especially along the eastern flank, strategically shift NATO military assets eastward to support deterrence. All of these things and more need to be done.[3]

But describing NATO as a political and cultural organization was more common. On March 5, 2014, in the House of Representatives in a debate about Ukraine, Congressman Shimkus argued that NATO during the coming summit in Wales, UK, had to take a firm grip on the enlargement issue. The arguments were, as before, political and cultural rather than military:

I call upon members of NATO to now do what they should have done in the last summit. NATO now must offer membership action plans to those aspirational countries that are moving towards democracy, freedom, and the rule of law. In particular, they need to grant membership action plans to Ukraine, Georgia, and Moldova… It is difficult times as you know, Mr. Speaker, but the coalition of free democratic countries must stand united against totalitarianism.[4]

The same day Congresswoman Marcy Kaptur (D, Ohio) expressed a similar argument in the chamber. She argued that NATO should create "a new category of provisional membership for nations whose military has fought alongside NATO member forces in the war on terrorism." Ukraine had done that, and according to her the "free world" had to "walk with Ukraine as she moves toward a more free and democratic future."[5]

---

[3] CRS, March 27, 2014, "Providing for the Costs of Loan Guarantees for Ukraine," p. S 1787. See also Senator Robert "Bob" Menendez (D, New Jersey) argumentation in the same debate, p. S 1791: "We need to ensure that NATO continues to be a vibrant entity for the collective security of the United States and of Europe."

[4] CRHR, March 5, 2014, "Ukraine," p. H2151.

[5] CRHR, March 5, 2014, "Supporting Ukraine's Future," p. H2155.

And in a hearing in the House of Representatives on Ukraine the day after, Congressman Brian Higgins (D, New York) summarized NATO's character, as he saw it: "NATO, which is 28 countries including the United States and Canada and 26 European countries, was essentially established to safeguard the freedom and security through political and military means. It was a vehicle through which democratic principles could be promoted."[6]

So to sum up, the debate in Congress about what NATO is and should be, was similar to the debate during the earlier periods: moderate to maximalist. It was argued that NATO should be a political and cultural organization.

Regarding NATO's mission, what NATO should do, the focus was, as during previous periods, on collective security and values. In a debate about the Ukraine Crisis in Senate, March 4, 2014, Senator "Dan" Coats (R, Indiana) wanted the United States to use NATO as an instrument to punish Russia for its actions against Ukraine:

> The United States should propose to NATO that the alliance immediately suspend operation of the Russian-NATO council. The Russian military and diplomatic representation at NATO should be expelled. A close relationship with Russian's defense officials during a time when that country has invaded and occupied a neighbor contravenes the founding purpose of NATO. How could we possibly meet on a Russian-NATO council basis when Russia has invaded and occupied a neighbor?[7]

In a debate in the House of Representatives about Ukraine on March 11, 2014, Congressman "Steve" King (R, Iowa) talked about US and NATO reactions to the Ukraine Crisis. He wanted to see more NATO joint exercises on the ground in Poland, and more in general "on the west side of the new Iron Curtain that Putin has essentially announced by his invasion into the Crimea." He also suggested inviting Georgia into NATO—"We should have done that back in 2008—'and eventually also Ukraine.' We need to build our defenses up along those borders," he argued.[8]

---

[6] HFAC, *U.S. Foreign Policy Toward Ukraine*, No. 113–129, Washington, DC: USGPO, 2014, p. 32.
[7] CRS, March 4, 2014, "Ukraine Crisis," p. S 1273.
[8] CRHR, March 11, 2014, "Historical Implications of the Situation in Ukraine," p. H 2297.

Senator Marco Rubio (R, Florida) expressed a similar opinion when he wrote in the *Washington Post* on March 20, 2014. The Russian invasion of Crimea "should dispel the myth that closing NATO's door to future allies would appease Russian aggression," he argued. Furthermore, the United States had to make clear "to all interested partners in Europe who wish to join NATO and meet the requirements that the alliance remains open for membership."[9]

And on March 25, 2014, when the "Ukraine Support Act" was discussed in the Senate, Senator Rubio suggested that the United States should work with its European NATO members to "help equip and train the Ukrainian military forces" so that they could protect the country. Rubio suggested that the United States had to "reassess the role that NATO plays in Europe," because "the facts on the ground in Europe have changed dramatically in the last 2 months":

> I think it is time for NATO to reevaluate its capabilities, given this new threat that is here to stay. Also, the time has come for NATO to reposition its assets to face this threat and this risk. I think and I hope that those conversations are happening now. I think for NATO, in many respects, it is time to reinvigorate this alliance. It has a clear and present danger in Europe in the form of the government of Vladimir Putin, who threatens his neighbors and the stability of Europe. So now I think NATO has found a reason to reinvigorate itself.[10]

On March 27, 2014, when the "Ukraine Support Act" was discussed in the House of Representatives, Congressman Eric Ivan Cantor (R, Virginia) said that he strongly supported the act: "Vladimir Putin's recent military invasion and illegal annexation of Crimea stand in direct violation of Ukraine's sovereignty and international law. His aggression may only continue unless we in America, along with our allies, respond with strength." It was of vital importance, he continued, that the United States, "in conjunction with our EU and NATO allies, send an unmistakable signal that this aggression will

---

[9]   Marco Rubio, "Making Russia Pay," *Washington Post*, March 20, 2014.

[10]   CRS, March 25, 2014, "Support for the Sovereignty, Integrity, Democracy, and Economic Stability of Ukraine Act of 2014—Motion to proceed," p. S 1704.

not be tolerated. Together we must be prepared to exact a significant cost for Russia's behavior and that Mr. Putin's actions will be met with the firmest of resolve."[11]

In a Senate hearing about transatlantic security challenges on April 10, 2014, Senator Chris Murphy (D, Connecticut) suggested that an increased NATO response could stop Russia's aggressive behavior. He also suggested increased US troop levels in Europe: "Secretary Hagel has already said that a third brigade is being considered, and it is time for the United States to reevaluate our historically low U.S. force strength in Europe. Even a small increase will send a clear message to our friends and our adversaries." Furthermore, it was time for NATO to approve a membership action plan for Georgia, according to Murphy. He hoped that the administration would make a map for Georgia "a priority at the upcoming NATO summit in Wales."[12]

On April 27, 2014, four republican Senators, John McCain (Arizona), John Barrasso (Wyoming), John Hoeven (North Dakota), and Ron Johnson (Wisconsin), wrote in the *Washington Post* that Putin's actions in Ukraine required "a strategic response." This did not mean, they argued, "a new Cold War," but it meant "recognizing Putin's geopolitical challenge to the post-Cold War order in Europe and preparing for a more competitive relationship with Russia." That would include, they continued, a focus in NATO on deterrence and collective defense, a rebalancing of the alliance's force posture and presence, and NATO enlargement: "The United States and Europe did not seek, or deserve, this challenge from Putin's Russia. But we must rise to it all the same. Our shared interests and values depend on our resolve."[13]

Congressman Engel's view of NATO's mission was also to promote collective security which was articulated in a hearing in the House of Representatives on May 8, 2014. NATO had to remain the guarantor of

---

[11] CRHR, March 27, 2014, "Ukraine Support Act," p. H 2725–2726.
[12] SFRC, *Transatlantic Security Challenges: Central and Eastern Europe*, April 10, No. 113–475, Washington, DC: USGPO, 2014, p. 2.
[13] John McCain, John Barrasso, John Hoeven, and Ron Johnson, "A New Strategy for the Real Russia," *Washington Post*, April 27, 2014.

peace and security in Europe, he argued: "NATO allies, especially those on the eastern side of the alliance, must be confident that Article 5 guarantees remain in force."[14]

Finally, on July 24, 2014, Congressman Coffman said that strengthening NATO alliance was also a critical component in "pushing back against Russian aggression." The alliance had been "the bedrock of stability in the region," according to him:

> We must provide immediate reassurance to our European allies that the United States remains firm in our commitment to security. We must also make a strong push for the further enlargement of NATO ... The United States, in partnership with our European allies, must respond strongly to the ongoing crisis in Ukraine. Reinforcing our defense relationships with Europe, particularly Ukraine and Eastern Europe, strengthening our strategic partnerships through NATO, and enhancing European and global energy security are critical components to bolstering the transatlantic alliance and deterring further Russian aggression in the region.[15]

So in sum, the debate in Congress about NATO's mission was quite similar to previous periods. The Congressmen and Congresswomen argued that NATO should promote collective security and universal Western values—a moderate to high level of importance for NATO in US long-term security policy.

Regarding NATO's guidance, the Ukraine Crisis animated stronger demands for US leadership in Congress. For example, in a debate about the Ukraine Crisis on March 4, 2014, Senator Coats said that:

> It is in our national interest, in my opinion, to lead the world toward solutions that we know are best for us all. No other country can manage it. We have seen that. Without that management, we risk things that could harm us in many ways and continue to undermine our role in this world in providing for peace and stability.[16]

---

[14] HFAC, *Russia's Destabilization of Ukraine*, May 8, No. 113–176, Washington, DC: USGPO, 2014, p. 4.

[15] CRER, July 24, 2014, "Strengthening the Transatlantic Alliance in the Face of Russian Aggression," p. E1224.

[16] CRS, March 4, 2014, "Ukraine Crisis," p. S 1273.

And in an article in the *New York Times* on March 15, 2014, Senator McCain argued that "Crimea must be the place where President Obama recognizes this reality and begins to restore the credibility of the United States as a world leader." This would require different kinds of responses, according to McCain; isolating Russia, increasing NATO's military presence and exercises especially on its eastern border, and supporting and resupplying Ukrainian patriots across the Crimea.[17]

So in sum, the focus has clearly been on the United States as a charismatic leader of NATO, which differs from the periods before, when there were some Congressmen and Congresswomen arguing for a rational readership as well. The result from the debate in Congress can thereby be summarized in Table 4.1.

Table 4.1 Results from the US NATO debate 2014 in Congress

Vision	Political and cultural
Mission	Collective security and values
Guidance	Charismatic

The tendency, compared to the two previous periods, is that the view of NATO in US security policy as described in the US Congress was still moderate to high (maximalist), but slightly higher than before since Congress more clearly called for a charismatic US leadership of NATO.

The political debate in the administration

Unlike in the previous periods, the Obama administration clearly described the vision of NATO as a military, political, *and* cultural tool during 2014, especially after the Russian annexation of the Crimean Peninsula.

Secretary Hagel's speech in Munich on February 1, 2014, was a relatively traditional description of NATO as a military and political organization:

---

[17] John McCain, "Obama Made America Look Weak," *New York Times*, March 15, 2014.

"The foundation of our collective security relationship with Europe has always been cooperation against common threats," he said, and continued:

> The centerpiece of our transatlantic defense partnership will continue to be NATO, the military alliance that has been called the greatest peace movement in history…We must continue to hone the capabilities we've fielded and sustain these deep and effective defense relationships. And NATO must continue to develop innovative ways to maintain alliance readiness as we apply our hard-earned skills to new security challenges … The United States will engage European allies to collaborate more closely, especially in helping build the capabilities of other global partners. We're developing strategies to address global threats as we build more joint capacity—joint capacity with European militaries. In the face of budget constraints here on this continent as well as in the United States, we must all invest more strategically to protect military capability and readiness.[18]

Hagel's views of NATO as a mainly military and political organization were also reflected in the QDR that were released on March 4, 2014. The US rebalancing to the Asia Pacific was reiterated—the DoD was "committed to implementing the President's objective of rebalancing U.S. engagement toward this critical region"[19]—and it had "deep and abiding interests in a European partner that is militarily capable and politically willing to join with the United States to address future security challenges." The US commitment to NATO was "steadfast and resolute:" "We will continue to adapt the U.S. defense posture in Europe to support U.S. military operations worldwide while also conducting a range of prevention, deterrence, and assurance-related activities in Europe itself."[20]

But the QDR had, in principle, been shaped before the Ukraine Crisis. After that, the argumentation from the Obama administration also contained descriptions of NATO as a political and cultural organization. In a hearing

---

[18] Chuck Hagel, "Munich Security Conference," February 1, 2014, http://www.defense.gov (homepage), date accessed February 3, 2014. See also John Kerry, "Remarks at Munich Security Conference," February 1, 2014, www.state.gov (homepage), date accessed February 3, 2014.

[19] Department of Defense, *Quadrennial Defense Review 2014*, Washington, DC: Department of Defense, 2014, p. 16.

[20] Ibid., p. 18.

regarding the Ukraine Crisis in the House of Representatives on March 6, 2014, Deputy Assistant Secretary Rubin said that it was the US first priority to support the alliance:

> Additionally, let me mention that it is our highest priority to ensure that the solemn commitments that we have under the North Atlantic Treaty to our allies in Europe are upheld. We take that obligation with the utmost seriousness. We have worked within NATO in the past several days to ensure that we are prepared within the alliance to support all its members. We have taken action to expand our Baltic air policing mission, our aviation detachment in Poland. The North Atlantic Council issued a very strong statement on behalf of all the allies and we will be working very closely with them in coming days and weeks to ensure that the alliance stands strong and united on this.[21]

Rubin also said that Ukraine had been a member of NATO's partnership for peace for two decades, "and we have a very extensive positive experience working together with Ukraine on training, on improving the readiness, on all sorts of questions that relate to building a modern military—civilian military control and that is something that we certainly hope to continue." According to Rubin, countries "need to be free to choose their memberships, their alliances, their commitments to other countries, that this is basic principle of sovereignty, and therefore as a matter of basic principle NATO is an open alliance."[22]

And Susan E. Rice, National Security Advisor to President Obama, said in a speech in State Department on March 11, 2014, that Europe was the United States' "partner of first resort on almost every critical global challenge," and that partnership delivered results around the world:

> As the world's pre-eminent security alliance, NATO is a bulwark for peace and security—of its members and partners alike. Particularly in light of recent events, the NATO alliance and our summit this September will fortify the unshakable bond between Europe and the United States.[23]

---

[21] HFAC, *U.S. Foreign Policy Toward Ukraine*, March 6, p. 32.

[22] Ibid., p. 36.

[23] Susan E. Rice, "Remarks by Security Advisor Susan E. Rice at the Department of State's Global Chiefs of Mission Conference," Speech March 11, 2014, www.whitehouse.gov (homepage), date accessed July 1, 2014.

Furthermore, as the Ukraine Crisis escalated, the emphasis on NATO's political and cultural features became more frequently articulated. On March 31, 2014, when Secretary Kerry spoke in Washington, DC, celebrating the 15th (the Czech Republic, Hungary, Poland), the 10th (Bulgaria, Estonia, Latvia, Lithuania, Romania, Slovakia, Slovenia), and the 5th (Albania, Croatia) anniversaries of NATO enlargement, he said that NATO was strong "because of the common values that all its members share." NATO's open door policy had "expanded democracy, prosperity and stability in Europe," he said, and around the globe: "Our challenge today is to work toward a Europe that is whole, free, and at peace—and to use the power of the planet's strongest alliance to promote peace and security for people all over the world."[24]

But a more traditional view of NATO, NATO as a military and political tool, was also given by the representatives of the administration. In a Senate hearing on April 10 Derek Chollet, Assistant Secretary of Defense for International Security Affairs, said that the Wales summit would have to balance multiple competing issues and priorities, and that United States had to "reenergize the political will of our allies to invest in defense capabilities." According to Chollet, Russia's actions in the Ukraine reminded the United States of "the importance of the transatlantic alliance and the benefits that comes from many years of investment to ensure that this remains strong." "Simply put," he said, "if NATO did not exist, we would have to invent it."[25]

When Kerry spoke in Rome on May 13, 2014, he used the Ukraine Crisis to characterize NATO as a cultural tool. "We also want to be clear," he said: "There are still threats to a Europe whole, free and at peace."[26] And when Vice President Biden held a speech in Romania a week after, on May 21, 2014, he said that it was a shared value system that was "the foundation of the Western

[24] John Kerry, "Anniversaries of NATO Enlargement," March 31, 2014, www.state.gov (homepage), date accessed April 1, 2014.

[25] SFRC, *Transatlantic Security Challenges*, pp. 8–9. See also Chuck Hagel, "Submitted Statement—Senate Appropriations Committee-Defense (Budget Request)," June 18, 2014, http://www.defense .gov (homepage), date accessed June 30, 2014.

[26] John Kerry, "Remarks with Italian Foreign Minister Federica Mogherini After Their Meeting," March 31, 2014, www.state.gov (homepage), date accessed May 21, 2014.

alliance." The most fundamental of these values was not free markets, Biden continued, it was "an open, free, and transparent society, where corruption is viewed as the enemy, where government is honest and accountable, and people are given a fair opportunity at success and all—regardless of their station—are treated with dignity." He also took the opportunity to declare US commitment to NATO allies:

> America's commitment to the collective defense under Article 5 of the NATO Treaty is absolutely ironclad. It's a sacred commitment in the eyes of the President and myself. As President Obama said, "NATO nations never stand alone." NATO nations never stand alone. We protect one another.[27]

Furthermore, on June 4, 2014, in Poland, Obama said that:

> Article 5 is clear—an attack on one is an attack on all. And as allies, we have a solemn duty—a binding treaty obligation—to defend your territorial integrity. And we will. We stand together—now and forever—for your freedom is ours. Poland will never stand alone. But not just Poland—Estonia will never stand alone. Latvia will never stand alone. Lithuania will never stand alone. Romania will never stand alone. These are not just words. They're unbreakable commitments backed by the strongest alliance in the world and the armed forces of the United States of America—the most powerful military in history.[28]

Obama also said that he had, together with Congress, "announced a new initiative to bolster the security of our NATO allies and increase America's military presence in Europe," an initiative that would mean "more pre-positioned equipment to respond quickly in a crisis, and exercises and training to keep our forces ready; additional U.S. forces—in the air, and sea, and on land, including here in Poland." That would mean, however, that other NATO states must follow that example:

> Every NATO member is protected by our alliance, and every NATO member must carry its share in our alliance. This is the responsibility we have to each

---

[27] Joe Biden, "Remarks by Vice President Joe Biden to Romanian Civil Society Groups and Students," Speech May 21, 2014, www.whitehouse.gov (homepage), date accessed July 1, 2014.

[28] Barack Obama, "Remarks by President Obama at 25th Anniversary of Freedom Day," Speech June 4, 2014, www.whitehouse.gov (homepage), date accessed July 1, 2014.

other. Finally, as free peoples, we join together, not simply to safeguard our own security but to advance the freedom of others. Today we affirm the principles for which we stand. We stand together because we believe that people and nations have the right to determine their own destiny. And that includes the people of Ukraine.[29]

"Ukraine must be free to choose its own future for itself and by itself," Obama continued. He rejected "the zero-sum thinking of the past," because the people of Ukraine wanted the same freedom and opportunities and progress that the West had:

> Bigger nations must not be allowed to bully the small, or impose their will at the barrel of a gun or with masked men taking over buildings. And the stroke of a pen can never legitimize the theft of a neighbor's land. So we will not accept Russia's occupation of Crimea or its violation of Ukraine's sovereignty. Our free nations will stand united so that further Russian provocations will only mean more isolation and costs for Russia. Because after investing so much blood and treasure to bring Europe together, how can we allow the dark tactics of the 20th century to define this new century?[30]

In the end, Obama said, "tanks and troops are no match for the force of our ideals."[31]

On September 3, 2014, when the president came to Estonia, he held a joint press conference with the Estonian president, and said that Estonia was a "model ally." Furthermore, President Obama wanted to "commend" Estonia "for being such a strong voice both in NATO and the EU on behalf of the Ukrainian people." Estonia had, according to the president, "provided assistance as Ukrainians work to strengthen their democratic institutions and reform their economy," and NATO was "poised" to do more to help Ukraine. Estonia, a nation of 1.3 million people, "truly punches above its weight," he said.[32]

---

[29] Barack Obama, "Remarks by President Obama at 25th Anniversary of Freedom Day," Speech June 4, 2014, www.whitehouse.gov (homepage), date accessed July 1, 2014.

[30] Ibid.

[31] Ibid.

[32] Barack Obama, "Remarks by President Obama and President Ilves of Estonia in Joint Press Conference," September 3, 2014, www.whitehouse.gov (homepage), date accessed September 6, 2014.

Later that day, September 3, 2014, Obama was speaking to the Estonian people. We are stronger "because we stand together," he said. There was no doubt that the Baltic states had made NATO stronger, according to Obama:

> And your progress reflects a larger truth: Because of the work of generations, because we've stood together in a great alliance, because people across this continent have forged a European Union dedicated to cooperation and peace, we have made historic progress toward the vision we share—a Europe that is whole and free and at peace. And yet, as we gather here today, we know that this vision is threatened by Russia's aggression against Ukraine… It challenges that most basic of principles of our international system—that borders cannot be redrawn at the barrel of a gun; that nations have the right to determine their own future. It undermines an international order where the rights of peoples and nations are upheld and can't simply be taken away by brute force. This is what's at stake in Ukraine. This is why we stand with the people of Ukraine today. Now, let's put to rest, once and for all, the distortions or outdated thinking that has caused this crisis. Our NATO Alliance is not aimed "against" any other nation; we're an alliance of democracies dedicated to our own collective defense. Countries like Estonia and Latvia and Lithuania are not "post-Soviet territory." You are sovereign and independent nations with the right to make your own decisions. No other nation gets to veto your security decisions.[33]

So as shown, the Obama administration argued for a slightly more maximalist view of NATO's importance, incorporating, more often, cultural aspects of the vision of NATO.

Regarding NATO's mission, the Obama administration continued to focus on collective security, but also—more than before—on promoting values.

In his Munich speech on February 2, 2014, Kerry said that the transatlantic mission was to fight for values, for freedom. For more than 70 years, he said, the United States and Europe had fought "side by side for freedom, and that

---

[33] Barack Obama, "Remarks by President Obama to the People of Estonia," September 3, 2014, www.whitehouse.gov (homepage), date accessed September 7, 2014.

is what binds us." And those ties had grown even stronger after the Cold War, he argued.[34] And in a Senate hearing on budget on March 5, 2014, Secretary Hagel underscored that the United States worked through several institutional frameworks, among them NATO, to de-escalate the Ukraine Crisis.[35]

And the focus on working the crisis out through NATO, through collective action, continued. In a hearing in the Senate on March 13, 2014, Secretary Hagel said that:

> Chairman Dempsey and I have spoken with our Ukrainian counterparts, our NATO counterparts, as well as our Russian counterparts, and Chairman Dempsey and I will meet with NATO Secretary General Rasmussen here in Washington next week. Last week, we put a hold on all military-to-military engagements and exercises with Russia, and directed actions to reinforce NATO allies during this crisis.[36]

Also President Obama himself underlined NATO's institutional value in a speech on Ukraine on March 17, 2014:

> … we're continuing our close consultations with our European partners, who today in Brussels moved ahead with their own sanctions against Russia. Tonight, Vice President Biden departs for Europe, where he will meet with the leaders of our NATO allies—Poland, Estonia, Latvia and Lithuania. And I'll be traveling to Europe next week. Our message will be clear. As NATO allies, we have a solemn commitment to our collective defense, and we will uphold this commitment.[37]

And when Biden talked in Warsaw, Poland, the day after, together with the Polish prime minister, he said that the United States joined Poland and the international community "condemning the continuing assault on Ukraine's sovereignty and territorial integrity," and the "blatant" violation of international

---

[34] Kerry, "Remarks at Munich Security Conference."

[35] Chuck Hagel, "Opening Summary—Senate Armed Services Committee (Budget Request)," March 5, 2014, http://www.defense.gov (homepage), date accessed March 14, 2014.

[36] Chuck Hagel, "Opening Summary—House Appropriations Committee-Defense (Budget Request)," March 13, 2014, http://www.defense.gov (homepage), date accessed March 14, 2014.

[37] Barack Obama, "Statement by the President on Ukraine," Speech March 17, 2014, www.whitehouse .gov (homepage), date accessed July 1, 2014.

law by Russia. He said that the recent events in Ukraine had reminded the alliance members "that the bedrock of our alliance remains collective self-defense, as enshrined in Article 5 of the NATO Treaty."[38]

The same day, on March 18, 2014, Biden also spoke in Warsaw with the Estonian president, and made similar statements:

> I came here today and will travel to Vilnius tomorrow to stand with our NATO allies and reconfirm and reaffirm our shared commitment to collective self-defense, to Article 5. I want to make it absolutely clear what it means to the Estonian people and all the people of the Baltics. President Obama and I view Article 5 of the NATO Treaty as an absolutely solemn commitment which we will honor—we will honor.[39]

The day after, he met with Latvian and Lithuanian presidents in Vilnius, and said that the United States reaffirmed its commitment to Article 5 of the NATO treaty: "We will respond to any aggression against a NATO ally."[40] Before Obama went to Europe, on March 20, 2014, he made a statement on Ukraine where he also underscored NATO's mission as promoting collective security:

> America's support for our NATO allies is unwavering. We're bound together by our profound Article 5 commitment to defend one another, and by a set of shared values that so many generations sacrificed for. We've already increased our support for our Eastern European allies, and we will continue to strengthen NATO's collective defense, and we will step up our cooperation with Europe on economic and energy issues as well.[41]

And when he had arrived to Europe, on March 24, he held a speech with the prime minister of Netherlands, in which he said that the Netherlands was "one of our closest allies," and that it underscored a larger point, that the

---

[38] Joe Biden, "Remarks to the Press by Vice President Joe Biden with Prime Minister Donald Tusk of Poland," Speech March 18, 2014, www.whitehouse.gov (homepage), date accessed July 1, 2014.

[39] Joe Biden, "Remarks to the Press by Vice President Joe Biden and President Toomas Ilves of Estonia," Speech March 18, 2014, www.whitehouse.gov (homepage), date accessed July 1, 2014.

[40] Joe Biden, "Remarks to the Press by Vice President Joe Biden, President Dalia Grybauskaite, and President Andris Berzins of Latvia," Speech March 19, 2014, www.whitehouse.gov (homepage), date accessed July 1, 2014.

[41] Barack Obama, "Statement by the President on Ukraine," Speech March 20, 2014, www.whitehouse.gov (homepage), date accessed July 1, 2014.

NATO allies were the "closest partners on the world stage" for the United States: "Europe is the cornerstone of America's engagement with the world." Europe and the United States were united in their support of the Ukrainian government and the Ukrainian people. They were "united in imposing a cost on Russia for its actions so far."[42]

Two days after, on March 26, 2014, Obama met with Secretary General Rasmussen. Before their meeting, Obama argued that the Ukraine Crisis had "focused everyone's attention on the importance of the transatlantic relationships," and reaffirmed the importance of NATO, "the bedrock of America's security as well as European security." The United States and Europe shared the view that that Russia's actions in Ukraine had to be condemned, but it also reminded that "Article 5 are something that are not just items on a piece of paper, but are critically important to all NATO members."[43]

Furthermore, when Kerry spoke in Brussels on April 1, 2014, he was as clear, underscoring NATO's mission as to promote collective security and values. It was time, he said, to "come together and to reaffirm our commitment to each other, to the transatlantic treaty and transatlantic security, and especially to our common values." It was the critical moment, he continued, when "some of the basic principles underlying the international system have been violated and, frankly, our alliance has been put to the test:"

> Today, NATO allies tasked the Supreme Allied Commander to provide visible reassurance with respect to our Central and Eastern European allies, assurance that Article 5 of NATO's treaty means what it says on land, air, and sea… Just as importantly, Europe and North America have stood together in defense of Ukraine's right to choose its future and in defense of international law. Together, we have rejected any notion that there is any legality in Russia's efforts to annex Crimea… As free nations, we will continue to stand together and stand always in defense of international law, of our mutual security, and of the right of nations and

---

[42] Barack Obama, "Remarks by President Obama and Prime Minister Rutte of the Netherlands After Bilateral Meeting," Speech March 24, 2014, www.whitehouse.gov (homepage), date accessed July 1, 2014.

[43] Barack Obama, "Remarks by President Obama and NATO Secretary General Rasmussen Before Meeting," Speech March 26, 2014, www.whitehouse.gov (homepage), date accessed July 1, 2014.

people everywhere to freely choose their own destiny. Our meeting today underscored these principles in both words and in deeds.[44]

And in Brussels, on April 1, 2014, when Kerry answered a question about NATO's reactions on the Ukraine Crisis, he said that it was "important for everybody in the world to understand that the NATO alliance takes seriously this attempt to change borders by use of force." "And as a result," he continued, "people here today made a commitment to be able to strengthen visibly, as a matter of deterrence and as a matter of reality, the cooperation, the deployment, and the efforts of those who are members of this alliance."[45]

In Washington, DC, on May 2, 2014, Obama gave a talk with the German Chancellor Angela Merkel on Ukraine, and he said that the United States and Germany were "united in our unwavering Article 5 commitment to the security of our NATO allies, including German aircraft joining NATO patrols over the Baltics."[46]

Also other representatives of the administration underscored NATO's collective defense. In a hearing in the House of Representatives, May 8, 2014, Victoria Nuland said that the United States was: "working intensively" with its NATO allies "to provide visible reassurance on land, on sea, and in the air that Article 5 of the NATO treaty means what it says." Our message to Russia is clear, she said: "NATO territory is inviolable. We will defend every piece of it and we are mounting a visible deterrent to any Russian efforts to test that."[47]

And when Vice President Biden gave a talk in Romania on May 20, 2014, he said that the United States "commitment to collective defense under Article 5 of NATO" was a "sacred obligation… not just for now, but for all time":

> You can count on us. Period. We do what we say, and we mean what we say. Today aggression in Crimea, less than 250 miles from Romanian territory, from NATO's borders reminds us why we need NATO and why Romania belongs to NATO. What Russia has done violates not just Ukraine's

---

[44] John Kerry, "Press Availability at NATO," April 1, 2014.

[45] John Kerry, "Press Availability at NATO," April 1, 2014.

[46] Obama, Barack, "Remarks by President Obama and German Chancellor Merkel in Joint Press Conference," Speech May 2, 2014, www.whitehouse.gov (homepage), date accessed July 1, 2014.

[47] HFAC, *Russia's Destabilization of Ukraine*, p. 10.

sovereignty, but a fundamental principle we fought for in the 20th century and thought we had clearly established. Europe's borders should never again be changed at the point of a gun ...[48]

And the pattern of underscoring collective security and values carried on. On May 28, 2014, Secretary Kerry was interviewed by the CNN about the Ukraine Crisis, and he said:

> NATO has been strengthened. NATO has been awakened. NATO is doing a full assurance program right now with additional troops throughout the NATO countries ... I think the President's policy has worked. I think the European alliance has been strengthened. The unity between Europe and the United States is what has empowered this election to take place and made it clear to Russia that the West is unified and there will be a very severe price to pay for further interference in Ukraine.[49]

A week later, on June 3, 2014, Obama spoke twice in Poland. In the first speech, he said that he started his European visit there because the US commitment to Poland, "as well as the security of our allies in Central and Eastern Europe," was "a cornerstone of our own security and it is sacrosanct."[50] In the second speech, he said that the 25th anniversary of Polish freedom reminded of the transformation that had taken place all across the region: "The countries represented here have all undertaken hard reforms, have built democratic institutions, have delivered greater prosperity for their citizens, and underlying this progress is the security guarantee that comes from NATO membership."[51]

In Brussels on June 25, 2014, Secretary Kerry said that NATO had "taken measures" that demonstrate that the Article 5 commitment is "absolutely rock solid." The United States also, he continued, "affirmed NATO's open door

---

[48] Joe Biden, "Remarks by Vice President Joe Biden to Joint United States and Romanian Participants in Carpathian Spring Military Exercise," Speech May 20, 2014, www.whitehouse.gov (homepage), date accessed July 1, 2014.

[49] CNN, "Interview with Chris Cuomo of CNN New Day," May 28, 2014, www.state.gov (homepage), date accessed May 29, 2014.

[50] Barack Obama, "Remarks by President Obama and President Komorowski to U.S. and Polish Armed Forces," Speech June 3, 2014, www.whitehouse.gov (homepage), date accessed July 1, 2014.

[51] Barack Obama, "Remarks by President Obama Before a Meeting with Central and Eastern European Leaders," Speech June 3, 2014, www.whitehouse.gov (homepage), date accessed July 1, 2014.

policy as well as the vital importance of having strong, capable partners." In addition, NATO "sustained support for Ukraine's sovereignty and the right of its people to determine their own future." He also talked about the upcoming NATO Summit in Wales, and the necessity for a more fair transatlantic burden sharing:

> As we head to the Wales summit, every ally spending less than 2 percent of their GDP needs to dig deeper and make a concrete commitment to do more. And all you have to do is look at a map in order to understand why— Ukraine, Iraq, Syria—all threats to peace and to security, and they surround the region.[52]

"At a time when people doubt the ability of multilateral efforts to make a difference," he said, "the meeting here today stands in stark testimony to the contrary."[53]

On July 16, 2014, Obama said regarding Ukraine, that he had approved a new set of sanctions on Russia. "Along with our allies," he continued, "with whom I've been coordinating closely the last several days and weeks, I've repeatedly made it clear that Russia must halt the flow of weapons and fighters across the border into Ukraine; that Russia must urge separatists to release their hostages and support a cease-fire; that Russia needs to pursue internationally-mediated talks and agree to meaningful monitors on the border."[54]

And on July 18, 2014, President Obama said that he did not see "a U.S. military role beyond what we've already been doing in working with our NATO partners and some of the Baltic States, giving them reassurances that we are prepared to do whatever is required to meet our alliance obligations."[55]

The week before the Wales Summit started, on July 28, 2014, Obama again declared that the Ukraine Crisis would be solved collectively:

---

[52] John Kerry, "Press Availability at NATO Headquarters," June 25, 2014, www.state.gov (homepage), date accessed June 30, 2014.

[53] Ibid.

[54] Barack Obama, "Remarks by the President on Foreign Policy," Speech July 16, 2014, www .whitehouse.gov (homepage), date accessed July 31, 2014.

[55] Barack Obama, "Statement by the President on Ukraine," Speech July 18, 2014, www.whitehouse.gov (homepage), date accessed July 31, 2014.

As a result of the actions Russia has already taken, and the major sanctions we've imposed with our European and international partners, Russia is already more isolated than at any time since the end of the Cold War. Capital is fleeing. Investors are increasingly staying out. Its economy is in decline. And this ongoing Russian incursion into Ukraine will only bring more costs and consequences for Russia. Next week, I'll be in Europe to coordinate with our closest allies and partners.[56]

There were more examples of the view that NATO's mission was to promote collective security. In a statement on August 28, just one week before the NATO Summit in Wales, President Obama said that:

In Estonia, I will reaffirm our unwavering commitment to the defense of our NATO allies. At the NATO Summit in the United Kingdom, we'll focus on the additional steps we can take to ensure the Alliance remains prepared for any challenge. Our meeting of the NATO-Ukraine Commission will be another opportunity for our alliance to continue our partnership with Ukraine. And I look forward to reaffirming the unwavering commitment of the United States to Ukraine and its people when I welcome President Poroshenko to the White House next month.[57]

President Obama also said, as an answer to a question about the Ukraine Crisis, that:

We are not taking military action to solve the Ukrainian problem … Keep in mind, however, that I'm about to go to a NATO conference. Ukraine is not a member of NATO, but a number of those states that are close by are. And we take our Article 5 commitments to defend each other very seriously, and that includes the smallest NATO member, as well as the largest NATO member. And so part of the reason I think this NATO meeting is going to be so important is to refocus attention on the critical function that NATO plays to make sure that every country is contributing in order to deliver on the promise of our Article 5 assurances. Part of the reason I'll be going to Estonia is to let the Estonians know that we mean

[56] Barack Obama, "Statement by the President," August 28, 2014, www.whitehouse.gov (homepage), date accessed September 6, 2014.
[57] Ibid.

what we say with respect to our treaty obligations. We don't have those treaty obligations with Ukraine.[58]

And on September 3, when President Obama came to Estonia, he held a joint press conference with the Estonian president. Estonian forces had served "with courage and skill in Iraq and Afghanistan," and the United States honored that. Furthermore, the Estonians contributed to "its full share," that is, 2 percent of GDP, to NATO and was an example of "how every NATO member needs to do its fair share" for the collective defense. Obama had come to Estonia to "reaffirm the commitment" of the United States to Estonia, and to signalize that Article 5 was "unbreakable," "unwavering," and "eternal." "Estonia will never stand alone," the president said.[59]

The question of how to handle the "Islamic State" (IS) was also a matter for collective action, according the administration.[60] On a question related to what NATO could contribute to regarding the handling of ISIL, the president said at the press conference on September 3 that one of the US goals was to "get NATO to work with us to help create the kinds of partnerships regionally that can combat not just ISIL, but these kinds of networks as they arise and potentially destabilize allies and partners of ours in the region":

> What we hope to do at the NATO Summit is to make sure that we are more systematic about how we do it, that we're more focused about how we do it. NATO is unique in the annals of history as a successful alliance. But we have to recognize that threats evolve, and threats have evolved as a consequence of what we've seen in Ukraine, but threats are also evolving in the Middle East that have a direct effect on Europe.[61]

Later that day, on September 3, 2014, when Obama was speaking to the Estonian people, and he was forcefully underscoring NATO's mission to

[58] Barack Obama, "Statement by the President," August 28, 2014, www.whitehouse.gov (homepage), date accessed September 6, 2014.
[59] Barack Obama, "Remarks by President Obama and President Ilves of Estonia in Joint Press Conference."
[60] See also John Kerry, "To Defeat Terror, We Need the World's Help," *New York Times*, August 29, 2014.
[61] Barack Obama, "Remarks by President Obama and President Ilves of Estonia in Joint Press Conference."

promote collective security. "As free peoples, as an Alliance, we will stand firm and united to meet the test of this moment," he said. The United States would defend its NATO allies, he continued, "and that means every Ally." There were no "old members or new members, no junior partners or senior partners" in the alliance, according to him, "just Allies, pure and simple. And we will defend the territorial integrity of every single Ally." Article 5 was crystal clear:

> An attack on one is an attack on all. So if, in such a moment, you ever ask again, "who will come to help," you'll know the answer—the NATO Alliance, including the Armed Forces of the United States of America, "right here, [at] present, now!" We'll be here for Estonia. We will be here for Latvia. We will be here for Lithuania. You lost your independence once before. With NATO, you will never lose it again.[62]

At the press conference at the Wales Summit, on September 5, 2014, Obama continued to underscore NATO's mission as promoting collective security. He said that the alliance had "reaffirmed the central mission of the Alliance," Article 5: "This is a binding, treaty obligation. It is non-negotiable." The alliance had also "agreed to be resolute in reassuring our Allies in Eastern Europe," he said.[63]

Secretary Kerry followed that up and connected it to the handling of the IS, when he said that:

> There is no contain policy for ISIL. They're an ambitious, avowed genocidal, territorial-grabbing, Caliphate-desiring, quasi state within a regular army. And leaving them in some capacity intact anywhere would leave a cancer in place that will ultimately come back to haunt us. So there is no issue in our minds about our determination to build this coalition, go after this. I'll give you a quick take at what we are looking for and what we're going to do. When we say holistic, we mean every aspect of this group, and I think this could become conceivably a model that can help us with Boko Haram, could help us with Shabaab, with other groups if we can do this

---

[62] Barack Obama, "Remarks by President Obama to the People of Estonia," September 3, 2014, www.whitehouse.gov (homepage), date accessed September 7, 2014.

[63] Barack Obama, "Remarks by President Obama at NATO Summit Press Conference," September 5, 2014, www.whitehouse.gov (homepage), date accessed September 7, 2014.

successfully. And NATO needs to think of it that way as we consider sort of our role in this new world we're living in.[64]

And at the press conference in Wales on September 5, President Obama more specifically said that the NATO Allies and partners were "prepared to join in a broad, international effort to combat the threat posed by ISIL":

> Already, Allies have joined us in Iraq, where we have stopped ISIL's advances; we've equipped our Iraqi partners, and helped them go on offense. NATO has agreed to play a role in providing security and humanitarian assistance to those who are on the front lines. Key NATO Allies stand ready to confront this terrorist threat through military, intelligence and law enforcement, as well as diplomatic efforts.[65]

On a question about how to fight the IS, Obama once again underscored the collective effort. The threat posed by them was "a significant threat to NATO members," and the NATO members recognized that they had a "critical role to play in rolling back this savage organization." It was "encouraging," he said that the allies were prepared to act "as part of the international community to degrade and ultimately destroy ISIL." On another question, regarding the same topic, the president replied that the IS could not be contained:

> You can't contain an organization that is running roughshod through that much territory, causing that much havoc, displacing that many people, killing that many innocents, enslaving that many women. The goal has to be to dismantle them.[66]

Obama was "pleased" to see that there was "unanimity" in NATO to achieve that goal. He also reiterated that the United States would not be placing ground troops in Syria: "We are going to have to find effective partners on the ground to push back against ISIL."[67]

---

[64] John Kerry, "Remarks at Top of Meeting on Building an Anti-ISIL Coalition Chaired by Defense Secretary Chuck Hagel, U.K. Foreign Secretary Phillip Hammond and U.K. Defense Secretary Michael Fallon," September 5, 2014, www.state.gov (homepage), date accessed September 6, 2014.

[65] Barack Obama, "Remarks by President Obama at NATO Summit Press Conference".

[66] Ibid.

[67] Ibid.

So in sum, the tendency is clear. The administration continued to focus on collective security, but it also, in a more direct way, talked about NATO's mission to promote values.

Regarding NATO's guidance, the same main pattern appeared within the Obama administration as before. The administration argued that the United States should lead, but rational leadership was the preferred strategy of leadership. In Munich on February 2, 2014, Secretary Kerry underlined that when he said that:

> The task of building a Europe that is whole and free and at peace is not complete. And in order to meet today's challenges both near and far, America needs a strong Europe, and Europe needs a committed and engaged America. And that means turning inward is not an option for any of us. When we lead together, others will join us. But when we don't, the simple fact is that few are prepared or willing to step up. That's just a fact. And leading, I say respectfully, does not mean meeting in Munich for good discussions. It means committing resources even in a difficult time to make certain that we are helping countries to fight back against the complex, vexing challenges of our day.[68]

And Secretary Hagel filled in the same day, when he said that:

> This is a partnership. Partnerships mean partnership. Everybody has to participate. Everyone has to contribute. Everybody has a role to play. Because not only is something new today with restrained resources in everyone's budgets. I get that, the realities of what we're each dealing with in our own respective countries, own respective political dynamics and dimensions—but if your nation's security is not worth an investment, is not worth leadership in fighting for that investment, then you've got the wrong leadership or—again, history's been instructive on this point—then the future of that country is in some peril. It's going to take some courage and vision and strong leadership to make this point clear to all of our constituents. And the Europeans must play their role as well.[69]

---

[68] Kerry, "Remarks at Munich Security Conference".
[69] Hagel, "Munich Security Conference."

The administration made quite clear that leading together also meant sharing the burdens together. When Obama spoke with the Italian prime minister on March 27 in Rome, he took the opportunity to address the burden sharing issue through the Ukraine Crisis. "We can't have a situation," he said, "in which the United States is consistently spending over 3 percent of our GDP on defense," and Europe is spending 1 percent. "The gap becomes too large," he continued, and the alliance needed to make sure that everybody was doing their fair share.[70]

Obama's "West Point speech," on May 28, 2014, was in many ways summarizing his philosophy of leadership since the Libya war. "America must always lead on the world stage," he said: "If we don't, no one else will." The United States would use military force, "unilaterally if necessary," but it preferred to do it within a multilateral frame:

> After World War II, America had the wisdom to shape institutions to keep the peace and support human progress—from NATO and the United Nations, to the World Bank and IMF. These institutions are not perfect, but they have been a force multiplier. They reduce the need for unilateral American action and increase restraint among other nations... Now, there are a lot of folks, a lot of skeptics, who often downplay the effectiveness of multilateral action. For them, working through international institutions like the U.N. or respecting international law is a sign of weakness. I think they're wrong.[71]

It is important to underline that leading in a rational way does not mean not leading. Secretary Kerry emphasized that on July 20, 2014, when he said that "I think, to greater effect than at any time in recent memory, and I can't think of a time when the United States has been engaged in more places where people are worried not about our staying, but they don't want us to leave, and they recognize that American leadership is critical."[72]

[70] Obama, Barack, "Remarks by President Obama and Prime Minister Renzi of Italy in Joint Press Conference," Speech March 27, 2014, www.whitehouse.gov (homepage), date accessed July 1, 2014.

[71] Barack Obama, "Remarks by President Obama at the United States Military Academy Commencement Ceremony," Speech May 28, 2014, www.whitehouse.gov (homepage), date accessed July 1, 2014.

[72] John Kerry, "Interview with George Stephanopoulos of ABC's This Week," July 20, 2014, www.state.gov (homepage), date accessed July 29, 2014.

In an even more general statement the same day, he said that "The United States of America has never been more engaged in helping to lead in more places than we are now."[73] And President Obama said in a press conference on August 1, 2014, in Washington, DC, that:

> ... there's a big world out there, and that as indispensable as we are to try to lead it, there's still going to be tragedies out there and there are going to be conflicts. And our job is to just make sure that we continue to project what's right, what's just, and that we're building coalitions of like-minded countries and partners in order to advance not only our core security interests but also the interests of the world as a whole.[74]

In sum, no principal differences in the expressed views of the Obama administration occurred regarding the leadership of NATO during 2014. The administration still argued that NATO should be led in a rational way—a minimalist view. On the other hand, the administration did not use concepts such as leading from behind to describe their preferred guidance of NATO, and that is a slight difference compared to previous periods.

All in all, the Ukraine Crisis moved the Obama administration in a maximalist direction: from a moderate to low view of NATO's importance in US security policy to a moderate to high view. The results are summarized in Table 4.2.

Table 4.2 Results from the US NATO debate 2014 in the administration

Vision	Political and cultural
Mission	Collective security and values
Guidance	Rational

The administration was emphasizing a vision of NATO that was more maximalist when it included cultural aspect. Furthermore it was more clearly arguing that NATO's mission included promoting universal values. And

---

[73] John Kerry, "Interview with David Gregory of NBC's Meet the Press," July 20, 2014, www.state.gov (homepage), date accessed July 29, 2014.

[74] Barack Obama, "Press Conference by the President," August 1, 2014, www.whitehouse.gov (homepage), date accessed September 6, 2014.

lastly it pointed at the necessity of US leadership, although not a charismatic (maximalist) leadership but a rational (minimalist) one.

The policy debate in the think tank and elite media environment

The policy debate about NATO during the Ukraine Crisis was slightly more maximalist than before. The vision of NATO was described as military, political, and cultural, the mission of NATO as promoting collective security and values, and the guidance of NATO as charismatic.

Regarding the *vision* of NATO, an editorial in the *Washington Post* on March 20, 2014, argued that Russia's claim that it should have a say in the political orientation of its neighbors, and whether they join alliances such as the European Union or NATO, was "equally unacceptable." The editorial board found it perverse that "some in the West are echoing Mr. Putin's argument that his aggression is an understandable response to Western encouragement of the former Soviet Bloc states that embraced democracy and free markets and sought NATO and European Union membership." The crisis in Europe had not been caused by Western institutions enlarging they argued, "but because they did not fulfill their post-Cold War promise of 'a Europe whole and free.' "[75]

Lilia Shevtsova, Senior Associate at the Carnegie Moscow Center, argued in a similar way in the *Washington Post* on May 9, 2014: "By refusing to offer Ukraine real prospects for joining the Euro-Atlantic community through either European Union and/or NATO membership, the West is leaving Ukraine in a gray zone of uncertainty, vulnerable to falling into the Russian orbit."[76] Thomas L. Friedman, columnist in the *New York Times*, did not seem to be that worried, when he on May 28, 2014, wrote in a column:

> Let's add it up: Putin's seizure of Crimea has weakened the Russian economy, led to China getting a bargain gas deal, revived NATO, spurred Europe to

---

[75] "A Dangerous Russian Doctrine," Editorial, *Washington Post*, March 20, 2014.
[76] Lilia Shevtsova, "Putin's New World Order," *Washington Post*, May 9, 2014.

start ending its addiction to Russian gas and begun a debate across Europe about increasing defense spending. Nice work, Vladimir.[77]

On June 5, 2014, Anthony H. Cordesman at the CSIS discussed NATO and Ukraine in a commentary. He clearly saw NATO as a military and political tool:

> Events in Ukraine have made it all too clear that NATO's primary function remains deterring war in Europe … The practical problem for both the United States and Europe is now to create a level of deterrence that can secure the NATO countries nearest Russia without needlessly recreating some new form of Cold War. It is also to help the non-NATO states on Russia's borders in ways that help them develop without provoking Russia, but that still give Russia a strong incentive not to repeat what happened in Ukraine, Georgia, and Moldavia.[78]

And Michael Haltzel at the CTR wrote in the *Washington Post* on June 29, 2014, that President Obama had reassured Poland, Lithuania, Latvia, and Estonia of US support, "but he has shown little inclination to show needed leadership by putting another integral element of NATO policy on the agenda of September's Cardiff summit: enlargement of the alliance." According to Halzel, that was "unwise and unnecessary," since NATO enlargement "has been one of the most successful U.S. foreign policy achievements of the past two decades": "As a result of their countries joining NATO," he continued, "more than 100 million Central and Eastern Europeans in 12 nations from Estonia to Albania can freely elect their own governments and pursue national priorities without fear of foreign invasion."[79]

In September 2014, Alexandra de Hoop Scheffer, Senior Transatlantic Fellow and Director of GMF's Paris Office, and Bruno Lété, Senior Program Officer for Foreign and Security Policy in GMF's Brussels Office, argued that NATO had to go back to its military and political roots:

---

[77] Thomas L. Friedman, "Putin Blinked," *New York Times*, May 28, 2014.

[78] Anthony H. Cordesman, "NATO and Ukraine: The Need for Real World Strategies and for European Partners Rather Than Parasites," CSIS Commentary, June 5, 2014, www.csis.org (homepage), date accessed January 8, 2015. Regarding NATO as a military and political tool, see also Stanley R. Sloan and Sten Rynning, "Securing the Transatlantic Community: NATO Is Not Enough," ACUS Article, March 17, 2014, www.atlanticcouncil.org (homepage), date accessed January 8, 2015.

[79] Michael Haltzel, "Extenting NATO's Umbrella," *Washington Post*, June 29, 2014.

In the long run, NATO's credibility as a powerful, even formidable military machine has to be restored in the eyes of its members, its publics, its partners, and antagonists. After years of trying to be loved, the Alliance has to go back to being respected, and perhaps even feared. Solidarity can no longer be presumed, it has to be demonstrated, both within the Alliance and toward the outside world. Allies need to recommit to NATO on the understanding that they can trust it—and each other— to be there for them ... Hence, NATO should continue to improve its force-multiplying functions and offer effective command, enablers, and enhanced interoperability between allies and partners. In comparison to the past, the security challenges of today require quick responses— necessitating flexible policy frameworks in which quick coercive reactions can be decided among networked actors.[80]

In October 2014, in a GMF Policy Brief by Sinan Ülgen, Visiting Scholar at Carnegie Europe in Brussels, similar views were expressed. "The Ukraine crisis had helped to firmly reset the priorities of the Alliance," he argued, since it had "unraveled a debate on the credibility of Article 5." The crisis had also, he continued, "demonstrated the continued commitment of the United States to the security of the European continent, but also more importantly to the credibility of Article 5, and has helped eradicate some of the uneasiness the 'pivot to Asia' introduced in the debate."[81]

So the vision of NATO expressed in the policy debate was, just as before, pluralistic and moderate to high (maximalist): NATO was described as a military, political, and cultural tool.

Regarding NATO's mission, the focus was clearly on collective security and promoting universal values. In an article in the *Washington Post* on March 3, 2014, after Russia's annexation of Crimea, William B. Taylor, Steven K. Pifer, and John E. Herbst—all former US Ambassadors to Ukraine—wrote that "NATO can play a role by recognizing the threat a rogue Russia poses to

---

[80] Alexandra de Hoop Scheffer and Bruno Lété, "Rethinking NATO's Strategy in a Changing World: Recommendations for the Next Secretary General", *GMF Policy Brief*, September 2014, www.gmfus .org (homepage), date accessed January 8, 2015, p. 4.

[81] Sinan Ülgen, "Deterrence Beyond NATO Borders", *GMF Policy Brief*, October 2014, www.gmfus.org (homepage), date accessed January 8, 2015, p. 1.

member states, especially the Baltics."[82] On March 4, 2014, Roger Cohen, a columnist in the *New York Times*, argued along the same lines:

> Pivot to Asia cannot mean abandonment of Ukraine. Every form of diplomatic, trade and economic pressure should now be mustered by Obama to isolate Putin…every political means used to buttress the Kiev government; and NATO's readiness to defend its members should be ostentatiously underscored.[83]

On March 4 the editorial team in the *Washington Post* also argued for US show of force through NATO, so that Putin did not try to "replicate his Ukrainian adventure" in NATO's member states Rumania, and the Baltic States. "An obvious first step," they wrote, was to "dedicate greater NATO resources to training, exercises and defense planning in members along the border with Russia, starting with the Baltic States and extending to Romania and other former Warsaw Pact countries." NATO should also, they argued, "reinvigorate its glacial move to expand to nations in southeastern Europe," at the Wales Summit: "Mr. Putin must get the message that his aggression will not retard the integration into Western security structures of new European democracies."[84]

And in an article in the *Washington Post* the same day by Stephen J. Hadley, former US National Security Advisor, and Damon Wilson also argued that the United States needed to develop "a strategy for reassuring allies in Central and Eastern Europe… and for deterring Putin from seeking again to extend Russia's reach by force." The United States should reinforce its military engagement in Poland, the Baltic States, and Romania, they argued, and work through NATO for enlargement. "If Putin concludes he can get away with occupying Crimea," they argued, "he won't stop there."[85]

Former US National Security Advisor Zbigniew Brzezinski also called for US action through NATO in an article in the *Washington Post* on March 4.

[87] William D. Taylor, Steven K. Pifer, and John E. Herbst, "Ukraine Will Fight," Editorial, *Washington Post*, March 3, 2014.

[83] Roger Cohen, "Putin's Crimean Crime," *New York Times*, March 4, 2014.

[84] "Ukrainan Aftershocks," Editorial, *Washington Post*, March 4, 2014.

[85] Stephen J. Hadley, and Damon Wilson, "Putin's Long Game," *Washington Post*, March 4, 2014. For a similar argument, see David Ignatius, "The Cost of Adventurism," *Washington Post*, April 16, 2014.

"NATO cannot be passive," he wrote, "if war erupts in Europe." If Ukraine was crushed, he continued, "the new freedom and security in bordering Romania, Poland and the three Baltic republics would also be threatened."[86]

And Obama's critics also took the opportunity to blame the president for the crisis. Krauthammer, for example, wrote in the *Washington Post* on March 14, 2014, that:

> For the past five years, Obama's fruitless accommodationism has invited the kind of aggressiveness demonstrated by Iran in Syria, China in the East China Sea and Russia in Ukraine. But what's done is done … What is to be done now? Reassure NATO … Declare that any further Russian military incursion beyond Crimea will lead to a rapid and favorable response from NATO to any request from Kiev for weapons. These would be accompanied by significant numbers of NATO trainers and advisers … Any Russian push into western Ukraine would then engage a thin tripwire of NATO trainer/advisers. That is something the most rabid Soviet expansionist never risked. Nor would Putin… Obama is not the first president to conduct a weak foreign policy. Jimmy Carter [US President 1977–81] was similarly inclined—until Russia invaded Afghanistan, at which point the scales fell from Carter's eyes … Invasion woke Carter from his illusions. Will it wake Obama?[87]

Anne Applebaum also argued for NATO forward deployment in the *Washington Post* on March 21, 2014: "We need to re-imagine NATO, to move its forces from Germany to the alliance's eastern borders."[88] As did the editorial board in the *Washington Post* a week later, the March 27, 2014:

> Russia's seizure of Crimea and Vladimir Putin's dangerous revanchism will require an overhaul of NATO's deployments and strategy in Europe. That should mean more forward deployments in front-line states such as Poland, Estonia and Latvia and better preparation for Moscow-initiated cyber-attacks.[89]

---

[86] Zbigniew Brzezinski, "What Is to Be Done?" *Washington Post*, March 4, 2014.

[87] Charles Krauthammer, "How to Stop Putin," *Washington Post*, March 14, 2014. See also James P. Rubin, "Reassuring Eastern Europe," *New York Times*, June 12, 2014.

[88] Anne Applebaum, "Russia, Unveiled," *Washington Post*, March 21, 2014.

[89] "The Long Game," Editorial, *Washington Post*, March 27, 2014.

Applebaum had a more value oriented approach in the *Washington Post* on March 30, when she wrote that President Obama's speech in Georgia, when he said that Georgia is not on a path to NATO membership, he strengthened the anti-Western arguments there: "An alignment with Russia can bring Russian-style corruption and can inspire the rise of Russian-style xenophobia and homophobia, too." The alternative, an alignment with the West, had the opposite consequences, according to her.[90]

Ignatius was, however, supporting President Obama's policy in the *Washington Post* on May 7, 2014, when he wrote that the president should "stay the course:" "With sanctions, diplomatic pressure, NATO resolve. If Obama can hold the Western alliance together with these measured policies, the essential weakness of Putin's position will be obvious in a few years."[91]

And the editorial team in the *New York Times* was of the same opinion when they, June 5, 2014, wrote that President Obama's decision to commit $1 billion "to bolster security in Central and Eastern Europe" sent important messages, both to NATO allies and Russia. The initiative, they continued, was meant to "assure Central and Eastern European states within Russia's shadow of America's willingness to help in times of trouble," and the Russians needed to know that "continued attempts to destabilize Ukraine or aggressively extend Russia's reach" would not be unanswered.[92]

Furthermore, Magnus Nordenman, Snowcroft Center Deputy Director at ACUS, wrote about NATO's mission to promote collective security and values in an ACUS Report, in June 2014:

> At heart, NATO is an alliance of nations that share similar values and ideals, even despite occasional differences in policies. A NATO that confidently takes on the new challenges and equips, trains, plans, and politically prepares for the era of global competition will not only defend transatlantic security but also advance its ideals globally.[93]

---

[90] Anne Appelbaum, "Russia's Anti-western Thinking Takes Hold," *Washington Post*, March 30, 2014. See also *The Washington Post*, "Caught in the Middle," *Washington Post*, April 26, 2014.

[91] David Ignatius, "Say Less and Do More," *Washington Post*, May 7, 2014.

[92] "Standing Up to Mr. Putin," Editorial, *New York Times*, June 5, 2014.

[93] Magnus Nordenman, "NATO in an Era of Global Competition," ACUS Report, June 2014, www .atlanticcouncil.org (homepage), date accessed January 8, 2015, p. 12.

Finally Anne Applebaum wrote in the *Washington Post* on October 19, and argued for collective security:

> Our mistake was not to humiliate Russia but to underrate Russia's revanchist, revisionist, disruptive potential. If the only real Western achievement of the past quarter-century is now under threat, that's because we have failed to ensure that NATO continues to do in Europe what it was always meant to do: deter. Deterrence is not an aggressive policy; it is a defensive policy. But in order to work, deterrence has to be real. It requires investment, consolidation and support from all of the West, and especially the United States.[94]

So the focus in the policy debate about NATO's mission was clearly on promoting collective security and universal values: a moderate to high (maximalist) view of NATO in US security policy.

Regarding NATO's guidance, finally, the policy debate contained both minimalist (rational leadership) and maximalist (charismatic leadership) arguments, just as previous periods. But the focus was more clearly on charismatic leadership than before, so the view of how NATO should be led was slightly more maximalist than before.

Opinion writer Fareed Zakaria, for example, was representative, when he in the *Washington Post* on March 14, 2014, wrote that the Ukraine Crisis was "the most significant geopolitical problem since the Cold War." It involved a great power and a global principle, "whether national boundaries can be changed by brute force." If it became acceptable to change border by force, he argued, the consequences, not least in Asia, could be huge. The United States had to lead the way, according to him: "Obama must rally the world, push the Europeans and negotiate with the Russians. In this crisis, the United States truly is the indispensable nation."[95]

However, on June 5, 2014, Cordesman at the CSIS discussed NATO and Ukraine in a commentary, and he was clearly arguing for a rational US

---

[94] Anne Applebaum, "The Myth of Russian humiliation," *Washington Post*, October 19, 2014.
[95] Fareed Zakaria, "Obama's Mandate on Ukraine," *Washington Post*, March 14, 2014.

leadership of NATO. According to Cordesman, Russia needed to see that Europe could "react and not wait on, or passively exploit American leadership." So far, Europe has failed to do so, according to him:

> Both the United States and the rest of NATO should make it clear that they are fully committed to the defense of the NATO states nearest Russia. The United States needs to make good on President Obama's June 3rd pledge of $1 billion to boost the military presence in Eastern Europe, not simply pledge or spend the money on military exercises. It is the rest of Europe, however, that should really be taking the lead... But, this will only work if Europe stops being a parasite, steps up to doing its share in defense, and stops whining about American "decline." ... If anyone should whine about decline, it should be the United States ... It is Europe that should be taking the lead in Europe—with solid American backing. It is Europe that should worry about its own decline, and its Europe that should remember the words of a European named Edmund Burke, "The only thing necessary for the triumph of evil is for good men to do nothing."[96]

More common, however, was to argue for a charismatic US leadership. In the *Washington Post*, on August 24, 2014, Anne Applebaum argued that "Obama might not have the power to make Congress do what he wants, but he does have the power to relaunch the Western alliance."[97] And in an editorial in the *Washington Post* on August 30, 2014, the editorial board argued that:

> Allies are vital; the United States overstretched in the Bush years; it can't solve every problem. All true. But it's also true that none of the basic challenges to world order can be met without U.S. leadership: not Russia's aggression, not the Islamic State's expansion, not Iran's nuclear ambition nor China's territorial bullying. Each demands a different policy response, with military action and deterrence only two tools in a basket that includes diplomatic and economic measures. It's time Mr. Obama started emphasizing what the United States can do instead of what it cannot.[98]

[96] Cordesman, "NATO and Ukraine."
[97] Anne Applebaum, "Here's a Legacy: Shaking up NATO," *Washington Post*, August 24, 2014.
[98] "A Can't Do Attitude," Editorial, *Washington Post*, August 30, 2014.

In their report from September 2014, de Hoop Scheffer and Lété argued that the "centrality" of US leadership in NATO must be "prominently discussed and is essential to the future of the Alliance." Since Libya, they argued, the United States had been more reluctant to take the political lead of any military intervention. That had to change: "No other power can replace today the unique U.S. capacity to build coalitions, and in the absence of U.S. leadership, any coalition-building effort within NATO will become much more difficult."[99]

In December 2014, Christopher Musselman, US Navy Commander and 2014 US Navy Fellow at ACUS, published an ACUS Issue Brief, in which he argued that "steadfast American leadership" was necessary:

> NATO must firmly and credibly demonstrate an enduring undertaking to defend the allies. Putin will not be dissuaded by rhetoric, and he will thrive on European and transatlantic disunity. The Ukraine crisis exposed a challenge to Washington's cornerstone of American leadership—coalition building… Washington's leadership through action is necessary to advance Europe's security and identify ways to work with Russia on those mutual interests where Moscow's influence is needed.[100]

So to sum up the view from the think tank and elite media environment about how NATO should be led, the arguments for a charismatic leadership dominated, but there are also examples of arguments for a rational leadership. All in all that means a moderate to high (maximalist) view of how NATO should be guided by the United States.

To conclude, the results from the policy debate shows that the actors within this arena argued that NATO's importance in US long-term security policy was moderate to high (maximalist), slightly higher than in previous periods. The debate is summarized in Table 4.3.

---

[99] de Hoop Scheffer and Lété, "Rethinking NATO's Strategy in a Changing World".
[100] Christopher Musselman, "The Die Is Cast: Confronting Russian Aggression in Eastern Europe," Atlantic Council Issue Brief, December 2014, www.atlanticcouncil.org (homepage), date accessed January 8, 2015, p. 9.

Table 4.3 Results from the US NATO debate 2014 in the think tanks and elite media

Vision	Political and cultural
Mission	Collective security and values
Guidance	Charismatic

The actors of the policy debate argued that NATO was a political and cultural tool (vision), that it should promote collective security and values (mission) and that it should be led in a charismatic way (guidance).

Summary and reflections

As has been demonstrated in this chapter, US Congress, think tanks, and elite media expressed a similar view of NATO's importance in US long-term security policy—a moderate to high importance—actually more similar than before and also slightly more maximalist than before. Most important, the Obama administration went from a moderate to low view of NATO's role in US security policy to a moderate to high view. The results of the empirical investigation are summarized in Table 4.4.

Table 4.4 The US NATO debate during 2014

Issue/Arena	The Political Debate		The Policy Debate
	Congress	*Administration*	*Think tanks and elite media*
Vision	Political and cultural	Political and cultural	Political and cultural
Mission	Collective security and values	Collective security and values	Collective security and values
Guidance	Charismatic	Rational	Charismatic
Importance	Moderate to high	Moderate to high	Moderate to high

As the table shows, taken as a whole, the debate indicates a slightly increased importance of the role for NATO in US security policy during the Ukraine Crisis and the Wales Summit. The administration still argued that

NATO should be led in a rational (minimalist) way, but concepts such as leading from behind was not used anymore in its vocabulary.

Despite the slightly increased importance of NATO in US security policy, as expressed in the US NATO debate, it is still relatively moderate. The importance of NATO in US long-term security policy during 2014 thereby reinforces the results from the previous periods and the arguments made in scholarly literature on NATO, that the importance of the alliance in US long-term security policy is decreasing.

Conclusions

What is the present status of NATO in US security thinking? In this book the importance of NATO in US long-term security policy, as it has been manifested in the US NATO debate, from the Libya War in 2011 to the Ukrainian Crisis in 2014, has been scrutinized. The debates in US Congress, within the Administration, and in the think tank and elite media environment have been systematically described, categorized, and analyzed. The overall result is that the importance of NATO in US security policy has been described as slightly higher since the Ukraine Crisis started, but the long-term trend is still that the importance of the alliance—especially within the administration—is seen as moderate, rather than high. And that differs from how NATO's importance was described during the Cold War and the 1990s.

The results of the analysis

Before, during, and after the Libya War in 2011, Congress and the policy environment (think tanks and elite media) expressed a moderate to high (maximalist) view of what NATO should be (vision), what NATO should do (mission), and how NATO should be led (guidance).

First, the *vision* of NATO was described as not just military and political, but also as cultural. Senator Jeanne Shaheen (D, New Hampshire), for example, argued that it would be wrong "to underestimate the transatlantic influence in the international community," and that "the most open, transparent, and democratic societies in the world today, the United States and Europe still represent a model for citizens everywhere who support the rule of law and want their voices heard and their legitimate needs met."[1]

---

[1] US Congress, Senate, Foreign Relations Committee (SFRC), *Administration Priorities for Europe in the 112th Congress*, May 18, 2011, No. 112–84, Washington, DC: USGPO, 2011, p. 4.

And the editorial board in the *Washington Post* was expressing the opinion that NATO was a bearer of Western culture and democracy and that it was rightful to intervene in Libya: "We believed that Mr. Obama was right to support NATO's intervention in Libya not only because of the risk that Mr. Gaddafi would carry out massacres but because defeating the dictator is crucial to the larger cause of democratic change in the Middle East."[2]

The Obama administration was more moderate and minimalist in its views, and usually described its vision of NATO as military and political tool. For example, in the British Parliament in May 2011, President Obama said that "At its core, NATO is rooted in the simple concept of Article Five: that no NATO nation will have to fend on its own; that allies will stand by one another, always." He also said that "a revitalized NATO will continue to hew to that original vision of its founders, allowing us to rally collective action for the defense of our people."[3]

The trend that Congress, think tanks, and elite media described NATO's vision in moderate to maximalist terms, and the administration described it in moderate to minimalist terms, continued during 2012–2013, when NATO's Chicago Summit and the Syria Conflict animated the debate about NATO in the US.

In Congress, NATO was described as a military and political tool, but also as a force for good spreading Western culture. Senator Benjamin L. Cardin (D, Maryland), for example, argued that NATO enlargement was driving cultural change: "It has been that ability or desire to join either the European Union or NATO that has been a motivating factor to accelerate democratic reforms in many countries of Europe. And we have seen that work very successfully."[4]

Examples of how NATO was perceived as a cultural tool was also common within the think tank and elite press environment. In an Issue Brief from the Atlantic Council, Nancy DeViney and Edgar Buckley wrote that NATO should revisit its core values to "provide the cultural foundation that will enable

[2] "The Libya Stalemate," Editorial, *Washington Post*, April 17, 2011.
[3] Barack Obama, "Remarks by the President to Parliament in London, United Kingdom." Speech May 25, 2011, www.whitehouse.gov (homepage), date accessed February 20, 2013.
[4] SFRC, *NATO: Chicago and Beyond*, May 10, No. 112–601, Washington, DC: USGPO, 2012, p. 19.

NATO to adapt and execute new strategies in an every changing world, while remaining true to its mission and identity."[5]

The Obama administration continued to be more restrictive in its descriptions of its more military vision of NATO. For example, in a speech at King's College in London in January 2013, Defense Secretary Leon Panetta said that the NATO members must work more cost-effectively together to be able to meet "the most relevant security challenges that we face today and tomorrow." According to Panetta, NATO had to "be prepared to quickly respond to a wide range of threats in an era of fiscal constraint, we have got to build an innovative, flexible, and rotational model for forward-developed presence and training."[6]

During the Ukraine Crisis, however, the administration became more maximalist in its descriptions of its vision of NATO, and it started to describe NATO as a cultural tool as well. For example, Secretary of State John Kerry said in a speech in the end of March 2014 that NATO was strong "because of the common values that all its members share." NATO's open door policy had "expanded democracy, prosperity and stability in Europe," he said, and around the globe: "Our challenge today is to work toward a Europe that is whole, free, and at peace—and to use the power of the planet's strongest alliance to promote peace and security for people all over the world."[7]

In Congress and the policy environment, the description of what NATO should be was not changing much: it was still described in moderate to maximalist terms, as a political and cultural tool.

In Congress, Congressman John Mondy Shimkus (R, Illinois) argued that NATO should take a firm grip of the enlargement issue during its Summit in Wales, UK: "I call upon members of NATO to now do what they should have done in the last summit. NATO now must offer membership action plans to

---

[5] Nancy DeViney and Edgar Buckley, "Change Management and Cultural Transformation in NATO: Lessons from the Public and Private Sectors," Atlantic Council Issue Brief, May 2012, http://www.atlanticcouncil.org (homepage), date accessed January 5, 2014, p. 4.

[6] Leon E. Panetta, "King's College London," Speech January 18, 2013, http://www.defense.gov (homepage), date accessed January 22, 2013.

[7] John Kerry, "Anniversaries of NATO Enlargement," March 31, 2014, www.state.gov (homepage), date accessed April 1, 2014.

those aspirational countries that are moving towards democracy, freedom, and the rule of law...the coalition of free democratic countries must stand united against totalitarianism."[8]

And in the *Washington Post*, the editorial team found it unacceptable that Russia could claim that it should have a say in the political orientation of its neighbors, and whether they join alliances such as the European Union or NATO. According to them, the crisis in Europe had not been caused by Western institutions enlarging, "but because they [the institutions] did not fulfill their post-Cold War promise of 'a Europe whole and free.'"[9]

Second, the views of NATO's *mission* (what NATO should do) in the US NATO debate underwent a similar slight change from the Libya War to the Ukraine Crisis. In Congress and the policy environment it was described as moderate to maximalist during the whole period, as promoting collective security *and* universal values. The administration expressed a more moderate view, emphasizing first and foremost collective security, during 2011–2013, but started to describe it more and more in terms of promoting universal values during the Ukraine Crisis.

Before, during, and after the Libya War, representatives of Congress—especially Democrats—often argued that NATO's mission was something more than just promoting US interests; it was to promote collective security and central Western values. Congresswoman Allyson Schwartz (D, Pennsylvania), for example, argued that NATO's mission was to conduct cost-effective, legitimate, military operations to protect central values:

> President Obama has emphasized the military mission in response to potential humanitarian crises be both limited and have the support of a broad international coalition .... The fact that the call to action by the broad international coalition is there has been absolutely critical. There is a clear regional and international agreement on the use of military force to protect civilian, and the coalition leadership helps ensure that we do not assume sole responsibilities for operations or costs.[10]

---

[8] CRHR, March 5, 2014, "Ukraine," p. H2151.
[9] "A Dangerous Russian Doctrine," Editorial, *Washington Post*, March 20, 2014.
[10] HFAC, *Libya: Defining US National Security Interests*, March 31, 2011, No. 112–25, Washington, DC: USGPO, 2011, p. 14.

Within the think tank and elite media environment, the focus was slightly more moderate, underscoring NATO's role in promoting collective security. Meghan O'Sullivan at Harvard University's Kennedy School of Government, for example, argued in the *Washington Post* in April that it served US interests to use NATO's framework and NATO partners in military operations to create legitimate, collectively based security: "The political benefits of a coalition", she argued, "are enormous in an intervention such as the one in Libya."[11]

The administration seldom argued for a maximalist NATO mission, including promotion of universal values, during the Libya War. Rather it emphasized a more moderate view, promoting collective security. In October in Brussels, Secretary Panetta took the opportunity to underscore the importance of NATO partners around the world: "A look at the composition of NATO's ongoing operations—in Libya, Afghanistan, off the coast of Somalia—makes it clear that non-NATO partners will be increasingly central to NATO's future activities, particularly as we all strive to more broadly share the burden of defending our common interests." "Security," Panetta said, "will not be achieved by each nation marching to its own drummer." It could only be achieved "by a willingness to fight together to defend our common security interests."[12]

During 2012–2013 the pattern continued; Congress and the policy environment described NATO's mission in more maximalist terms than the administration. The administration did not solely see NATO's mission as supporting US interests (the minimalist view), but they were rather emphasizing NATO's promotion of collective security than universal values. For example, when Secretary Panetta presented the new US defense strategy in January 2012, he said that the close political and military cooperation with the European NATO allies and partners was "critical." We will, he said, "invest in the shared capabilities and responsibilities of NATO, our most effective military alliance." We are, he argued, "committed to sustaining a presence that

---

[11] Meghan O'Sullivan, "Will Libya Become Obama's Iraq?," *Washington Post*, April 3, 2011.
[12] Leon E. Panetta, "Carnegie Europe (NATO)," Speech October 5, 2011, http://www.defense.gov (homepage), date accessed January 24, 2013.

will meet our Article 5 commitments, deter aggression, and the U.S. military will work closely with our allies to allow for the kinds of coalition operations that NATO has undertaken in Libya and Afghanistan."[13]

In Congress and in the policy environment it was more common to argue for a more comprehensive (maximalist) mission for NATO that included promotion of universal values.

In the end of May 2012, the editorial team in the *Washington Post* argued that NATO was the solution to the Syria Conflict, and they were complaining that the administration and NATO itself did not look at the issue in that way. The Libya war had been described as a "model intervention," and a "teachable moment," they argued. And yet nobody of the NATO leaders at the Chicago Summit had raised the subject of Syria. "Why not?" they asked, "What happened to the 'teachable moment,' just one year old?" The humanitarian stakes were as great in Syria as in Libya, they argued and as with Libya, NATO could "support the Syrian opposition without putting its own troops at risk."[14]

And when the debate about the Syria Conflict peaked in the US, in September 2013, Congressman Gregory W. Meeks (D, New York) warned against using force unilaterally. If force should be used, it should be used within a multilateral framework, that is, through NATO, according to him. He believed that the use of chemical weapons by the Assad regime was a "flagrant violation of international norms," which was contradictory to US interests: "But it is not only against U.S. interests; it is also against the international interests. So if we act in a unilateral way, I have huge concerns; that if there is a violation, we should act, especially militarily, in a multilateral way."[15]

Third, regarding NATO's *guidance*, the picture was more polarized in Congress and the policy environment during the Libya War and the Syria Conflict; the actors argued either that NATO should be led in a rational (minimalist) way, or that the alliance should be led in a charismatic way.

---

[13] Leon E. Panetta, "Statement on Defense Strategic Guidance," Speech January 5, 2012, http://www
.defense.gov (homepage), date accessed January 23, 2013.

[14] "NATO's Blind Spot," Editorial, *Washington Post*, May 22, 2012.

[15] HFAC, *Syria: Weighing the Obama Administration's Response*, September 4, No. 113, Washington,
DC: USGPO, 2013, pp. 28–29.

The arguing for a charismatic US leadership increased, however, during the Ukraine Crisis. In the administration the view of how NATO should be led did not seem to change much over time; it was argued during the whole period that NATO should be guided in a minimalist, rational way, rather than in a maximalist, charismatic way. A slight difference can be tracked, however, during the Ukraine Crisis; the administration did not normally use concepts like "leading from behind" to describe its view of how NATO should be led.

Before, during, and after the Libya War, the debate in Congress and in think tanks and elite media was polarized. Congresswoman Lynn Woolsey (D, California), for example, was not "comforted" by the fact that NATO was leading the Libya mission because the US was "the dominant force within NATO." Therefore, she argued, the US had an "enormous responsibility" for any NATO-led operation.[16] And in April 2011, Senator John McCain (R, Arizona), said that "America must lead. NATO is America. We need to be leading in a strong and sustained way, not sitting on the side lines or playing a supporting role."[17]

On the other hand, Senator John Kerry (D, Massachusetts) was satisfied with the US minor role: "here is the alliance leading. Here is the alliance doing what we have wanted them to do for years."[18] Furthermore, Congressman Barnett Frank (D, Massachusetts) argued that "America can no longer be asked to be the one that does everything, everywhere, every time. Our allies have to step up."[19] And Congressman David Adam Smith (D, Washington) said that "For once, NATO is actually carrying the bulk of the mission."[20]

The same pattern appeared in the policy environment. The actors were either arguing for a maximalist or a minimalist US leadership of NATO. The editorial team in the *New York Times* was arguing for the rational (minimalist) view, when they wrote that other NATO members' leadership best served

---

[16] CRHR, March 30, "Is Two Wars in the Middle East Not Enough?," p. H2045.

[17] CRS, April 8, 2011, "Libya," pp. S 2305–S2306.

[18] CRS, June 21, 2011, "Libya," pp. S3945–3946. See also Kerry's statement in SFRC, *Libya and War Powers*, June 28, No. 112–89, Washington, DC: USGPO, 2011, p. 3.

[19] CRHR, June 24, 2011, "Limiting Use of Funds for Armed Forces in Libya," p. H 4560.

[20] Ibid., p. H 4563.

American interests: "The United States took the lead in knocking out Libyan air defenses. That made sense because it alone has the cruise missiles for the job. Now the Obama administration rightly wants to hand off military leadership to its NATO partners."[21] Charles Krauthammer of the *Washington Post*, was of the opposite view, when he was complaining about Obama's lack of leadership. "Obama seems equally obsessed with handing off the lead role," he wrote:

> No primus inter pares for him. Even the Clinton administration spoke of America as the indispensable nation. And it remains so. Yet at a time when the world is hungry for America to lead—no one has anything near our capabilities, experience and resources—America is led by a man determined that it should not.[22]

And it is fair to say that the administration was quite reluctant to argue that it strived for a charismatic (maximalist) leading role in NATO. In Brussels in October 2011, Secretary Panetta praised the European leadership in the Libya operation. France and the UK had engaged on a large scale, "flying one third of the overall sorties and attacking forty percent of the targets." They had also "exercised leadership roles politically and diplomatically."[23] Later on, in Washington, DC, Panetta said that the US had "helped" NATO achieve its mission in Libya.[24] The Obama Administration's arguments of how NATO should be led during the Libya operation were definitely minimalist in character, and it should continue like that during 2012–2013.

In a budget hearing in the Senate in the end of February 2012, Secretary Clinton, for example, said that the modernization of US and NATO forces was "an opportunity for our European allies to take on greater responsibility."[25] But the actual rate of defense spending was not the only criteria when the US valued its allies, according to her. The value of allied and partner contributions

[21] "Discord Among Allies," Editorial, *New York Times*, March 24, 2011.

[22] Krauthammer, Charles, "The Professor's War," *Washington Post*, March 25, 2011.

[23] Panetta, "Carnegie Europe (NATO)."

[24] Panetta, "Lee H. Hamilton Lecture," Speech October 11, 2011, http://www.defense.gov (homepage), date accessed January 24, 2013.

[25] SFRC, *National Security and Foreign Policy Priorities in the FY 2013 International Affairs Budget*, p. 103.

had been clear in Afghanistan and more recently in Libya, "where the United States was able to provide operational support while other allies and partners took the lead in combat efforts."[26]

In the media and think tank environment, and in Congress, the debate continued to be more polarized during 2012–2013. In Congress, some argued that the US should lead in a "rational way" (the minimalist view), and others argued that the US should lead in a "charismatic way," that the US should lead as NATO's primus inter pares (the maximalist view).[27]

In the policy environment, the debate was slightly less polarized than before, and more actors argued for a rational (minimalist) US guidance of NATO. In an ACUS Brief from June 2012, Barry Pavel and Jeff Lightfoot, for example, argued that "Washington will look to its European allies to take a leading role in managing certain crises and contingency operations on their own periphery." The US will do what it must, they continued, "and Europe will bear the rest of the burden for operations that are more in its own interests than those of the United States."[28]

During the Ukraine Crisis in 2014, the policy environment changed its view to a rather charismatic (maximalist) view of US NATO leadership. In the *Washington Post*, Anne Applebaum argued that "Obama might not have the power to make Congress do what he wants, but he does have the power to relaunch the Western alliance."[29] And in the end of August 2014, the editorial team of the *Washington Post* was arguing that although the US cannot solve every problem, "none" of the basic challenges to world order can be met without US leadership: "not Russia's aggression, not the Islamic State's expansion, not Iran's nuclear ambition nor China's territorial bullying."[30]

Also in Congress, the representatives argued for a charismatic (maximalist) US leadership of NATO more clearly than before. In an article in the *New*

---

[26] SFRC, *National Security and Foreign Policy Priorities in the FY 2013 International Affairs Budget*, p. 135.

[27] See, for example, SFRC, *National Security and Foreign Policy Priorities in the FY 2013 International Affairs Budget*, p. 140; and SASC, *Department of Defense Authorization for Appropriations for Fiscal Year 2013 and the Future Years Defense Program*, Pt. 1, p. 267

[28] Barry Pavel and Jeff Lightfoot, "The Transatlantic Bargain After 'the Pivot,'" Atlantic Council Issue Brief, June 2012, http://www.atlanticcouncil.org (homepage), date accessed February 5, 2014, p. 2.

[29] Anne Applebaum, "Here's a Legacy: Shaking up NATO," *Washington Post*, August 24, 2014.

[30] "A Can't Do Attitude," Editorial, *Washington Post*, August 30, 2014.

York Times in March 2014, Senator McCain, for example, argued that "Crimea must be the place where President Obama recognizes this reality and begins to restore the credibility of the United States as a world leader."[31]

The administration, however, continued to play down the US leadership role in NATO and emphasized other allies' responsibility both to lead and to share the burdens within the alliance. Obama's speech at West Point in the end of May 2014 was a clear case. The US should lead, he argued, but it preferred to do it within a multilateral frame. After World War II the US had "the wisdom" to shape institutions to keep the peace and support human progress. These institutions were not perfect, but they had been "a force multiplier," according to the president:

> They reduce the need for unilateral American action and increase restraint among other nations...Now, there are a lot of folks, a lot of skeptics, who often downplay the effectiveness of multilateral action. For them, working through international institutions like the U.N. or respecting international law is a sign of weakness. I think they're wrong.[32]

Although the view of NATO's importance in long-term US security policy, as manifested in the US NATO debate, increased slightly during the Ukraine Crisis, the results in this book show that the importance of the alliance has decreased since the Libya War, and clearly since the Cold War. NATO's importance is viewed as moderate, rather than high. And that did not change because of the Ukraine Crisis.

The wider implications of the results

This book has been focusing on the importance of NATO in US security thinking as it is expressed in the political and policy debate in the US, from the Libya War to the present. The overall result is that the importance of NATO has been viewed as relatively moderate. The book has also shown that there

---

[31] John McCain, "Obama Made America Look Weak," *New York Times*, March 15, 2014.

[32] Barack Obama, "Remarks by President Obama at the United States Military Academy Commencement Ceremony," Speech May 28, 2014, www.whitehouse.gov (homepage), date accessed July 1, 2014.

are significant differences of how to view NATO in the different debate arenas in the US. In Congress, NATO's importance has been described as relatively high (maximalist) during the whole period. In the Obama Administration the importance of NATO has been described as relatively moderate, except from the Ukraine Crisis and onwards when it can be described as moderate to high. In the think tank and elite media environment it has been described as moderate to high, especially since the Ukraine Crisis started.

It is difficult to know if the elevation of NATO's importance in the US NATO debate since the Ukraine Crisis is permanent or ephemeral. What seems to be clear, however, is that the Obama Administration does not want to lead NATO in the charismatic or traditional way that the US used to do. That has also been manifested in the discussion about the burden sharing within the alliance; that the European members must step up both concerning the leadership of the alliance in European affairs, and concerning actual defense spending. There are support of such a policy in Congress and the policy world as well, although not as clear.

The support for a more traditional, charismatic US leadership of NATO is also demonstrated in Congress. But it is reasonable to believe that the US focus on allies and partners, combined with the focus on the Asia Pacific, and the decreasing US defense budget, will make the long-term trend work in the direction of even less ability and will to lead NATO in a charismatic (maximalist) way from the US side. Kenneth B. Moss, Professor at National Defense University in Washington, DC, for example, argues that:

> The United States seeks to maintain enough military power to defend itself alone, but the lessons of the Iraq War and Afghanistan have shown that it cannot act alone in all the dimensions of such operations. The U.S. approach to NATO action in Libya, especially its willingness to allow other NATO members highly visible roles in shaping and executing the decisions, suggests appreciation of these circumstances.[33]

Damon Coletta and Sten Rynning do not see anything wrong with a less manifest US NATO leadership. They argue that NATO should be seen as

---

[33] Kenneth B. Moss, "War Powers and the Atlantic Divide," *Orbis*, Spring (2012), p. 306.

a congress. "A congress", they argue, "notably one without a strong chief executive, pulls together representatives of several states, each capable in its own right of discharging basic government functions, each jealous of its sovereign prerogatives, and yet committed to the security of a union that may act beyond the simple aggregation of state preferences."[34]

That trend might also be strengthened by the European NATO members' unwillingness to engage with the US outside Europe. The end of the Afghanistan operation and the Ukraine Crisis are probably two elements that reinforce each other in that direction. Even before the Ukraine Crisis several scholars and analyst were quite skeptical to European contributions in the Asia Pacific. Europe has "no role to play in the U.S. pivot to Asia," wrote Gideon Rachman at the *Financial Times* in a GMF policy brief in May 2013. "In fact," he continued, "U.S. ambitions seem to be limited to hoping that the Europeans do not actively undermine U.S. policy in Asia."[35]

The US would certainly be more than happy if the Europeans could take care of their own security problems. The most important question is, however, if that is possible. Jamie Shea, deputy assistant secretary general for emerging security challenges at NATO HQ, sees to possible answers: Either can the changed US role in Europe "counter-balance the European defense budget meltdown," and stimulate "a truly credible and operational European Security and Defense Policy." Or can the Europeans "drift" when they are no longer "operating in a U.S.-defined (and dominated) framework."[36]

Although the Ukraine Crisis in many ways has been in focus of US security policy during 2014, the events in the Middle East, IS' actions especially, have shown that the US attention and priorities can change

---

[34] Coletta and Rynning, "NATO from Kabul to Earth Orbit," p. 27.

[35] Gideon Rachman, "The Pivot: Test of Europe as a Security Actor?," *GMF Policy Brief*, May 2013, http://www.gmfus.org (homepage), date accessed March 12, 2014, p. 1. See also Robert S. Ross, "What the Pivot Means for Transatlantic Relations: Separate Course or New Opportunity for Engagement?," *GMF Policy Brief*, May 2013, http://www.gmfus.org (homepage), date accessed March 12, 2014, p. 2; and Michel Foucher, "For a New Transatlantic Strategic Sequence: In, Near, and Beyond Europe," *GMF Policy Brief*, May 2013, http://www.gmfus.org (homepage), date accessed February 21, 2014, p. 6.

[36] Jamie Shea, "NATO and the US Pivot to Asia: To Follow or Not to Follow", *GMF Policy Brief*, May 2013, http://www.gmfus.org (homepage), date accessed March 12, 2014, p. 3.

fast and that Europe is no longer the US first priority.[37] The Obama Administration has also used the Ukraine Crisis to animate its European allies to step up and do more. For example, Vice President Biden said in a speech at the Harvard Kennedy School in the beginning of October 2014 that "the transatlantic relationship does not sustain itself by itself," that it could not be sustained by the US alone, and that it required "investment and sacrifice on both sides of the Atlantic."[38] And in Brussels in the beginning of December 2014, Secretary Kerry said:

> Overall, I am very satisfied that NATO is on track to meet any challenge to our collective security; but in order to do so, every ally has to pull their weight, and that was part of my message today. We can't have 21st century security on the cheap. All nations, all members of the alliance, need to be increasing their capacity to be able to meet the challenges that we face today.[39]

The US Administration has also been very eager to separate the sixty-member coalition of the willing against IS from a NATO frame. When Kerry made a statement in NATO's Headquarters in Brussels December 3, 2014, he demonstratively said that he just wanted to begin the meeting by stressing that "despite the location, this is not a NATO event."[40]

But at the same time, the Obama Administration, and not least President Obama himself, has underscored the US will—and responsibility— to lead, much more during 2014 than before. In his weekly address on September 27, 2014, Obama said that American leadership was "the one constant in an uncertain world," that the people of the world wanted the US to lead, and that the US was prepared to do so.[41] The same message

---

[37] See, for example, Barack Obama, "Remarks by the President After Meeting with Chiefs of Defense," October 14, 2014, www.whitehouse.gov (homepage), date accessed January 6, 2015; and John Kerry, "Remarks at the Brooking Institution's 2014 Saban Forum," December 7, 2014, www.state.gov (homepage), date accessed January 6, 2015.

[38] Joe Biden, "Remarks by Vice President at the John F. Kennedy Forum," Speech October 3, 2014, www.whitehouse.gov (homepage), date accessed January 6, 2015.

[39] John Kerry, "Solo Press Availability at NATO Headquarters," December 2, 2014, www.state.gov (homepage), date accessed January 6, 2015.

[40] John Kerry, "Remarks at the Counter-ISIL Meeting," December 3, 2014, www.state.gov (homepage), date accessed January 6, 2015.

[41] Barack Obama, "Weekly Address: America Is Leading the World," September 27, 2014, www .whitehouse.gov (homepage), date accessed January 6, 2015.

could be heard from Congress. In Senate on November 20, 2014, Senator Rob Portman (R, Ohio) said:

> When America is strong, when we stand unequivocally for freedom and justice, when we don't back down in the face of threats and intimidation, that is when we see a world that is more stable, less dangerous, and more free. That is because we stand with our allies. More wars, more conflicts, more threats to our security—these do not arise from American strength; these arise from American weakness. Let's be strong again. Let's lead again. Let's help Ukraine. The world is watching.[42]

---

[42] CRS, November 20, 2014, "Russian Encroachment into Ukraine," S6167.

Name Index

Ackerman, Bruce	Professor of Law at Yale University
Andrews, Robert E.	US Congressman (D, New Jersey)
Applebaum, Anne	Opinion Writer at the *Washington Post*
Asmus, Ronald D.	US Diplomat and political analyst
Aybet, Gülnur	Professor of Political Science and International Relations at Bahçeşehir University, Istanbul, Turkey
Barrasso, John	US Senator (R, Wyoming)
Barry, Charles	Distinguished Research Fellow, Center for Transatlantic Security Studies, Institute for National Strategic Studies (INSS), National Defense University (NDU)
Bashar al-Assad	Syria's Dictator (since 2000)
Baum, Matthew A.	Professor of Global Communications, Harvard UniversityBensahel, Nora * Deputy director of studies and a senior fellow at the Center for a New American Security (CNAS)
Biddle, Steven	Roger Hertog Senior Fellow for Defense Policy at the Council on Foreign Relations, Washington, DC
Biden, Joe	US Vice President
Binnendijk, Hans	Vice President for Research and Applied Learning and Director of the Institute for National Strategic Studies (INSS), National Defense University (NDU). After that Senior Fellow at Johns Hopkins' Center for Transatlantic Relations.
Boot, Max	Senior Fellow in National Security Studies at the CFR
Brzezinski, Zbigniew	Former US National Security Advisor
Buckley, Edgar	Former Assistant Secretary General of NATO
Burns, Nicholas	Former US Ambassador to NATO, Board Member of ACUS
Cantor, Eric Ivan	US Congressman (R, Virginia)
Cardin, Benjamin L.	US Senator (D, Maryland)
Carothers, Thomas	Vice President for Studies at the Carnegie Endowment for International Peace

List of Abbreviations

ACUS	Atlantic Council of the United States, Washington, DC, USA
AQIM	al-Qaeda in Islamic Maghreb
AU	American University, Washington, DC, USA, *or* African Union
BMD	Ballistic Missile Defense
BU	Boston University, Boston, Massachusetts, USA
CFR	Council on Foreign Relations, Washington, DC, USA
CNAS	Center for a New American Security, Washington, DC, USA
CRER	US Congressional Record, Extensions of Remarks
CRHR	US Congressional Record, House of Representatives
CRS	US Congressional Record, Senate
CSDP	EU's Common Security and Defence Policy
CSIS	Center for Strategic and International Studies, Washington, DC, USA
CTR	Center for Transatlantic Relations, The Paul H. Nitze School of Advanced International Studies (SAIS), Johns Hopkins University, Washington, DC, USA
DDPR	NATO's Deterrence and Defence Posture Review (initiated at the Lisbon agreed upon at the Lisbon Summit in 2010)
DoD	US Department of Defense
ECOWAS	Economic Community of West African States
EIU	Eastern Illinois University, Charleston, Illinois, USA
ELN	European Leadership Network, London, UK
EU	European Union
EUCOM	US European Command
EUTM	European Union Training mission in Mali
FRIDE	Foundation for International Relations and Foreign Dialogue, Brussels, Belgium, and Madrid, Spain
GMF	German Marshall Fund of the United States, Washington, DC, USA
HASC	US Congress, House of Representatives, Armed Services Committee, "House Armed Services Committee"
HFAC	US Congress, House of Representatives, Foreign Affairs Committee, "House Foreign Affairs Committee"
IHEDN	Institute for Higher National Defense Studies, Paris, France
IS/ISIS/ISIL	Islamic State

MIT	Massachusetts Institute of Technology, Cambridge, Massachusetts, USA
NATO	North Atlantic Treaty Organization
NDU	National Defense University, Washington, DC, USA
OWU	Ohio Wesleyan University, Delaware, Ohio, USA
QDR	Quadrennial Defense Review, a strategic study by the US DoD, regularly revised
SACEUR	Supreme Allied [NATO] Commander Europe
SAIS	The Paul H. Nitze School of Advanced International Studies, Johns Hopkins University, Washington, DC, USA
SASC	US Congress, Senate, Armed Services Committee, "Senate Armed Services Committee"
SFRC	US Congress, Senate, Foreign Relations Committee, "Senate Foreign Relations Committee"
UN	United Nations
UNSCR	UN Security Council Resolution
USIP	the United States Institute for Peace
USMCU	U.S. Marine Corps University, Quantico, Virginia, USA

Bibliography

Since the sources of this book comes from relatively different places and are connected to different parts of the study, I have found it relevant to divide them into US official sources (sources from Congress and the Administration), media sources (mainly the *New York Times* and the *Washington Post*), think-tank sources (such as policy briefs, reports, etc.), and other sources (mainly books and journal articles).

Congress sources

CRER, March 13, 2013, "The Nagorno Karabakh."

CRER, June 11, 2013, "Regarding American Leadership in the Balkans."

CRER, July 24, 2014, "Strengthening the Transatlantic Alliance in the Face of Russian Aggression."

CRHR, March 30, 2011, "Is Two Wars in the Middle East Not Enough?"

CRHR, March 30, 2011, "What's So Special About Libya?"

CRHR, June 21, 2011, "The way it is on American Involvement in Libya."

CRHR, June 24, 2011, "Limiting Use of Funds for Armed Forces in Libya."

CRHR, July 7, 2011, "Department of Defense Appropriations Act, 2012."

CRHR, January 25, 2012, "High-Level Nuclear Waste."

CRHR, May 10, 2012, "Reducing America's Military Footprint and Spending in Europe."

CRHR, March 5, 2014, "Ukraine."

CRHR, March 5, 2014, "Supporting Ukraine's Future."

CRHR, March 27, 2014, "Ukraine Support Act."

CRS, April 8, 2011, "Libya."

CRS, June 15, 2011, "NATO."

CRS, July 5, 2011, "Shared Sacrifice in Resolving the Budget Deficit – Motion to Proceed."

CRS, March 4, 2014, "Ukraine Crisis."

CRS, March 25, 2014, "Support for the Sovereignty, Integrity, Democracy, and Economic Stability of Ukraine Act of 2014 – Motion to Proceed."

CRS, March 27, 2014, "Providing for the Costs of Loan Guarantees for Ukraine."

CRS, March 29, 2012, "Expressing Sense of Senate in Support of NATO and NATO Summit Being Held May 20 Through 21, 2012."

CRS, November 20, 2014, "Russian Encroachment into Ukraine."

HASC, *The Status of United States Strategic Forces*, March 2, 2011, No. 112–12, Washington, DC: USGPO, 2011.

HASC, *Operation Odyssey Dawn and US Military Operations in Libya*, No. 112–31, Washington, DC: USGPO, 2011.

HASC, *The Future of National Defense and the United States Military Ten Years After 9/11: Perspectives of Secretary of Defense Leon Panetta and Chairman of the Joint Chiefs of Staff General Martin Dempsey*, October 13, 2011, No. 112–76, Washington, DC: USGPO, 2011.

HASC, *The Current Status and Future Direction for US Nuclear Weapons and Policy and Posture*, No. 112–88, November 2, 2011, Washington, DC: USGPO, 2011.

HASC, *Framework for Building Partnership Capacity Programs and Authorities to Meet 21ˢᵗ Century Challenges*, No. 113–5, Washington, DC: USGPO, 2013.

HASC, *The Posture of the U.S. European Command and U.S. Africa Command*, March 15, No. 113–19, Washington, DC: USGPO, 2013.

HASC, *Budget Request from the Department of Defense*, No. 113–25, Washington, DC: USGPO, 2013.

HASC, *Budget Request for Missile Defense Programs*, May 8, No. 113–44, Washington, DC: USGPO, 2013.

HFAC, *Overview of US Relations with Europe and Eurasia*, March 10, 2011, No. 112–20, Washington, DC: USGPO, 2011.

HFAC, *Libya: Defining US National Security Interests*, March 31, 2011, No. 112–25, Washington, DC: USGPO, 2011.

HFAC, *War Powers, United States Operations in Libya, and Related Legislation*, May 25, 2011, No. 112–38, Washington, DC: USGPO, 2011.

HFAC, *Budget Oversight: Examining the President's 2012 Budget Request for Europe and Eurasia*, April 14, 2011, No. 112–43, Washington, DC: USGPO, 2011.

HFAC, *Overview of Security Issues in Europe and Eurasia*, May 5, 2011, No. 112–44, Washington, DC: USGPO, 2011.

HFAC, *The State of Affairs in the Balkans*, November 15, 2011, No. 112–112, Washington, DC: USGPO, 2011.

HFAC, *Cyber Attacks: An Unprecedented Threat to U.S. National Security*, March 21, No. 113–8, Washington, DC: USGPO, 2013.

HFAC, *Kosovo and Serbia: A Pathway to Peace*, No. 113–23, Washington, DC: USGPO, 2013.

HFAC, *Syria: Weighing the Obama Administration's Response*, September 4,
   No. 113–113, Washington, DC: USGPO, 2013.

HFAC, *U.S. Foreign Policy Toward Ukraine*, March 6, No. 113–129, Washington, DC:
   USGPO, 2014.

HFAC, *Russia's Destabilization of Ukraine*, May 8, No. 113–176, Washington, DC:
   USGPO, 2014.

SASC, *Department of Defense Authorization for Appropriations for Fiscal Year 2012
   and the Future Years Defense Program*, February 17; March 1, 8, 17, 29, 31; April 5,
   7, 12; May 19, 2011, No. 112–80, Pt. 1, Washington, DC: USGPO, 2011.

SASC, *Department of Defense Authorization for Appropriations for Fiscal Year 2013
   and the Future Years Defense Program*, February 14, 28; March 1, 6, 8, 13, 15, 20,
   27, No. 112–590, Pt. 1, Washington, DC: USGPO, 2012.

SASC, *Department of Defense Authorization for Appropriations for Fiscal Year 2013 and
   the Future Years Defense Program*, No. 112–590, Pt. 7, Washington, DC: USGPO, 2012.

SASC, *Department of Defense Authorization for Appropriations for Fiscal Year 2014
   and the Future Years Defense Program*, No. 113–108, Pt. 7, Washington, DC:
   USGPO, 2013.

SASC, *Nominations Before The Senate Armed Service Committee, First Session, 113th
   Congress*, January 31; February 12, 14, 28; April 11; July 18, 25, 30; September 19;
   October 10, No. 113–270, Washington, DC: USGPO, 2013.

SFRC, *Administration Priorities for Europe in the 112th Congress*, May 18, 2011,
   No. 112–84, Washington, DC: USGPO, 2011.

SFRC, *Libya and War Powers*, June 28, No. 112–89, Washington, DC: USGPO, 2011.

SFRC, *National Security and Foreign Policy Priorities in the FY 2013 International
   Affairs Budget*, February 28, No. 112–599, Washington, DC: USGPO, 2012.

SFRC, *NATO: Chicago and Beyond*, May 10, No. 112–601, Washington, DC: USGPO, 2012.

SFRC, *Rebalance to Asia II: Security and Defense; Cooperation and Challenges*, April
   25, No. 113–138, Washington, DC: USGPO, 2013.

SFRC, *Nomination of John F. Kerry to Be Secretary of State*, January 24, No. 113–163,
   Washington, DC: USGPO, 2013.

SFRC, *Transatlantic Security Challenges: Central and Eastern Europe*, April 10,
   No. 113–475, Washington, DC: USGPO, 2014.

Sources from the Administration

Biden, Joe, "Remarks by the Vice President at the Atlantic Council's 50th Anniversary
   Dinner," Speech May 4, 2011, www.whitehouse.gov (homepage), date accessed
   February 17, 2013.

Biden, Joe, "Remarks by the Vice President to the Munich Security Conference," Speech February 2, 2013, www.whitehouse.gov (homepage), date accessed July 1, 2014.

Biden, Joe, "Remarks by the Vice President Joe Biden on Asia-Pacific Policy," Speech July 19, 2013, www.whitehouse.gov (homepage), date accessed July 1, 2014.

Biden, Joe, "Remarks to the Press by Vice President Joe Biden with Prime Minister Donald Tusk of Poland," Speech March 18, 2014, www.whitehouse.gov (homepage), date accessed July 1, 2014.

Biden, Joe, "Remarks to the Press by Vice President Joe Biden and President Toomas Ilves of Estonia," Speech March 18, 2014, www.whitehouse.gov (homepage), date accessed July 1, 2014.

Biden, Joe, "Remarks to the Press by Vice President Joe Biden, President Dalia Grybauskaite, and President Andris Berzins of Latvia," Speech March 19, 2014, www.whitehouse.gov (homepage), date accessed July 1, 2014.

Biden, Joe, "Remarks by Vice President Joe Biden to Joint United States and Romanian Participants in Carpathian Spring Military Exercise," Speech May 20, 2014, www.whitehouse.gov (homepage), date accessed July 1, 2014.

Biden, Joe, "Remarks by Vice President Joe Biden to Romanian Civil Society Groups and Students," Speech May 21, 2014, www.whitehouse.gov (homepage), date accessed July 1, 2014.

Biden, Joe, "Remarks by Vice President at the John F. Kennedy Forum," Speech October 3, 2014, www.whitehouse.gov (homepage), date accessed January 6, 2015

Clinton, Hillary R., "Munich Security Conference Plenary Session Remarks", February 5, 2011, www.state.gov (homepage), date accessed February 21, 2013.

Clinton, Hillary R., "Remarks after the International Conference on the Libyan Crisis," March 29, 2011, www.state.gov (homepage), date accessed February 21, 2013.

Clinton, Hillary R., "Remarks with British Foreign Secretary William Hague", May 23, 2011, www.state.gov (homepage), date accessed February 21, 2013.

Clinton, Hillary R., "Press Availability on Libya," September 1, 2011, www.state.gov (homepage), date accessed March 4, 2013.

Clinton, Hillary R., "America's Pacific Century," November 10, 2011, www.state.gov (homepage), date accessed October 26, 2013.

Clinton, Hillary R., "America's Pacific Century," *Foreign Policy*, November (2011).

Clinton, Hillary R., "Remarks With Danish Foreign Minister Villy Sovndal After Their Meeting," December 15, 2011, www.state.gov (homepage), date accessed March 4, 2013.

Clinton, Hillary R., "Remarks With German Foreign Minister Guido Westerwelle," January 20, 2012, www.state.gov (homepage), date accessed March 11, 2013.

Clinton, Hillary R., "Remarks at Euro-Atlantic Security Community Initiative and Keynote Session Q&A", February 4, 2012, www.state.gov (homepage), date accessed March 11, 2013.

Clinton, Hillary R., "Remarks to the World Affairs Council 2012 NATO Conference", April 3, 2012, www.state.gov (homepage), date accessed February 22, 2013.

Clinton, Hillary R., "Press Availability Following Ministerial Meetings at NATO Headquarters", December 5, 2012, www.state.gov (homepage), date accessed March 16, 2013.

Clinton, Hillary R., "Secretary Clinton Holds a Global Townterview," January 29, 2013, www.state.gov (homepage), date accessed January 29, 2013.

Department of Defense, *Sustaining US Global Leadership: Priorities for the 21st Century*, Washington, DC: Department of Defense, 2012.

Department of Defense, *Quadrennial Defense Review 2014*, Washington, DC: Department of Defense, 2014.

Donilon, Tom, "Remarks by National Security Advisor Tom Donilon", Speech November 15, 2012, www.whitehouse.gov (homepage), date accessed July 1, 2014.

Gates, Robert M., "Statement to NATO Defense Ministers", Speech March 11, 2011, http://www.defense.gov (homepage), date accessed January 24, 2013.

Gates, Robert M., "Statement on Libya – House Armed Service Committee," Speech March 31, 2011, http://www.defense.gov (homepage), date accessed January 24, 2013.

Gates, Robert M., "The Security and Defense Agenda (Future of NATO)," Speech June 10, 2011, http://www.defense.gov (homepage), date accessed September 18, 2011.

Hagel, Chuck, "Pentagon All-Hands Meeting," Speech February 27, 2013, http://www.defense.gov (homepage), date accessed March 2, 2013.

Hagel, C., "Message to the Department from Secretary of Defense Chuck Hagel", Speech February 27, http://www.defense.gov (homepage), date accessed March 2, 2013.

Hagel, C., "International Institute for Strategic Studies (Shangri-La Dialogue)", Speech June 1, http://www.defense.gov (homepage), date accessed June 6, 2013.

Hagel, Chuck, "Munich Security Conference," February 1, 2014, http://www.defense.gov (homepage), date accessed February 3, 2014.

Hagel, Chuck, "Opening Summary – Senate Armed Services Committee (Budget Request)," March 5 2014, http://www.defense.gov (homepage), date accessed March 14, 2014.

Hagel, Chuck, "Opening Summary – House Appropriations Committee-Defense (Budget Request)," March 13 2014, http://www.defense.gov (homepage), date accessed March 14, 2014.

Hagel, Chuck, "Submitted Statement – Senate Appropriations Committee-Defense (Budget Request)," June 18, 2014, http://www.defense.gov (homepage), date accessed June 30, 2014.

Kerry, John, "Remarks with French Foreign Minister Laurent Fabius," Speech February 27, 2013, www.state.gov (homepage), date accessed March 2, 2013.

Kerry, John, "Press Availability After NATO Ministerial," April 23, 2013, www.state.gov (homepage), date accessed May 2, 2013.

Kerry, John, "Remarks with Italian Foreign Minister Emma Bonino Before Their Meeting", May 9, 2013, www.state.gov (homepage), date accessed May 10, 2013.

Kerry, John, "Remarks with Polish Foreign Minister Radoslaw Sikorski After Their Meeting," June 3, 2013, www.state.gov (homepage), date accessed June 6, 2013.

Kerry, John, "Secretary's Remarks: Swearing-in Ceremony for Victoria Nuland as Assistant Secretary of State for European and Eurasian Affairs," September 18, 2013, www.state.gov (homepage), date accessed September 25, 2013.

Kerry, John, "Remarks at the APEC CEO Summit", October 7, 2013, www.state.gov (homepage), date accessed November 19, 2013.

Kerry, John, "Solo Press Availability at NATO," December 3, 2013, www.state.gov (homepage), date accessed December 4, 2013.

Kerry, John, "Remarks at Munich Security Conference," February 1, 2014, www.state.gov (homepage), date accessed February 3, 2014.

Kerry, John, "Anniversaries of NATO Enlargement," March 31, 2014, www.state.gov (homepage), date accessed April 1, 2014.

Kerry, John, "Press Availability at NATO", April 1, 2014, www.state.gov (homepage), date accessed April 2, 2014.

Kerry, John, "Remarks with Italian Foreign Minister Federica Mogherini after Their Meeting," March 31, 2014, www.state.gov (homepage), date accessed May 21, 2014.

Kerry, John, "Remarks at Pacific Day Policy Seminar," June 18, 2014, www.state.gov (homepage), date accessed June 30, 2014

Kerry, John, "Press Availability at NATO Headquarters," June 25, 2014, www.state.gov (homepage), date accessed June 30, 2014.

Kerry, John, "Interview with Chris Wallace of Fox News Sunday," July 20, 2014, www.state.gov (homepage), date accessed July 29, 2014.

Kerry, John, "Interview with George Stephanopoulos of ABC's This Week," July 20, 2014, www.state.gov (homepage), date accessed July 29, 2014.

Kerry, John, "Interview with David Gregory of NBC's Meet the Press," July 20, 2014, www.state.gov (homepage), date accessed July 29, 2014.

Kerry, John, "Interview with Bob Schieffer of CBS's Face the Nation," July 20, 2014, www.state.gov (homepage), date accessed July 29, 2014.

Kerry, John, "U.S. Vision for Asia-Pacific Engagement," August 13, 2014, www.state
.gov (homepage), date accessed September 6, 2014.

Kerry, John, "Remarks at Top of Meeting on Building an Anti-ISIL Coalition Chaired
by Defense Secretary Chuck Hagel, U.K. Foreign Secretary Phillip Hammond
and U.K. Defense Secretary Michael Fallon," September 5, 2014, www.state.gov
(homepage), date accessed September 6, 2014.

Kerry, John, "Solo Press Availability at NATO Headquarters," December 2, 2014,
www.state.gov (homepage), date accessed January 6, 2015

Kerry, John, "Remarks at the Counter-ISIL Meeting," December 3, 2014, www.state
.gov (homepage), date accessed January 6, 2015.

Kerry, John, "Remarks at the Brooking Institution's 2014 Saban Forum," December 7,
2014, www.state.gov (homepage), date accessed January 6, 2015.

Obama, Barack, "Remarks by the President on Libya," Speech February 23, 2011,
www.whitehouse.gov (homepage), date accessed February 17, 2013.

Obama, Barack, "Remarks by the President on the Situation in Libya," Speech March
18, 2011, www.whitehouse.gov (homepage), date accessed February 17, 2013.

Obama, Barack, "Remarks by the President on Libya," Speech March 19, 2011, www
.whitehouse.gov (homepage), date accessed February 17, 2013.

Obama, Barack, "Remarks by the President in Address to the Nation on Libya,"
Speech March 28, 2011, www.whitehouse.gov (homepage), date accessed February
17, 2013.

Obama, Barack, "Remarks by the President to Parliament in London, United
Kingdom," Speech May 25, 2011, www.whitehouse.gov (homepage), date accessed
February 20, 2013.

Obama, Barack, "Remarks by President Obama at High-Level Meeting on Libya,"
Speech September 20, 2011, www.whitehouse.gov (homepage), date accessed
February 20, 2013.

Obama, Barack, "Remarks by President Obama in Honoring the Alliance Between
the United states and France," Speech November 4, 2011, www.whitehouse.gov
(homepage), date accessed February 20, 2013.

Obama, Barack, "Remarks by President Obama at Opening NAC Meeting," Speech
May 20, 2012, www.whitehouse.gov (homepage), date accessed February 21, 2013.

Obama, Barack, "Remarks by President Obama and NATO Secretary General Anders
Rasmussen after Bilateral Meeting," Speech May 31, 2013, www.whitehouse.gov
(homepage), date accessed July 1, 2014.

Obama, Barack, "Remarks by President Obama and German Chancellor Merkel in
Joint Press Conference," Speech June 19, 2013, www.whitehouse.gov (homepage),
date accessed July 1, 2014.

Obama, Barack, "Statement by the President on Ukraine," Speech March 17, 2014, www.whitehouse.gov (homepage), date accessed July 1, 2014.

Obama, Barack, "Statement by the President on Ukraine," Speech March 20, 2014, www.whitehouse.gov (homepage), date accessed July 1, 2014.

Obama, Barack, "Remarks by President Obama and Prime Minister Rutte of the Netherlands After Bilateral Meeting," Speech March 24, 2014, www.whitehouse.gov (homepage), date accessed July 1, 2014.

Obama, Barack, "Remarks by President Obama and NATO Secretary General Rasmussen Before Meeting," Speech March 26, 2014, www.whitehouse.gov (homepage), date accessed July 1, 2014.

Obama, Barack, "Remarks by President Obama and Prime Minister Renzi of Italy in Joint Press Conference," Speech March 27, 2014, www.whitehouse.gov (homepage), date accessed July 1, 2014.

Obama, Barack, "Remarks by President Obama and German Chancellor Merkel in Joint Press Conference," Speech May 2, 2014, www.whitehouse.gov (homepage), date accessed July 1, 2014.

Obama, Barack, "Remarks by President Obama and President Komorowski to U.S. and Polish Armed Forces," Speech June 3, 2014, www.whitehouse.gov (homepage), date accessed July 1, 2014.

Obama, Barack, "Remarks by President Obama Before a Meeting with Central and Eastern European Leaders," Speech June 3, 2014, www.whitehouse.gov (homepage), date accessed July 1, 2014.

Obama, Barack, "Remarks by President Obama at 25th Anniversary of Freedom Day," Speech June 4, 2014, www.whitehouse.gov (homepage), date accessed July 1, 2014.

Obama, Barack, "Remarks by President Obama at the United States Mlitary Academy Commencement Ceremony," Speech May 28, 2014, www.whitehouse.gov (homepage), date accessed July 1, 2014.

Obama, Barack, "Remarks by the President on Foreign Policy," Speech July 16, 2014, www.whitehouse.gov (homepage), date accessed July 31, 2014.

Obama, Barack, "Statement by the President on Ukraine," Speech July 18, 2014, www.whitehouse.gov (homepage), date accessed July 31, 2014.

Obama, Barack, "Press Conference by the President," August 1, 2014, www.whitehouse.gov (homepage), date accessed September 6, 2014.

Obama, Barack, "Statement by the President," August 28, 2014, www.whitehouse.gov (homepage), date accessed September 6, 2014

Obama, Barack, "Remarks by President Obama and President Ilves of Estonia in Joint Press Conference," September 3, 2014, www.whitehouse.gov (homepage), date accessed September 6, 2014.

Obama, Barack, "Remarks by President Obama to the People of Estonia," September 3, 2014, www.whitehouse.gov (homepage), date accessed September 7, 2014.

Obama, Barack, "Remarks by President Obama at NATO Summit Press Conference," September 5, 2014, www.whitehouse.gov (homepage), date accessed September 7, 2014.

Obama, Barack, "Statement by the President on Airstrikes in Syria," September 23, 2014, www.whitehouse.gov (homepage), date accessed January 6, 2015.

Obama, Barack, "Weekly Address: America Is Leading the World," September 27, 2014, www.whitehouse.gov (homepage), date accessed January 6, 2015

Obama, Barack, "Remarks by the President After Meeting with Chiefs of Defense," October 14, 2014, www.whitehouse.gov (homepage), date accessed January 6, 2015

Panetta, Leon E., "Carnegie Europe (NATO)", Speech October 5, 2011, http://www.defense.gov (homepage), date accessed January 24, 2013.

Panetta, Leon E., "Lee H. Hamilton Lecture," Speech October 11, 2011, http://www.defense.gov (homepage), date accessed January 24, 2013.

Panetta, Leon E., "Halifax International Security Forum", Speech November 18, 2011, http://www.defense.gov (homepage), date accessed January 24, 2013.

Panetta, Leon E., "Statement on Defense Strategic Guidance," Speech January 5, 2012, http://www.defense.gov (homepage), date accessed January 23, 2013.

Panetta, Leon E., "Munich Security Conference", Speech February 4, 2012, http://www.defense.gov (homepage), date accessed January 23, 2013.

Panetta, Leon E., "Building Partnership in the 21st Century," Speech June 28, 2012, http://www.defense.gov (homepage), date accessed January 23, 2013.

Panetta, Leon E., "Statement to NATO Defense Ministers", Speech October 10, http://www.defense.gov (homepage), date accessed January 25, 2013.

Panetta, Leon E., "King's College London", Speech January 18, 2013, http://www.defense.gov (homepage), date accessed January 22, 2013.

Panetta, Leon E., "Farewell Ceremony", Speech February 8, http://www.defense.gov (homepage), date accessed February 11, 2013.

Panetta, Leon E., "Pentagon Community Farewell Event", Speech February 12, http://www.defense.gov (homepage), date accessed February 11, 2013.

Rice, Susan E., "Remarks by Security Advisor Susan E. Rice at the Department of State's Global Chiefs of Mission Conference," Speech March 11, 2014, www.whitehouse.gov (homepage), date accessed July 1, 2014.

Media sources

"A Can't Do Attitude," Editorial, *Washington Post*, August 30, 2014.

"A Dangerous Russian Doctrine," Editorial, *Washington Post*, March 20, 2014.

"A Deadline on Libya," Editorial, *Washington Post*, May 20, 2011.

"A Hungarian Power Grab," Editorial, *Washington Post*, March 14, 2013.

"A Strategy of Slowness," Editorial, *Washington Post*, May 1, 2011.

ABC, "Interview With Cynthia McFadden of ABC," January 29, 2013, www.state.gov (homepage), date accessed January 29, 2013.

"Absent on Syria," Editorial, *New York Times*, August 31, 2013.

Ackerman, Bruce and Hathaway, Oona, "Libya's looming deadline," *Washington Post*, May 18, 2011.

Applebaum, Anne, "NATO's Last Mission?" *Washington Post*, April 12, 2011.

Applebaum, Anne, "Let Libya Take Charge of Its Revolution," *Washington Post*, August 24, 2011.

Applebaum, Anne, "A New Cop on the Beat?" *Washington Post*, January 25, 2013.

Applebaum, Anne, "Russia, Unveiled," *Washington Post*, March 21, 2014

Applebaum, Anne, "Russia's Anti-western Thinking Takes Hold," *Washington Post*, March 30, 2014.

Applebaum, Anne, "Here's a Legacy: Shaking Up NATO," *Washington Post*, August 24, 2014.

Applebaum, Anne, "The Myth of Russian Humiliation," *Washington Post*, October 19, 2014.

"At Odds Over Libya," Editorial, *Washington Post*, May 26, 2011.

BBC, "US Military to Close 15 Bases in Europe," January 8, 2015, www.bbc.com (homepage), date accessed January 9, 2015.

"Beginning of the End," Editorial, *New York Times*, February 19, 2012.

Biddle, Steven, "What Bombs Can't Do in Libya," *Washington Post*, March 26, 2011.

Binnendijk, Hans, "Rethinking U.S. Security Strategy," *New York Times*, March 25, 2013.

Boot, Max: "Planning for a Post-Quaddafi Libya," *New York Times*, March 22, 2011

"Bracing in Aleppo," Editorial, *Washington Post*, July 29, 2012.

Brunnstrom, David, and Croft, Adrian, "Analysis: Looming end of Afghan Mission Leaves NATO with Identity Crisis", http://www.reuters.com (homepage), date accessed October 1, 2012.

Brzezinski, Zbigniew, "What Is to Be Done?" *Washington Post*, March 4, 2014

"Caught in the Middle," Editorial, *Washington Post*, April 26, 2014.

CNN, "Interview with Elise Labbot and Jill Dougherty of CNN," January 29, 2013, www.state.gov (homepage), date accessed January 29, 2013.

CNN, "Interview with Chris Cuomo of CNN New Day," May 28, 2014, www.state.gov (homepage), date accessed May 29, 2014.

Cohen, Richard, "Paul's Amoral Policy", *Washington Post*, January 3, 2012.

Cohen, Richard, "Our Share of Syria's Misery," *Washington Post*, January 20, 2013

Cohen, Richard, "Looking the Other Way," *Washington Post*, February 12, 2013.

Cohen, Roger, "Putin's Crimean Crime," *New York Times*, March 4, 2014

Dao, James, "A Recap of the Pentagon Briefing on Defense Cuts", *New York Times*, January 5 (2012).

"Democracy in the Former Soviet Republics," Editorial, *New York Times*, September 30, 2012.

Diehl, Jackson, "Who Needs the US?" *Washington Post*, April 30, 2012.

"Discord Among Allies," Editorial, *New York Times*, March 24, 2011.

Donilon, Tom, "The Continuing Need for a Strong NATO," *Washington Post*, October 28, 2011.

Doran, Michael and Boot, Max, "Five Reasons to Intervene in Syria Now," *New York Times*, September 27, 2012

Douthat, Ross, "A War by Any Name," *New York Times*, March 28, 2011.

Douthat, Ross, "The Diminished President," *New York Times*, August 1, 2011.

Dubik, James M., "Finish the Job," *New York Times*, April 26, 2011.

Dunne, Charles, Kramer, David J. and Taft IV, William H., "Our Role in Saving Syria," *Washington Post*, July 15, 2012.

Erlanger, Steven, "Libya's Dark Lesson for NATO," *New York Times*, September 4, 2011.

"Facing Failure in Syria," Editorial, *Washington Post*, April 10, 2012.

Finn, Peter and Jaffe, Greg, "U.S. Jets Strike Gadaffi's Ground Forces," *Washington Post*, March 21, 2011.

FoxNews, "Interview With Greta Van Susteren of Fox News," January 29, 2013, www.state.gov (homepage), date accessed January 29, 2013.

Friedman, Thomas L., "Putin Blinked," *New York Times*, May 28, 2014

Gearan, Anne, "U.S. Offical Apalogizes for Blunt Remark," *Washington Post*, February 7, 2014.

"Georgia Speaks Its Mind," Editorial, *New York Times*, October 2, 2012.

Goldgeier, James, "Don't Forget NATO," *New York Times*, October 17, 2012

Haass, Richard N., "Continental Drift," *Washington Post*, June 19, 2011.

Hadley, Stephen J., and Wilson, Damon, "Putin's Long Game," *Washington Post*, March 4, 2014.

Haltzel, Michael, "Extending NATO's Umbrella," *Washington Post*, June 29, 2014

Hiatt, Fred, "Choosing Decline," in *Washington Post*, June 27, 2011.

Hoagland, Jim, "A Burden Worth Bearing," *Washington Post*, March 30, 2011.

Hoagland, Jim, "An Uncertain Alliance," *Washington Post*, July 17, 2011.

Hoagland, Jim, "What We've Learned in Libya," *Washington Post*, August 25, 2011.

Hoagland, Jim, "America the Hesitant," *Washington Post*, January 20, 2013.

Howorth, Jolyon, "NATO, Bicycles and Training Wheels," Guest Post 20130619, http://www.foreignpolicy.com (homepage), date accessed July 23, 2014

Ignatius, David, "Where Are the Allies?" *Washington Post*, June 12, 2011.

Ignatius, David, "A Foreign Policy that Works," *Washington Post*, September 4, 2011.

Ignatius, David, "A Moment to Savor," *Washington Post*, October 21, 2011.

Ignatius, David, "The Cost of Adventurism," *Washington Post*, April 16, 2014

Ignatius, David, "'Say Less and Do More'," *Washington Post*, May 7, 2014

Jaffe, Greg, "2 Army Brigades to Leave Europe in Cost-Cutting Move," *Washington Post*, January 12, 2012

John Kerry, "To Defeat Terror, We Need the World's Help," *New York Times*, August 29, 2014.

Kagan, Robert, "An Imperfect Triumph in Libya," *Washington Post*, August 28, 2011.

"Keeping Ahead of Quaddafi," Editorial, *New York Times*, April 8, 2011.

Kerry, John, "Libya: An Iraq Redux?" *Washington Post*, March 11, 2011.

Khalilsad, Zalmay, "Five Things the U.S. Can Do in Syria," *Washington Post*, August 8, 2012.

Krauthammer, Charles, "The Professor's War," *Washington Post*, March 25, 2011.

Krauthammer, Charles, "How to Stop Putin," *Washington Post*, March 14, 2014.

"Leaderless in Europe: The List of Crises Is Frightening, So Is the Lack of Vision," Editorial, *New York Times*, June 29, 2011.

"Libya's Achievement," Editorial, *Washington Post*, July 10, 2012.

Marcus, Jonathan, "Transcript of Leaked Nuland-Pyatt Call," *BBC News Europe*, February 7, 2014, www.bbc.com (homepage), date accessed May 29, 2014

McCain, John, "Obama Made America Look Weak," *New York Times*, March 15, 2014.

McCain, John, Barrasso, John, Hoeven, John, and Johnson, Ron, "A New Strategy for the Real Russia," *Washington Post*, April 27, 2014.

Meyerson, Harold, "The GOP Misses Its Bogeyman," *Washington Post*, February 10, 2012.

"Moore Answers Needed on Syria," Editorial, *New York Times*, August 29, 2013.

"Mr. Gate's Sermon," Editorial, *Washington Post*, June 14, 2011.

"NATO After Libya," Editorial, *New York Times*, April 19, 2012.

"NATO's Blind Spot", Editorial, *Washington Post*, May 22, 2012.

NBC, "Interview with Andrea Mitchell of NBC," January 29, 2013, www.state.gov (homepage), date accessed January 29, 2013.

NPR, "Interview with Michele Kelemen of NPR", January 29, 2013, www.state.gov (homepage), date accessed January 29, 2013.

O'Sullivan, Meghan, "Will Libya Become Obama's Iraq?" *Washington Post*, April 3, 2011.

"On Syria's Sidelines", Editorial, *Washington Post*, August 14, 2012.

Pape, Robert A., "Why We Shouldn't Attack Syria (Yet)," *New York Times*, February 3, 2012.

Pollack, Kenneth M., "How. When. Whether. Stopping Syria's War," *Washington Post*, August 12, 2012.

Robinson, Eugene, "Lost in a Libyan Fog," *Washington Post*, March 25, 2011.

Rubin, James P., "Reassuring Eastern Europe," *New York Times*, June 12, 2014.

Rubio, Marco, "Making Russia Pay," *Washington Post*, March 20, 2014.

"Saving Lives in Libya," Editorial, *Washington Post*, April 28,.

Serwer, Daniel, "Once Gaddafi is Gone...," *Washington Post*, August 23, 2011.

Shevtsova, Lilia, "Putin's New World Order," *Washington Post*, May 9, 2014

"Standing up to Mr. Putin," Editorial, *New York Times*, June 5, 2014.

Stravidis, James G., "The Dark Side of Globalization," *Washington Post*, June 2, 2013.

Stravidis, James G., "NATO Must Help Obama on Syria," *New York Times*, September 3, 2013.

"Syria's Hard Core," Editorial, *Washington Post*, August 9, 2012.

Taylor, William B., Pifer, Steven K., and Herbst, John E., "Ukraine Will Fight," Editorial, *Washington Post*, March 3, 2014.

"Teachable Moment: The Alliance Helped Topple Quaddafi – But had to Struggle to Keep Up the Campaign," Editorial, *New York Times*, August 30, 2011.

"The Libya Stalemate," Editorial, *Washington Post*, April 17, 2011.

"The Long Game," Editorial, *Washington Post*, March 27, 2014.

"Ukrainian Aftershocks," Editorial, *Washington Post*, March 4, 2014.

Valasek, Tomas, "Europe and the 'Asia Pivot'," in *New York Times*, October 26, 2012.

Volker, Kurt, "Afghanistan and Libya Point NATO to Five Lessons," *The Christian Science Monitor*, July 28, 2011.

Volker, Kurt, "Beyond Afghanistan, a Weakened NATO Can Still Write Its Own Future," *The Christian Science Monitor*, May 21, 2012.

"War by Any Other Name," Editorial, *Washington Post*, June 18, 2011.

Will, George F., "Obama's Illegal War," *Washington Post*, May 29, 2011.

Will, George F., "Lawless war", *Washington Post*, June 19, 2011.

Zakaria, Fareed, "Obama's Mandate on Ukraine," *Washington Post*, March 14, 2014.

Think tank sources

Barry, Charles and Binnendijk, Hans, "Widening Gaps in U.S. and European Defense Capabilities and Cooperation", *Transatlantic Current*, No. 6, July 2012, www.ndu .edu (homepage), date accessed February 10, 2014.

Bensahel, Nora and Stokes, Jacob, "The U.S. Defense Budget and the Future of Alliance Burden Sharing", *GMF Policy Brief*, November 2013, www.gmfus.org (homepage), date accessed February 21, 2014.

Burns, Nicholas, Wilson, Damon and Lightfoot, Jeff, "Anchoring the Alliance", Atlantic Council Report, May 2012, www.atlanticcouncil.org (homepage), date accessed January 15, 2014.

Coffey, Luke, "The Future of U.S. Bases in Europe: A View from America," Lecture, No. 1233, July 15, 2013, http://www.heritage.org (homepage), date accessed January 9, 2015.

Conley, Heather, *Beware the Backburner: The Risk of a Neglected Europe*, Washington, DC: CSIS, 2012, www.csis.org (homepage), date accessed February 6, 2014.

Conley, Heather and Leed, Maren, "NATO in the Land of Pretend", CSIS Commentary, June 26, 2013, www.csis.org (homepage), date accessed February 6, 2014.

Cordesman, Anthony H., "NATO and Ukraine: The Need for Real World Strategies and for European Partners Rather than Parasites," CSIS Commentary, June 5, 2014, www.csis.org (homepage), date accessed January 8, 2015

CSIS, *European Defense Trends 2012: Budgets, Regulatory Frameworks, and the Industrial Base*, Washington, DC: CSIS, 2012, www.csis.org (homepage), date accessed February 6, 2014.

de Hoop Scheffer, Alexandra and Lété, Bruno, "Rethinking NATO's Strategy in a Changing World: Recommendations for the Next Secretary General", *GMF Policy Brief*, September 2014, www.gmfus.org (homepage), date accessed January 8, 2015.

Deni, John R., "Mali: Another Chance to Lead from Behind", January 14, 2013, www. acus.org (homepage), date accessed January 17, 2013.

DeViney, Nancy and Buckley, Edgar, "Change Management and Cultural Transformation in NATO: Lessons from the Public and Private Sectors," Atlantic Council Issue Brief, May 2012, www.atlanticcouncil.org (homepage), date accessed January 5, 2014.

Di Paola, Giampaolo (2012) "Why NATO Needs to Play a Global Role", www. europesworld.org (homepage), date accessed October 30, 2012.

Frankenberger, Klaus-Dieter, "The Atlantic Imperative in an Era of a Global Power Shift", Transatlantic Academy Paper Series, April 2011, www.gmfus.org (homepage), date accessed February 21, 2014.

Gray, C. Boyden, "An Economic NATO: A New Alliance for a New Global Order", Atlantic Council Issue Brief, February 2013, www.atlanticcouncil.org (homepage), date accessed January 5, 2014.

Gros, Philippe, "Libya and Mali Operations," GMF Foreign Policy Paper, July 2014, www.gmfus.org (homepage), date accessed August 2, 2014

Healy, Jason and van Bochoven, Leendert, "NATO's Cyber Capabilities: Yesterday, Today, and Tomorrow," Atlantic Council Issue Brief, February 2012, www. atlanticcouncil.org (homepage), date accessed January 5, 2014.

Howorth, Jolyon, *CSDP and NATO Post-Libya: Towards the Rubicon*, Brussels: Egmont, 2012.

Jaishankar, Dhruva, "Engaging Rising Powers in the Maritime, Space, and Cyber Domains", *GMF Policy Brief*, May 2012, www.gmfus.org (homepage), date accessed February 21, 2014.

Jenkins, Brian Michael, *The Dynamics of Syria's Civil War*, RAND Corporation, Perspective, RAND: Santa Monica, CA, 2014, www.rand.org (homepage), date accessed July 5, 2014

Kamp, Karl-Heinz, "Is NATO Set to Go on Standby?" Atlantic Council Issue Brief, September 2013, www.atlanticcouncil.org (homepage), date accessed January 5, 2014.

Kamp, Karl-Heinz and Volker, Kurt, "Toward a New Transatlantic Bargain", Carnegie Policy Outlook, February 1, 2012, carnegieendowment.org (homepage), date accessed January 10, 2014.

Keohane, Daniel, "Europeans Less Able, Americans Less Willing?" *GMF Policy Brief*, November 2013, www.gmfus.org (homepage), date accessed February 21, 2014.

Kramer, Franklin D., "Transatlantic Nations and Global Security: Pivoting and Partnerships", Atlantic Council Report, March 2012, www.atlanticcouncil.org (homepage), date accessed January 5, 2014.

Lunn, Simon and Kearns, Ian, "NATO's Deterrence and Defence Posture Review: A Status Report," European Leadership Network, NATO Policy Brief, February 2012, www.europeanleadershipnetwork.org (homepage), date accessed August 3, 2014.

Manning, Robert A., "Global Trends 2030: Challenges and Opportunities for Europe," Atlantic Council Report, May 2013, www.atlanticcouncil.org (homepage), date accessed February 5, 2014.

McGann, James G., *Think Tanks and Policy Advice in the US*, Philadelphia, PA: Foreign Policy Research Institute, 2005.

Musselman, Christopher, "The Die is Cast: Confronting Russian Aggression in Eastern Europe," Atlantic Council Issue Brief, December 2014, www.atlanticcouncil.org (homepage), date accessed January 8, 2015.

Nordenman, Magnus, "NATO in an Era of Global Competition," ACUS Report, June 2014, www.atlanticcouncil.org (homepage), date accessed January 8, 2015.

Pavel, Barry and Lightfoot, Jeff, "The Transatlantic Bargain After 'the Pivot'," Atlantic Council Issue Brief, June 2012, www.atlanticcouncil.org (homepage), date accessed February 5, 2014.

Rachman, Gideon, "The Pivot: Test of Europe as a Security Actor?," *GMF Policy Brief*, May 2013, www.gmfus.org (homepage), date accessed March 12, 2014.

Ross, Robert S., "What the Pivot Means for Transatlantic Relations: Separate Course or New Opportunity for Engagement?" *GMF Policy Brief*, May 2013, www.gmfus.org (homepage), date accessed March 12, 2014.

Schake, Kori, "EUCOM's Future Force Structure", Atlantic Council Issue Brief, June 2011, www.atlanticcouncil.org (homepage), date accessed February 3, 2014.

Shea, Jamie, "NATO and the US Pivot to Asia: To Follow or Not to Follow", *GMF Policy Brief*, May 2013, www.gmfus.org (homepage), date accessed March 12, 2014.

Simakovsky, Mark, Flexible Expansion: NATO Enlargement in an Era of Austerity and Uncertainty", GMF Foreign Policy Papers, 2013, www.gmfus.org (homepage), date accessed March 12, 2014.

Sloan, Stanley R. and Rynning, Sten, "Securing the Transatlantic Community: NATO Is Not Enough," ACUS Article, March 17, 2014, www.atlanticcouncil.org (homepage), date accessed January 8, 2015.

Stacey, Jeffrey, "The West at the Crossroads: Toward a New Transatlantic Bargain," Center for Transatlantic Relations Defense Policy Paper, June 4, 2012, www.transatlantic.sais-jhu.edu (homepage), date accessed February 10, 2014.

Szabo, Stephen F., "The Pacific Pivot and the West", Brussels Forum Paper Series, March 2012, http://www.gmfus.org (homepage), date accessed March 12, 2014.

Ullman, Harlan, "U.S. European Command and NATO's Strategic Concept: Post Afghanistan and Beyond", Atlantic Council Issue Brief, June 2011, http://www.atlanticcouncil.org (homepage), date accessed February 3, 2014.

Volker, Kurt, "Increasing Outreach, Public Understanding and Support for NATO across the Transatlantic Community," Atlantic Council Issue Brief, June 2011, www.atlanticcouncil.org (homepage), date accessed January 29, 2014.

Volker, Kurt and Green, Kevin P., "NATO Reform: Key principles," Atlantic Council Issue Brief, December 2011, www.atlanticcouncil.org (homepage), date accessed January 29, 2014.

Williams, John Allen, "Moving Toward a New NATO?", *National Strategic Forum Review*, Special Edition: Evaluation of the 2012 Chicago NATO Summit, pp. 12–15, nationalstrategy.com (homepage), date accessed October 1, 2012.

Wilson, Damon M., "Learning from Libya: The Right Lessons for NATO," Atlantic Council Issue Brief, September 2011, www.atlanticcouncil.org (homepage), date accessed January 29, 2014.

Ülgen, Sinan, "Deterrence Beyond NATO Borders", *GMF Policy Brief*, October 2014, www.gmfus.org (homepage), date accessed January 8, 2015.

Other sources

Asmus, Ronald D., *Opening NATO's Door: How the Alliance Remade itself for a New Era*, New York: Columbia University Press, 2002.

Asmus, Ronald D., "Having an Impact: Think Tanks and the NATO Enlargement-Debate," *The Quarterly Journal*, No. 1 (2003), pp. 91–94.

Auerbach, Yehudith and Bloch-Elkon, Yaeli, "Media Framing and Foreign Policy: The Elite Press Vis-à-Vis US Policy in Bosnia, 1992–95," *Journal of Peace Research*, Vol. 42, No. 1 (2005), pp. 83–99.

Aybet, Gülnur, "The NATO Strategy Concept Revisited: Grand Strategy and Emerging Issues," in *NATO: In Search for a Vision*, eds. Gülnur Aybet and Rebecca Moore, Washington, DC: Georgetown University Press, 2010, pp. 35–50.

Aybet, Gülnur and Moore, Rebecca, eds., *NATO: In Search for a Vision*, ed. Gülnur Aybet and Rebecca Moore, Washington, DC: Georgetown University Press, 2010.

Aybet, Gülnur and Moore, Rebecca, "Missions in Search for a Vision," in *NATO: In Search for a Vision*, eds. Gülnur Aybet and Rebecca Moore, Washington, DC: Georgetown University Press, 2010, pp. 1–10.

Baker, James A., "America in Asia: Emerging Architecture for a Pacific Community," *Foreign Affairs*, Vol. 70, No. 5 (1991), pp. 1–18.

Barany, Zoltan, "NATO's Post-Cold War Metamorphosis: From Sixteen to Twenty-Six and Counting," *International Studies Review*, Vol. 8, No. 1 (2006), pp. 165–178.

Baum, Matthew and Potter, Philip B. K., "The Relationship Between Mass Media, Public Opinion, and Foreign Policy: Toward a Theoretical Synthesis," *Annual Review of Political Science*, Vol. 11 (2008), pp. 39–65.

Bell, Joseph P. and Hendrickson, Ryan C., "NATO's Visegrad Allies and the Bombing of Quaddafi: The Consequence of Alliance Free-Riders," *The Journal of Slavic Military Studies*, Vol. 25, No. 2 (2012), pp. 149–161.

Berdal, Mats, *The United States, Norway and the Cold War, 1954–60*, Basingstoke: Macmillan, 1997.

Bertram, Christoph, "Europe's Security Dilemmas," *Foreign Affairs*, Vol. 65, No. 5 (1987), pp. 942–957.

Betts, Richard, "Should Strategic Studies Survive?" *World Politics*, Vol. 50, No. 1 (1997), pp. 7–33.

Bruthiaux, Paul, "Language Description, Language Prescription, and Language Planning," *Language Problems and Language Planning*, Vol. 16, No. 3 (1992), pp. 221–234.

Carothers, Thomas, "Barack Obama," in *US Foreign Policy and Democracy Promotion: From Theodore Roosevelt to Barack Obama*, eds. by Michael Cox, Timothy J. Lynch, and Nicholas Bouchet, London: Routledge, 2013.

Chokr, Nader, "Prescription vs Description in the Philosophy of Science, or Methodology vs History: A Critical assessment", *Metaphilosophy*, Vol. 17, No. 4 (1986), pp. 289–299.

Coker, Christopher, "A Farewell to Arms: Europe's Meritocracy and the Demilitarization of Europe," in *NATO's European Allies: Military Capability and Political Will*, eds. Janne Haaland Matlary and Magnus Petersson, Basingstoke: Palgrave Macmillan, 2013.

Coletta, Damon and Rynning, Sten, "NATO from Kabul to Earth Orbit: Can the Alliance Cope?" *Journal of Transatlantic Studies*, Vol. 10, No. 1 (2012), pp. 26–44.

Condit, Doris M., *The Test of War, 1950–1953*, Washington, DC: Historical Office, Office of the Secretary of Defense, 1988.

Deni, John R., "The American Role in European Defense Reform", *Orbis*, Fall (2012), pp. 530–546.

Deni, John R., "Maintaining Transatlantic Strategic, Operational and Tactical Interoperability in an Era of Austerity," *International Affairs*, Vol. 90, No. 3 (2014), pp. 583–600.

Derman, Joshua, "Max Weber and Charisma: A Transatlantic Affair", *New German Critique*, Vol. 38, No. 2 (2011), pp. 51–88.

Drath, Viola Herms, "Toward a New Atlanticism," *American Forign Policy Interests*, Vol. 28, No.6 (2006), pp. 425–431.

Dueck, Colin, "Strategies for Managing Rogue States", *Orbis*, Vol. 50, No. 2 (2006), pp. 223–241.

Edström, Håkan, Matlary, Janne Haaland and Petersson, Magnus, "Utility for
    NATO – Utility of NATO?" in *NATO: The Power of Partnerships*, eds. Håkan
    Edström, Janne Haaland Matlary and Magnus Petersson, Houndmills: Palgrave
    Macmillan, 2011.

Edström, Håkan and Gyllensporre, Dennis, eds., *Pursuing Strategy: NATO Operations
    from the Gulf War to Gaddafi*, Houndmills: Palgrave Macmillan, 2012.

Engelbrekt, Kjell, Mohlin, Marcus, and Wagnsson, Charlotte, eds., *The NATO
    Intervention in Libya: Lessons Learned from the Campaign*, London: Routledge, 2013.

Gaddis, John Lewis, *Strategies of Containment: A Critical Appraisal of American
    National Security Policy during the Cold War*, Oxford: Oxford University Press,
    2005.

Gasper, Des, "Analysing Policy Arguments", *The European Journal of Development
    Studies*, Vol. 8, No. 1 (1996), pp. 36–62.

Gates, Robert, *Duty: Memoirs of a Secretary at War*, London: WH Allen, 2014

Gilley, Bruce, *The Right to Rule: How States Win and Loose Legitimacy*, New York:
    Columbia University Press, 2009.

Hallams, Ellen, *The United States and NATO Since 9/11: The Transatlantic Alliance
    Renewed*, London: Routledge, 2009.

Hallams, Ellen, *A Transatlantic Bargain for the 21st Century: The United States, Europe,
    and the Transatlantic Alliance*, Carlisle Barracks: US Army War College Press,
    2013.

Hallams, Ellen, "Between Hope and Realism: The United States, NATO and
    a Transatlantic Bargain for the 21st Century," in *NATO Beyond 9/11: The
    Transformation of the Atlantic Alliance*, eds., Ellen Hallams, Luca Ratti, and
    Benjamin Zyla, Basingstoke: Palgrave Macmillan, 2013, pp. 217–238.

Hallams, Ellen and Schreer, Benjamin, "Towards a "Post-American" alliance?
    NATO Burden-Sharing After Libya," *International Affairs*, Vol. 88, No. 2 (2012),
    pp. 313–327.

Hallams, Ellen, Ratti, Luca and Zyla, Benjamin, eds., *NATO Beyond 9/11: The
    Transformation of the Atlantic Alliance*, Basingstoke: Palgrave Macmillan, 2013.

Heilman, Madeline E., Description and Prescription: How Gender Stereotypes
    Prevent Women's Ascent up the Organization Ladder", *Journal of Social Issues*,
    Vol. 57, No. 4 (2001), pp. 657–674.

Hendrickson, Ryan C., "Potential NATO Partners – Political and Military Utility for
    NATO", in *NATO: The Power of Partnerships*, eds. H. Edström, J. H. Matlary, and
    M. Petersson, Houndmills: Palgrave Macmillan, 2011.

Hodge, Carl C., "Full Circle: Two Decades of NATO Intervention", *Journal of
    Transatlantic Studies*, Vol. 11, No. 4 (2013), pp. 350–367.

Kaplan, Lawrence S., *NATO Divided, NATO United: The Evolution of an Alliance*, Westport, CT: Praeger, 2004.

Kaplan, Lawrence S., *NATO and the UN: A Peculiar Relationship*, Columbia, MO: University of Missouri Press, 2010

Kay, Sean, "No More Free-Riding: The Political Economy of Military Power and the Transatlantic Relationship," in *NATO's European Allies: Military Capability and Political Will*, eds. Janne Haaland Matlary and Magnus Petersson, Basingstoke: Palgrave Macmillan, 2013.

Kennedy, Paul, "Grand Strategy in War and Peace: Toward a Broader Definition," in *Grand Strategies in War and Peace*, ed. Paul Kennedy, New Haven, CT: Yale University Press, 1991.

Kitfield, James, "Hard Truths About Afghanistan," *National Journal*, May 26, 2012.

Klinkforth, Kristina, *NATO in US Policymaking and Debate – An Analysis: "Drawing the Map" of the US Think Tank Debate on NATO since 9/11*, Berlin: Osteuropa-Institut der Freien Universität Berlin, 2006.

Kupchan, Charles, "A Still-Strong Alliance," *Policy Review*, April & May (2012), pp. 59–70.

Larrabee, Stephen F., "The United States and Security in the Black Sea Region", *Southeast European and Black Sea Studies*, Vol. 9, No. 3 (2009), pp. 301–315.

Larsen, Henrik, "Danish Foreign Policy and the Balance Between the EU and the US: The Choice between Brussels and Washington after 2001," *Cooperation and Conflict*, Vol. 44, No. 2 (2009), pp. 209–230.

Lundestad, Geir, *United States and Western Europe Since 1945: From "Empire" by Invitation to Transatlantic Drift*, Oxford: Oxford University Press, 2005.

Medcalf, Jennifer, *NATO: A Beginners Guide*, Oxford: Oneworld, 2005.

Marsh, Steve and Dobson, Alan, "Fine Words, Few Answers: NATO's "Not so New" New Strategic Concept," in *NATO Beyond 9/11: The Transformation of the Atlantic Alliance*, eds. Ellen Hallams, Luca Ratti and Benjamin Zyla, Basingstoke: Palgrave Macmillan, 2013, pp. 155–177.

Matlary, Janne Haaland and Petersson, Magnus, eds., *NATO's European Allies: Military Capability and Political Will*, Basingstoke: Palgrave Macmillan, 2013.

Medcalf, Jennifer, *Going Global or Going Nowhere: NATO's Role in Contemporary International Security*, Bern: Peter Lang, 2008.

Melby, Svein, "NATO and U.S. Global Security Interests," in *The Future of NATO: Regional Defense and Global Security*, eds. Andrew Michta, and Paal Sigurd Hilde, Ann Arbor, MI: University of Michigan Press, 2014, pp. 36–54.

Michaels, Jeffrey, "NATO after Libya: Alliance Adrift?," *RUSI Journal*, Vol. 156, No. 6 (2011), pp. 56–61.

Michaels, Jeffrey, "A Model Intervention? Reflections on NATO's Libya 'Success', " in *NATO Beyond 9/11: The Transformation of the Atlantic Alliance*, eds. Ellen Hallams, Luca Ratti, and Benjamin Zyla, Basingstoke: Palgrave Macmillan, 2013, pp. 198–214.

Michta, Andrew, and Hilde, Paal Sigurd, eds., *The Future of NATO: Regional Defense and Global Security*, Ann Arbor, MI: University of Michigan Press, 2014.

Mitchell, R. Judson, "Atlanticism and Eurasianism in Reunified Germany," *Mediterrannean Quarterly*, Vol. 9, No. 1 (1998), pp. 92–113.

Moore, Rebecca, *NATO's New Mission: Projecting Stability in a Post-Cold War World*, Westport, CT: Praeger, 2007.

Moss, Kenneth B., "War Powers and the Atlantic Divide," *Orbis*, Spring (2012), pp. 289–307.

Murdock, Clark, A. and Smith, Becca, "The Libyan Intervention: A Study in U.S. Grand Strategy," in *Global Forecast 2011: International Security in a Time of Uncertainty*, eds. Craig Cohen and Josiane Gabel, Washington, DC: CSIS, 2011, pp. 61–63.

National Intelligence Council, *Global Trends 2030: Alternative Worlds*, Washington, DC: National Intelligence Council, 2012.

NATO, *The North Atlantic Treaty*, Washington, DC: NATO, April 4, 1949, www.nato .int (homepage), date accessed April 22, 2014.

NATO, *The Alliance's New Strategic Concept*, NATO: Brussels, 1991.

NATO, *The Alliance's Strategic Concept*, NATO: Brussels, 1999.

NATO, *Active Engagement, Modern Defence*, NATO: Brussels, 2010.

Nitze, Paul H., "Atoms, Strategy and Policy," *Foreign Affairs*, Vol. 34, No. 2 (January, 1956), pp. 187–198.

Noetzel, Timo and Schreer, Benjamin, "Does a Multi-Tier NATO Matter? The Atlantic Alliance and the Process of Strategic Change", *International Affairs*, Vol. 85, No. 2 (2009), pp. 211–226.

Petersson, Magnus, "The Forgotten Dimension? NATO and the Security of the Member States," in *Pursuing Strategy: NATO operations from the Gulf War to Gaddafi*, eds. Håkan Edström and Dennis Gyllensporre, Basingstoke: Palgrave Macmillan, 2012.

Magnus Petersson, "Just an "Internal Exercise?"": NATO and the "New" Security Challenges", in *NATO Beyond 9/11: The Transformation of the Atlantic Alliance*, eds. Ellen Hallams, Luca Ratti, and Ben Zyla, Basingstoke: Palgrave Macmillan, 2013.

Petersson, Magnus, "The US and the Wales Summit: Washington is Back, and NATO is Back to Basics", September 11, 2014, www.europeanleadershipnetwork.org (homepage), date accessed September 16, 2014.

Posen, Barry, "Pull Back", *Foreign Affairs*, Vol. 92, No. 1 (2013), pp. 116–128.

Posen, Barry, *Restraint: A New Foundation for U.S. Grand Strategy*, New York: Cornell University Press, 2014

Rasmussen, Anders Fogh, *The Secretary General's Annual Report 2012*, Brussels: NATO, 2013.

Rasmussen, Anders Fogh, "The Future of the Aliance: Revitalizing NATO for a Changing World," Speech at the Brookings Institution, March 19, 2014, www.brookings.edu (homepage), date accessed July 31, 2014.

Ringsmose, Jens and Rynning, Sten, "Introduction. Taking Stock of NATO's New Strategic Concept," in *NATO's New Strategic Concept: A Comprehensive Assessment*, eds. Jens Ringsmose and Sten Rynning, Copenhagen: DIIS, 2011.

Rosenberg, David Alan, "The Origins of Overkill: Nuclear Weapons and American Strategy, 1945–1960," *International Security*, Vol. 7, No. 4 (Spring, 1983), pp. 3–71.

Rosenberg, David Alan, "Reality and Responsibility: Power and Process in the Making of United States Nuclear Strategy, 1945–68," *The Journal of Strategic Studies*, Vol. 9, No. 1 (1986), pp. 35–52.

Rupp, Richard E., *NATO after 9/11: An Alliance in Continuing Decline*, New York: Macmillan, 2006.

Sauer, Tom and van der Swaan, Bob, "US Tactical Nuclear Weapons after NATO's Lisbon Summit: Why their Withdrawal is Desirable and Feasible," *International Relations*, Vol. 26, No. 1 (2012), pp. 78–100.

Siegel, Nicols, *The German Marshall Fund of the United States: A Brief History*, Washington, DC: GMF, 2012.

Sloan, Stanley, *Permanent Alliance? NATO and the Transatlantic Bargain from Truman to Obama*, London: Continuum, 2010.

Thies, Wallace J., *Why NATO Endures*, Cambridge: Cambridge University Press, 2009.

Volker, Kurt, "Reaffirming Transatlantic Unity", *Policy Review*, April & May (2012), pp. 109–118.

Walt, Stephen M., "Why Alliances Endure or Collapse," *Survival*, Vol. 39, No. 1 (1997), pp. 156–179.

Walt, Stephen M., "The End of the American Era", *The National Interest*, November/December (2011), pp. 6–16.

Webber, Mark, Hallams, Ellen and Smith, Martin A., "Repairing NATO's Motors," *International Affairs*, Vol. 90, No. 4 (2014), pp. 773–793.

Weber, Max, *The Theory of Social and Economic Organization*, New York: The Free Press, 1947.

Welsh, Jennifer, "The Responsibility to Protect: Dilemmas of a New Norm," *Current History*, November (2012).

Williams, Michael, *The Good War: NATO and the Liberal Conscience in Afghanistan*, Basingstoke: Palgrave Macmillan, 2011.

Yost, David, "The US Debate on NATO Nuclear Deterrence," *International Affairs*, Vol. 87, No. 6 (2011), pp. 1402–1438.

Index

Locators followed by n denote footnotes.